Gates to Asia

ALSO BY JAN MYRDAL

REPORT FROM A CHINESE VILLAGE
CONFESSIONS OF A DISLOYAL EUROPEAN

ALSO BY MYRDAL AND GUN KESSLE

CHINESE JOURNEY
ANGKOR: AN ESSAY ON ART AND IMPERIALISM
CHINA: THE REVOLUTION CONTINUED

OVERLEAF: *Sultan Mahmud of Ghazni built a residence at Lashkari bazaar. Of the Sultan, Firdausi said: "Being by birth not a prince but a boor, the praise of the noble he could not endure."*

JAN MYRDAL AND GUN KESSLE

GATES TO ASIA

A DIARY FROM A LONG JOURNEY

Translated from the Swedish by Paul Britten Austin

PANTHEON BOOKS
A Division of Random House, New York

ISBN: 0-394-47115-6

Library of Congress Catalog Card Number: 75-162580

Composition by Kingsport Press, Kingsport, Tennessee. Printed and bound by Halliday Lithograph Corp., West Hanover, Massachusetts

FIRST EDITION

Contents

Introduction

The subtitle of this book is: "A Diary from a Long Journey." That was not formulated as a phrase in general. This book was being written at different times and in different places. Thus not only does the scenery change from chapter to chapter; also the describer changes. The writer of the last chapter is the same person as the one who wrote the first chapter; but he is not the same writer.

But even if it is a diary from a long journey it is not the diary of Jan Myrdal, not a daily recording of matters affecting the writer personally. Insofar as such matters can be utilized in the general interest—and they can if treated as raw material only—I have utilized them in other works.

Written at different times and in different places, these are not jottings, not travel notes; these are reasoned comments during a long journey.

That journey took seven years. Three times during these years I returned to Sweden for a shorter or longer stay. The material from Sweden is not included. During these seven years I stayed a long time in China. Of that I have written in other books.

This book concerns mainly Afghanistan, Western India, and Soviet Central Asia. The title *Gates to Asia* thus has a geographical meaning for a traveler who is going overland from Europe. But during these seven years I also traveled in South India, Ceylon, Burma, Nepal. That is not included in this book.

I have made a geographical choice: the gates to Asia. But I have also made a choice in time. This journey lasted seven years. From 1958 to 1965. Those were the years from the landing of US troops in Lebanon to the stepping-up of the war in Vietnam.

During those years my perspectives shifted. If I had been asked whether I was in favor of social and national liberation in 1958 I would have answered: Yes. So I would have answered in 1965. But still the implications of this answer would have been different in 1965 from what they would have been in 1958. This is thus also a record of a journey toward understanding of the colonialist and imperialist legacy. To a large extent this book becomes a journey back to the source of present-day imperialism.

The first chapter in this book was written after the revolution in Iraq. Gun Kessle and I were in Teheran. It was toward the end of July, 1958. In the United Nations Security Council, Mr. Henry Cabot Lodge, Jr. had said:

> Observing the course of events in Lebanon and Iraq one is constrained to conclude that there are powers at work in the Middle East seeking, in total disregard for national sovereignty and independence, to substitute force or the threat of force for Law. (July 15, 1958)

And the British representative Sir Pierson Dixon had told the Security Council of the landing of British troops in Jordan:

> Not for the first time in our long history are we activated in what we have done by a sense of responsibility and a desire to see truly peaceful and stable conditions in the world. (July 17, 1958)

Coming to Teheran. Reading these statements. I started writing.

". . . And a month after the day when I had written about the figure of Eulenspiegel and Gun had opened her exhibition we drove southwards, out of Europe in a 2CV Citroën. Though we didn't know it, it would be several years before we returned. When we got back we should be quite different."

Gates to Asia

THE CAKE THE
CORPSE BAKED

"Back home I vote conservative," says the Swedish business-man. "But if I was born here I'd be a red-hot revolutionary."

The heat lies like a thick yellow mist over the plain, and the dust sticks in your throat. A big blond fellow, he sits drinking his whiskey.

Two days later there's a revolution. Nuri Said is hung up by the feet. Like Mussolini before him. But now the Swede is indignant.

"Can't carry on like that!"

The newspapers arrive from Sweden. We read them with amazement. They're all so serious and democratic, these pen-pushers! They count on their fingers, and build up pacts and bases and play with the map as if it were all nothing but one big game of chess.

"Sacrifice a pawn here, and an oil-derrick there, and white withdraws and black threatens . . ."

Further, they utter their warnings against Nasser, Nasserism, and Russian agents. Friendly words about Israel. Hopes of Western progress being maintained.

But all the fine words and all the pretty phrases are a lot of poetical poppycock. Because this isn't a game of chess, and no amount of sacrificed peasants can ever save the king.

Nuri Said gets hung up by his feet, and it's no good deceiving oneself. He won't be the only one. A good many thousands more are going to be shot and hanged, around here, in the next few years. And if I'm to be honest about it, then I can only say: "And a good thing too!"

Sweden is a well-to-do little country. Back home in Sweden they talk so prettily of reforms and progress—and aren't you much better off than your Dad was?

But who has footed the bill? Long ago the respectable Swedish labor newspapers have declared all that old stuff about "exploitation" and "impoverishment" and "the class war" hopelessly out of date, passé. Today we're all living in one big happy people's home. Yes. But who's had to pay for it all?

It's Hussein who has paid, and Ali who's had to foot the bill.

The poor man has become poorer, and the rich man has got richer. All this talk of progress is a confidence trick, a swindle. What has happened is this. Hussein has had to tighten his belt, work harder, and eat less. Total penury. Not just yesterday, nor since last year, either. But year after year. Decade after decade. The wealth of these countries' oil has meant ruin for their populations, luxury for their upper class, and some years peace and quiet in our tidy little social-democratic Swedish flats.

"Our western brothers." Today, as always, the mother of parliaments, like the descendants of the signatories of the Declaration of Independence, is supporting the exploiters, the feudal lords, serfdom.

The country is ruined, the people poverty-stricken, the rich man tramples on the poor man, judges can be bought, parliaments are a bad joke, high officials live to steal and petty officials steal to live, and the foreigner is always right. Even at home in social-democratic Sweden, whenever—even for a moment—the peace and quiet of this nefarious establishment is threatened, the labor leaders feel uneasy.

The rulers, having stolen all they need, have their bank accounts in Switzerland, their villas on the Riviera. And hope they'll have time to clear out when the big bang comes.

For my part I must say I hope they won't.

Nasser and the officer juntas seize power. That is to say, the petty bourgeois seizes power. This isn't a socialist revolution. It may be national liberation, but it's a petty bourgeois revolution.

When I listen to respectable Swedish democrats, sitting snug in their comfortable social-democratic *apparat,* talking about Nasserism, I feel like spewing up. Don't they know what they're talking about? If they do, then they're a pack of scoundrels.

To have got rid of even a small part of all the prevailing oppression and exploitation is a fine thing, to be sure. But to have given people, in addition—for the first time in a thousand years—a glimmer of hope that life may even become bearable, that's a truly staggering achievement.

Corruption isn't abolished in a day. Nor are competent administrators to be found overnight. That's why it doesn't surprise me in the least to read former friends of Nasser writing in the Swedish press of their "disappointment." The old familiar abuses (against others) are so very much easier to tolerate than improvements which don't instantly lead to a paradise on earth. Such "disappointment" is a coward's excuse for his treachery.

The remarkable thing isn't that so much of the bad old times still persists, but that there's so much of the good new time. There's nothing odd about many people plodding on in the old ruts. The miraculous thing (in the real sense of that word) is that so many are turning their footsteps into new paths. Liberation makes people grow.

The upper class in these countries have no amiable traits. They've sold out to the foreigner. They've pillaged their compatriots. As for the law, they've turned it into a bulwark for large-scale thieving. They have murdered and tortured without conscience. Long ago they have betrayed even feudalism's moral code: that the lord (however marginally) shall protect the interests of souls committed to his care. With the aid of foreign troops and foreign capital, they have succeeded in combining every means of oppression known to feudalism with the capitalist's impersonal exploitation.

No. I for one shan't shed any tears over their fate.

For—let us be quite clear about it. The bill, when it comes in, will be a bloody one. On the Riviera many a villa will stand empty.

5

Revolutions aren't set in motion by "agents." Armchair strategists, figuring out the positions of East and West and counting their divisions, ought to go home and read their history books more carefully.

Please take a cake; the corpse itself has baked it—as we say in Swedish at funerals.

Camels on the Bactrian plain

AFGHANISTAN

I

It's a summer night. We're driving toward Afghanistan. Half a year away from Sweden, we're still carrying our own country with us. Everything different still seems strange.

As we drive up out of the dry river bed, the stones rattle against the steel engine-guards. Ahead, the headlights light up the wheel-tracks, bathing the little prickly bushes in their light. More than five hundred species of thorny plant are said to grow in the deserts and steppes of the Iranian Plateau. The wheel-ruts are deep and the car shudders violently. I turn down the headlights, pointing their beams downward at the road, to be in time to spot holes and stones. Keep the speed down. Use the steering wheel to parry the road's surprises. The car chassis is screwed up as high as she'll go. In Teheran I got underneath and adjusted the clearance for rough-terrain driving. Now she's walking along like a mule on her four wheels.

"Didn't get as far as the border today, either," says Gun. We stop. I switch the engine off and get out. We've been driving since half past four this morning. Or, to be more exact, we started out from the little gendarme post out in the steppes at half past four this morning. All day we've been searching for ruins, monuments, and mosaics. Now Gun is pouring out tea from the thermos. All around us the night, the silence. In the dry air, the stars are immensely close. The Milky Way turns into a real white path across the heavens. I light a cigarette. Gun takes over at the wheel. And on we drive. Cones of light from our headlights sweep over the trail. Through the open windows the night air blows cool.

"As long as we're not on the wrong road," says Gun.

But this is the main route to Herat. The way taken by the mail vehicles and the trucks. Ahead, their wheel-tracks run on and on, leading us toward Afghanistan.

"Why just Afghanistan?" people had asked, when we'd left Sweden. To this question we had not been able to give any very clear answer.

For our ignorance was vast and representative of the ignorance prevailing in our own country about this part of the world. We knew Afghanistan lay on the watershed of Central Asia and the Indian Ocean. We had heard of the Hindu Kush mountains. We realized Afghanistan was more or less a neighbor of the Soviet Union, Pakistan, and Iran. We'd heard it even bordered on China. And we knew, too, that Afghanistan had never been under the dominion of any European colonial power; had kept its independence and was regarded as inaccessible. Kipling had sung of British heroism in the border wars:

> When you're wounded and left on Afghanistan's plains,
> An' the women come out to cut up what remains,
> Jest roll to your rifle an' blow out your brains
>   An' go to your Gawd like a soldier.
>   Go, go, go like a soldier.
>   Go, go, go like a soldier.
>   Go, go, go like a soldier.
>   So-oldier of the Queen!

And the first time Sherlock Holmes met his Watson, the latter had just come home from the Afghan Wars. That night, I suppose, we saw Afghanistan as a wild, perhaps even an exotic, land of wide deserts and high mountains.

In this ignorance we could have found an answer. We wished to see and experience for ourselves. Traveling is like falling in love; the world is made new. You recover your naïve hunger for reality, so easily abrased by the daily round and a home environment. Even the commonplace, all that has been worn into greyness becomes sharp, bright, colorful, clean. That autumn in a Stockholm heavy with rain, just home from one long journey and in every way we knew how struggling to scrape together money for another—and even longer— one, it is possible we came to say "Afghanistan" simply because the country was so remote and because we knew so little about it.

But there were other reasons. The romance of the steering wheel—motor-romanticism—for one. We wanted to drive our 2CV along roads where no private car had ever been before. Such roads we hoped to find in Afghanistan. There, despite all long-distance motor traffic, we reckoned there must be trails still only covered by jeeps. That areas still remain anywhere outside Antarctica which have never seen a motor vehicle of any kind we knew to be an illusion. Nevertheless, we longed to drive through torrential rivers, to force deserts and mountain ranges, to travel on our own responsibility, at our own hazard, relying entirely on our own wits, and achieve the Alpinist's bliss—the bliss of a satisfied craving. This motor-romanticism fused with a lust for purely physical adventure, which makes even the most insufferable conditions delightful, simply be-cause they're insufferable.

But this lure of the unknown, this romantic image of unblazed trails, was also rooted in a sense of solidarity with this unknown coun-try. A feeling it was a land for us. The more adverse the things we read of it, the stronger became this feeling. We read of banditry and ferocious acts, we saw journalistic phrases about a country where car tires were mended with camel dung and gearboxes had to be lubri-cated with goat's milk. But we belong to the war generation, which learned to read newspapers and reportages in much the same way as the Devil reads Holy Scripture. If a land is accused of being infested with bandits—always the accusation of rulers against those they haven't been able to subdue—then one begins to have a feeling of solidarity with the accused.

This growing sympathy with others' stiff-necked resistance was decked out in reminiscences of bold, colorful folk art, framed in recollections of photos of grand-style scenery.

Early next morning we drove out of Iran and into Afghanistan. In spite of the Iranian border guards' protests, we'd slept the night in the car. In the morning our eyes were red from lack of sleep and the dust tightened our skin. As yet the heat was not strong, and over the desert steppe the air was misty. Deep wheel-ruts led us on toward

9

the Afghan border station. Islam Kaleh. The fortress of Islam. We drove into the yard. The sun rose ever higher in the sky and the heat grew more intense. We mounted the brick steps and went into the verandah's shade. While we sat there amid the buzz of flies, men in wide white clothes looked at our passports and inscribed heavy ledgers with Arabic handwriting. Offered us tea. The customs officer in charge introduced us to his brethren. One by one they came up, and then withdrew more deeply into the shadow, politely reserved as they took part in the conversation. They said, "Sweden is a good country. Afghanistan is a good country."

They offered us tea, and we offered them cigarettes. The customs chief took one out of politeness. The others smoked a hubble-bubble. We smiled at each other and repeated that Sweden was a good and free country which had no wars, and that Afghanistan was a good country. No one bothered about our car or baggage. As they gave us back our passports, they said, "We never examine honest people's baggage."

We drove out of the yard, the knobbly customs barrier went up, and the yellow sun-scorched landscape stretched far and wide all around us. Gun said, "So—this is Afghanistan!"

Since then we've driven tens of thousands of miles in this country. What was to have been a tour became a stay. The differences ceased to seem strange to us. That summer we took the northern route along the Turkmen border and the Amu Darya, down via the Hindu Kush to Kabul. Toward winter's end we returned to Afghanistan, came up from the Indus Valley through the Khyber Pass and past Jalalabad, drove through sleet and slush over the Lataband Pass, and reached Kabul in a snowstorm, just as dusk was falling. Stayed in the country eight months. Had a little house in Kabul. (In the spring the peach tree in our garden bloomed and the mountains stood up white against the blue sky.) We drove around the country. Drove through the eastern river valleys, normally closed to foreigners, northward, until we reached Nuristan, the Land of Light. Drove up toward the Roof of the World, crossed two deserts, drove across rivers and over high mountains.

As for the romance of the steering wheel, we certainly got our bellyful! We've driven along more than twelve thousand miles of Afghan roads and over untracked terrain. We've driven to Munda-

10

gal in the Bashgul Valley. We've driven to Ish Kashim, where the Ab-i-Pandj comes down from Sarikol through Wakhan and turns northward as the Amu Darya. Wakhan, the yak route to China via Pamir. That time it proved impossible to reach High Pamir. We've stood on Ish Kashim's green meadows and seen the white mountains to the east. Were obliged to get back over the passes while the glaciers were still melting, wading for two or three miles at a time in water up to our windshield and the torrent so swift the wheels took off from the stony river bed and the car spun round and round in the rapids. At such times Gun sat inside, gripping the steering wheel while I stood in the icy foaming waters and made sure the rope held. Half a year later, stripping down the self-starter, I still found water in it.

We've learned how to drive along narrow ledges above rapids, to drive across deserts where hour after hour the wheels spin round and round in the loose sand as the car slowly creeps forward, the heat rises, and under the blazing sun the paintwork breaks out into a spider's web of wrinkles. You can fry eggs on the hood. Three times, driving up out of ravines, we ripped off the rear bumper. In the end we didn't even bother to weld it on again. The gas tank buckled like an old preserved-meat can. And though three of the car's four springs were broken, still we drove on.

To cross dry ravines where there is no road calls for a special technique. The river bed is stony, its banks steep and sandy. Gun drives. I sit beside her, ready to jump off. Skidding at top speed sideways down the steep slope, spin the wheel the other way, roar straight over the stones, with never a thought to tires, wheels, or suspension, just don't lose speed, a quick double-declutch, down into first, over-rev the engine, and up the other side. As the front wheels begin skidding and losing their grip on the loose sand and the engine roars dully and the slope rears up like the side of a house, I jump off, get a foothold in the sand, shove like hell, and jump back into the car again just as we reach the crest; Gun changes up to second; the engine quietens down; and on we go.

Yes, we've had our bellyful of the romance of the steering wheel. With our 12½ horsepower and all our baggage we have managed to get on where jeeps have stuck fast. In the monstrous July heat of the desert I've taken the carburetor to pieces and on a rainy night high

11

up in the mountains, gone through all the electrical circuits. I could take that car to pieces, into tiny pieces, in my sleep, like an erector set. Not because it was a bad car, because it broke down, or went on strike. No. Even when the bearings were worn, the springs had snapped, the bolts which hold the shock-absorbers were bent or broken off, the self-starter was full of rust, the steering connecting rod jerked all askew, and the piston rings done for, it always got us there. During two years of driving without access to a garage that car stood so much it had plenty of time to train me as a garage mechanic.

The desire for physical adventure, the instinct which finds pleasure in exertion, in extreme exhaustion—yes, we've had our bellyful of that, too. We stuck fast in sand dunes in the country around Kara Kum, east of Andkhui. I've had to dig the car out of the sand, working in the sun hour after hour with the shade temperature somewhere in the hundred-twenties Fahrenheit, and the air burning my throat and chest. In the course of our second year of travels we reached the point where tires and inner tubes had been burned up by the desert heat, the rubber had changed color and was so dark I could stick my thumb right through tread, cord, and inner. That point was reached six hundred miles beyond mountains and deserts, the other side of Kabul, where new tires and inner tubes were awaiting us. At that time we were having fourteen punctures in the course of a day's drive. The jack was worn out and could no longer be wound up—it had to be screwed up with a wrench. In the end the whole operation—carefully screw up the jack, remove the wheel, take off tire, take out inner tube, locate new hole, vulcanize, wait for patch to cool, check, refit the inner, work the tire on, pump it up, replace wheel and screw down the jack—was taking me sixteen minutes flat. Finally, in Badakhshan, I attained the ultimate goal of all lust for physical adventure: the day when one can truly say: One more step, and I collapse—and at the same time know you've several thousand miles still to go. The experience, perhaps, was worth it.

And of course we enjoyed the beauties of nature. High up in the mountains the sky becomes so deep and clear a blue it merges into mauve. The air so clear, that every contour is knife-sharp. The Afghan landscape's beauty is not of the late classical sort. It is grandiose. Nor is it romantic, Gothic, or swathed in Germanic mist. It is clear and firm. Central Asia's landscape is tremendous and clean. In these parts one's experience of nature is of the sort that makes everything else seem paltry and inessential. The Alps, tremendous though they are, seem pretty and hollow beside it. Even the deserted swampy barrenness and grandeur of the Swedish fells reveals itself as mere child's play beside such diamond-hard clarity.

It's not that the intensity of the light is different. It is the color scale, the clarity of the air, which make all the difference. Down here the light is yellower, the air clearer. In Sweden blues and greens predominate, standing out warmly against the strong shiny grey which is the Swedish national color. Our continent is poor in pure colors, but rich in nuances and airy perspectives. Down here the colors stand out sharp and isolated. The light eats color, and what in the Swedish air would be experienced as a dissonance here becomes a harmony. There was really no need to resort to ingenious religious explanations in order to understand the so-called lack of perspective of the Persian miniaturists. It was sheer realism.

Through the kaleidoscopic deserts and steppes, the little dust-devils wander. In their hundreds, in their immensity, they stand swaying all about us. Now, in late summer, the billowing steppe is a scorched yellow. From the steppe, up toward the dark mountains, through a narrow ravine where the rock-faces sheer up vertically toward a thin streak of sky, we drive in eternally unchanging shadow, the roar of our motor vibrant between the damp-gleaming rock walls and the green river frothing and foaming beside us. Mountains which open out, shifting in blue, green, white, red, mauve, a brilliant cascade of explosive color, of hot dry landscape broken by heavy coal-black cliffs. A pink mountain against the high white peaks of the Hindu Kush, and green narrowing valleys. Another sort of countryside is like what we have at home in Sweden in the province of Småland, with winding stone walls and trees weighed down with fruit, all at a height of six thousand feet above sea level.

But reality caught up with us on another plane. Deeper and more essential. The country which had looked so small on a Mercator projection of the world (a Belgium-in-Asia) and in international statistics only figured deep-buried in the footnotes, which in all our childhood history lessons and geography hours had hardly a word devoted to it, revealed to us its greatness, not merely its extent, but

13

also its significance. We reached a world, a culture, that was "otherwise." Yet similar. Our journeys through the country turned into intellectual adventures, of ever greater depth and ever more stirring to the emotions.

Cultures and history fell into a juster perspective; linked up; became close to us. We succeeded in freeing ourselves from exoticism and the romance of travel. Exoticism binds thought and feeling. Whatever is strange, it makes merely interesting. All that is "otherwise" is made to appear essentially different. Under its pretty talk of landscapes, customs, and folkways, the romance of travel conceals a deep scorn for other peoples.

The difference between myself and an Afghan farmer is minimal, smaller than between me and my own great-great-grandfather. A difference in technical progress. No sharp boundaries separate one people from another. Habit and custom can vary as sharply within my own country as between it and a country in Central Asia. We found it harder and harder to believe in differences in national mores. Behavior which gains me acceptance in our own northern mountain villages will gain me acceptance also in Afghanistan. The difference between a peasant in some Swedish village and a peasant in Bamian is so thin that anyone equally unfamiliar with both cultures wouldn't even notice it. Cultures differ. People don't. All travel writing which fails to recognize how much we all have in common is a glossy lie.

Only by recognizing our similarity can one begin to discuss our differences. Only common humanity lends them any meaning, or can fertilize them. Only on such terms are other peoples' art and culture anything but exotic ethnography.

A general in Iran told me Afghanistan was a poor and backward country. Later, a Pakistani police chief said the same. And so did a millionaire in India. Of course, they were quite right, this *is* a poor part of the world. Very poor. But—and this is the crux of the matter —an Afghan farmer lives better than an Iranian farmer, and a great deal better than a Pakistani or an Indian. The great Afghan landlord lives less well. And I must add: the Afghan farmer or shepherd knows his own worth as a human being. What is more, he's in a position to impress it on others. Wherein lies the crucial difference.

Freedom is not to be measured in parliaments. Nor does oppression simply mean a shortage of lawyers. Oppression and freedom are only to be measured in lives. In ownership of the soil. In the free man's right to carry weapons. Afghanistan was a country where the men bore themselves proudly. Where no one bowed obsequiously. Where beggars were few and the foreigner a guest, and as such in no position to behave like a sahib or great lord, or use his money to buy others' obsequiousness, friendship, or respect. A people never crushed retains its self-respect. Afghanistan is a poor country; but a country with hope for its future. A country which all generals, chiefs of police, and industrial magnates therefore regard as frighteningly backward.

One time, stuck fast in the desert and unable to get on, we saw a caravan approaching. It was hot. The sun blazed down, and I was tired. The men came up to us. Picked up our car, and carried it to firm ground. Then asked if they might turn back and follow us to the nearest town, to be of assistance if we got stuck again. I replied that this wouldn't be necessary; the road, as far as I remembered, would soon improve.

I I

Few nowadays amuse themselves with the old game of trying to locate paradise on a map. Long ago the very expression "paradise" became secularized for us. It means our pleasant Swedish summers—the little red wooden cottage, the wide blue lake; or some dream of an exotic technicolor paradise—an atoll in the South Seas, maybe, with palms and soft music, all made in USA. Not that the idea of paradise ever really took root among us Swedes, in frozen wintry Scandinavia. The prospect of being allowed to spend eternity sitting on a rainbow dressed only in a shift made scant appeal. Hell was swampy, autumnal, chilly, a drafty hole; and Valhalla a timber cottage exuding a pleasant odor of pork fat, its walls and ceiling deep-sooted with the smoke of silver-birch fires. The heavenly joys, for us, were incarnated in undrainable beer mugs and fights in which no one ever suffered lasting injury. Our hell was our own country, as anyone can experience it on a dark freezing autumn evening, when the icy wind whistles past your ears and the black rain comes lashing

Inside the shrine of Pir-i-Herat, the "Saint of Herat," the poet and mystic Khwaja Abdullah Ansari (c. 1006–c.1088)

down. Our heaven, likewise, was an everlasting market day. In another time and another environment this peasant myth later got into bad company, came to be exploited for strange ends (Herr Schicklgruber in his grey raincoat bidding Ludendorff *bon voyage* on his way to Valhalla), but this must not be allowed to obscure the myth's original dreamy longing for warmth, beer, and roast pork.

Not until one meets the great religions, the old countries where the world's cultures originated, does one come across the real paradises, whose streets—as in the Bible—are paved with gold, and which —the Koran says—are full of houris, melons, grapes, and cooling breezes.

Nor is it by any means certain that today's impatient traveler has the faculties necessary for recognizing and absorbing the heavenly beauty of such places. He arrives, perhaps, by air. Steps out into a yellow desert, sun-scorched and wind-swept. Is whisked off to the nearest oasis. In his eyes an oasis is the dreariest of all thinkable human habitations. Its bazaars are poor. Its trees few and dust-laden. Its streets full of stinking puddles. Over the grey-white houses of sun-dried clay the sun scorches down. The grey river bed stinks of filth and humanity. To few travelers is it granted to perceive in all this the purlieus of paradise.

Only he who is pure in heart and mind—any theologian will confirm—is worthy of the heavenly vision. To experience this culture as it was created, and in the terms in which it has in turn created its myth of paradise, then one must see it at the end of a long hot dusty journey. Then the myth again finds its natural setting; theology, stripped of speculation, becomes a legend of humanity; and as the desiccated and tormented body, doused with water, recovers its normal healthy hue in the hammam (bath) the old dogma of its resurrection becomes an everyday experience. For the caravan traveler, paradise is then a wish-dream as intimate and easily comprehensible as the crackling birch-logs, the tankards of frothing beer, and the roast pork swimming in fat are to anyone traveling in winter through the Swedish mountains.

Now, leaving Islam Kaleh behind us, we are driving through Dasht-i-Hamdam. The sun rises ever higher in the sky. The wind gets up. The Wind of a Hundred and Twenty Days blows hot and airless across steppe and desert in the direction of the salt lakes of

17

Seistan. The air, cruelly lacking in oxygen, is dry and thirsty. In long rolling dunes the landscape sweeps up to arid hillocks and scorched plains. The wind, coming against the car, filling our ears, nose, mouth, and eyes with dust. The wheels skid and the car lurches whenever the wind hits it. It is hot inside, getting steadily hotter. In the remote distances, hidden among hills, lie the villages. To our eyes this is still a strange, foreign landscape. A long time we've been driving through this high plateau country, sleeping at teahouses or in the car, and in the early morning driving on again into a landscape eternally poised between steppe and desert—and still we haven't grown used to it. Now we're really beginning to suffer from the heat. Even the water in our water-skin is scalding hot as we pour it over our necks, until its evaporation cools us. Driving with closed windows through which the dust is slowly forcing itself into our nostrils, we itch all over. The air parches our throats. If we open the windows the wind bursts in like tongues of fire.

Then, far ahead, the landscape begins to take on a greenish tinge. Against the pale hot dusty sky, factory chimneys stick up. After a while we fall in with the first irrigation canals. Trees come marching out to meet us. From time to time the car is gliding along in their shade. The factory chimneys take on definite shape, are transformed into minarets of shimmering blue mosaic. Now the road is skirted by trees. Through the waving treetops a glimpse of a Timurid cupola, heavenly blue. The verdure, the good air, is all around us. We drive into Herat.

Now the wind, which a little while ago was howling across the steppes and blowing smoky sand over the yellow scorched slopes before it, is whispering in the crowns of the conifers, sending the wavelets chasing across the watery shaded surfaces of the dams. The hot gusts, which a little while ago were causing us to itch in every dusty pore, have turned into a cool breeze, fanning my forehead. The dry and breathless air which was burning my lungs is now moist, gentle, life-giving, full of bracing ozone; intoxicating like a healthy acidulous *vin du pays*.

As we drive up in front of the hotel steps and step out onto its gravel forecourt, the whispering trees throw cool shadows.

In the washroom we douse each other in cool water. The water glitters silvery in the air. We stretch out our arms, voluptuously letting the water run down over our bodies. To wash, to soap oneself, letting the cool water wash away the soapsuds, is sensuous delight. And all the while this voluptuousness of water on skin!

We go back into our room. On the low table they have placed a big pewter bowl of grapes. We lie down on the old English iron beds, our windows wide open onto the garden. Among the treetops a glimpse of blue sky. We listen to the soughing of trees and the plash of running water; drink tea, eat grapes. Blue grapes, green grapes, violet grapes, sweet grapes, bitter grapes, big grapes, little grapes, grapes which melt like sugar in the mouth, and grapes which astringently tickle the lymph glands; oval grapes, round grapes. This is bliss. To reach Herat is to come to paradise.

Do not misunderstand me. Paradise, as defined by the dictionary: "Paradise, from Gr. *paradeisos,* garden; orig. early Persian word." Trees, tree-lined gardens, parks, set their stamp on Herat. The dust-laden, dirty, and decaying town described by travelers in the last century is changing. A town plan fraught with trees is linking it with its own great cultural traditions. The ancient bazaars with their narrow winding lanes are being forced to yield to shady new shopping streets, all lined with trees. This is a new city, dominated by wide parks and the massive new government buildings. Its whole architectonic perspective is one great ocean of swaying trees. Herat's dwelling houses disappear behind leafy curtains. Streets of rose bushes, avenues of conifers. The gravel street leading out to the bridge—still under construction—across the Hari Rud, is a Champs-Elysées walled with greenery. No paradise has a worthier architecture.

When a city in a poor agrarian country undergoes such transformation there is every reason to suspect it is at the expense of its peasantry. The work of the farmers and tax-paying peasantry in the agrarian uplands has had to pay for the landowners' new residences; all the beauty of the new seat of government. Out of their work the new esplanades are being built. It is their labor which is transforming Herat, the capital, into a paradise, a garden. One asks the Governor how much all these newly planted trees have cost. A glance of incomprehension: "Cost? They haven't cost anything. We just say, this is where the trees are to be planted. This is where they are to get their water from. Besides, everyone likes trees."

19

This is feudal. This is the corvée. Hitherto, beauty has never been created except by work. In most cases, other people's work.

Proudly, they showed me the parks. The shady trees leaning over the dams. The fountains playing, the glittering water. Families were sitting on their mats around melons and hubble-bubbles. Seeing me approach, the women lowered their veils. Outside the city we bathed in the huge new reservoir–swimming pool, also shaded; and again there were delightful flowers and it was swarming with people. All these parks were wide open. Not guarded by police, surrounded by fences, or bristling with FORBIDDEN notices. All that would have been superfluous. The parks are open to all. And everyone likes trees.

Prejudices are odd things. In front of a Persian miniature, for example: shady trees, a spring, flowers, a man reclining on a mat, eating a melon—many of us northerners only have to look at such a picture to be instantly seized with indignation. Words like effeminacy, decadence, luxury, good living. (Why should our Swedish word *vällust*—sensuousness—be as sure a source of antipathy in Scandinavia as the expression "to live by one's wits" is in Anglo-Saxon cultures? A nice subject for a thesis!) A color photo of Herr Svensson wearing blue bathing trunks, on the other hand, stretched out on a beach of yellow sand and eating a ham sandwich, is conducive to no moral indignation whatsoever. It just makes us feel happy, awakens associations with holidays. Summer. A day off.

But in these dry hot countries the Persian garden is a good deal more crucial to a decent existence than a bathing beach is to ours. On Thursday evenings and Fridays the poor man, who has no garden of his own, can seek refuge in one of the public gardens, rest, feel himself a human being among other human beings. The garden is more than an outdoor sitting room. It is his summer bedroom, too, planned to yield maximum comfort and relaxation. Its cool shade, the somnolent sound of running waters, its humid air, the light rustling of leaves, the scent of flowers; all is reposeful. The colors, the play of shadows, the glittering drops of water, the lovely cool respite from the burning heat outside, all these are basic.

Herat's beauty also bears the special stamp of Afghanistan's ancient feudalism. Between the landowner and his serf there is no inhuman gulf. Even in the Hari Rud Valley much of the land belongs to peasants. Less of it to landlords. The social gulf between classes is not quite impassable. Since the State of Afghanistan sprang from a free tribal barbarism two hundred years ago its whole apparatus has been developing a feudal system.

Feudalism's human relationships, too, are still intact. They have not yet been exploded and burst wide open by oil money, as in Iran; nor by foreign exploiters, Moguls, or the British. Nor codified into laws and regulations, or frozen into an icy pseudo-justice, as in India. This is still a society based on relations between people; not between things.

To make this thought clear—it is decidedly not understood by most "international experts":

In 1880 C. H. Crossby sent his book *The Garden of India: or Chapters on Oudh History and Affairs* to the German emigré Karl Marx "With the author's compliments." On reading this book Karl Marx used blue and green pencils to mark different passages. When he reached page 262 where Crossby quoted Raghbar Dyal, Kayath, karinda of Gulab Singh, zamindar, as saying: "The land was not worth cultivators' fighting about in the Nawabi, and consequently no one cared much whether they lost or held it," Marx exploded and wrote in the margin of the book:

> Such replies prove nothing atall with regard to social relationships prior to so-called rights!
>
> It seems very difficult for the English mind—having always before itself the examples of the small English and diminutive tenant at will—to understand that fixity of tenure may be considered a pest by the cultivator himself; even the fugitive slave or serf presupposes a society where, to get free, you have only to escape, to get rid of a man, but to get rid of, to escape from social interdependence, à s'échapper des rapports sociaux, is quite another thing.
>
> This is the thing, as soon as modern centralized government supersedes the much more "fluid" Asiatic despotism or feudal anarchy.
>
> Diese whole enquiry was so absurdly conducted as only English blockheads could contrive to do!

The poor man and the oppressed—a half-starved porter in the bazaar, for instance—still sleeps on the street under a lousy bedcover. But once a week, at least, he need not begrudge himself a bath in the hammam and the joys of the park. One Thursday afternoon we sat in a park outside the town, watching men coming in with their sons. They came walking up in their thousands toward the park, where they were going to spend the evening. They spread out their mats, lit their fires and, as they watched their tea-water come to the boil, made ready their skewers for the kebab. As night fell they sang songs and told stories, the park gleaming with their fires. The beauty of Herat!

Herat

Even the palaces of the rich, hiding behind their walls of green trees on the esplanades, are not palaces. The Governor is telling us about the Americans who wanted a contract to build roads in the Herat district: "They insisted on real western houses. They wanted to live as they do at home. They wanted air conditioning, canned foods, modern conveniences. We can't give them any of these things. So we had to call the whole deal off. Then along comes their ambassador and suspects me of being in Soviet pay. They can't under-

stand that the government simply won't allow such buildings in Herat."

Herat has an old wealthy upper class. By hook (or by crook) the government is trying to get them to invest their assets in the country's development. In Herat they have permission to build their big houses of sun-dried brick. But the day when air conditioning arrives in town—that day all available capital will be converted into luxuries for the upper class. The city would have to maintain an electric power station—just to cool off the upper class and the foreigners.

Beneath Herat's verdant paradisiac beauty a social drama is being enacted. Many are eating of the tree of the knowledge of good and evil, and know themselves naked. But refuse to be driven out.

III

In the morning light the dust swirls across the street. The bazaars are opening. The water-carriers are filling their water-skins. In the teahouses the day's first cups of steaming tea are being poured out. The street swarms with life and people. Civil servants in karakul caps and dark suits jostle with Tadzhiks, with Afghan nomads of the Durrani tribe, with Uzbeks and Turkmens, peasants come into town, businessmen from Iran in well-pressed suits and newly polished shoes, Hazaras with broad Mongoloid faces, learned mullahs adept in the scriptures, soldiers on leave, carpet-weavers, camel drivers, men from far and near. The samovars sing, the hubble-bubbles gurgle, and the street seethes with words in a multitude of tongues. Herat is fantastic. The fantastic thing about Herat is that it even exists.

Herat is an old city, a famous city, much fought over. It was already ancient when Alexander, who conquered the Achaemenids, passed this way on his way to the eastern satrapies of his new-won empire. Here, before marching on into world history, he founded an Alexandria. One among many. And when the clouds of dust raised by his departing soldiery had had time to settle behind the hills along the Seistan road, the daily round in Herat went on as before.

This city, ravaged, burned, and plundered, this city which seems to have stood right in the path of almost every military leader, every besieger, every conqueror, every adventurer, was always rebuilt, always rose to be wealthy enough to make it once again worth the plundering. Are human beings mere plant-lice, exuding a sweet juice for their plunderers?

In the end, cities usually find the effort too much for them. One conqueror is always the last. Then, desert and silence. Old Urgench, the great capital, and Balkh, the mother of cities, crumble to heaps of rubbish and clay. But Herat lives on. Is again conquered, again destroyed, and again rebuilt. This city which makes its appearance in written history with Zoroaster's *Avesta,* and even then had many long years and ancient traditions behind it—the multitudes still swarm its streets and markets. Here are the costliest of all carpets still woven. Here you can still sit in the teahouses and hear tales of distant lands.

Here, at its extreme eastern point, lies one of the richest agricultural areas of the high Persian plateau. Through this plain—at a height of somewhat over 2,500 feet above sea level and surrounded on three sides by mountain chains and on its fourth bordering on the desert steppe—the Hari Rud runs down from the Koh-i-Baba central massif. Here grow grapes and grain. Here are grazing grounds, and on the slopes of Paropamisus grow the pistaschio forests. It is a fertile land, with a good climate. Here irrigation schemes, canals, and kanats * were early developed.

This upland region has created the wealth of Herat.

And preserved it. Only in part is its agriculture based on irrigation. The conqueror, razing everything to the ground, could destroy the dams, fill in the wells, block up the kanats. But it was more than he could do to transform the Hari Rud Valley into a desert. Only half these farmlands depend on artificial irrigation. As long as the valley still bore crops no havoc, no destruction, could be definitive. In spite of all its disasters, Herat has remained the economic and administrative capital of a wealthy agricultural province.

But Herat is, and always has been, more than a mere well-to-do town in a farming district. Herat, at the foot of the mountains, was the high Persian plateau's gate to the east. Here the great trade routes have crossed. And here, each time its predecessor was razed to the ground, a new city grew up. These were the routes followed by the conquerors. But they too passed on, or else, having drunk their fill of pillage, turned to the ways of peace. And the routes remained. The Kingdom of the Achaemenids, shored up, collapses in chaos. The Empire of Alexander the Great turns out only to be the finale of an imperial drama. Seleucids, Parthians, Kushans, all in turn struggle for the city's possession. Herat flourishes, is razed, flourishes again. But always it remains a city, a center of trade and communications. During the millennium from Cyrus I to Yazdagard III, empires come and go, classical Persian antiquity reaches its climax and decays, migrations sweep past, nomads burst in through the valleys and settle down; new nomad tribes ride in and slough their skins—time and time again. But Herat remains.

Its conquest by the Arabs still further increases the city's importance. Herat becomes one of Islam's strongest religious and cultural fortresses. Still the conquerors ride by. Migrations and dynasties come and go. But in those days Herat is one of the richest and most cultivated cities in the richest and most cultivated region of the world —the world of Islam. The citizens of Herat are citizens of the world.

---

* An underground irrigation tunnel—Translator.

26

Their business houses and their men of learning are in regular touch with every civilized country on earth.

It was a tolerant and powerful city, in a tolerant culture. Its Nestorian Christians, exposed to no worse persecution than an obligation to pay taxes, had a bishop of their own. Islam has rarely lit fires for heretics. Religious life was not hierarchically organized.

Always open to impulses from every quarter of the compass, this city on the outskirts of Persian culture was also the city in which the new Persian culture, the synthesis of Islam's world culture and the Persian tradition, had its earliest beginnings. Here at the end of the ninth century the first Persian poems were written. This was before Herat was struck by the Mongol storm, a city said to have possessed 140,000,000 houses, 12,000 shops, 6,000 public baths and 350 schools.

In 1219 Herat submits to Jenghiz Khan. But in 1221 the city sides with Jalal-ud-din in his desperate fight against the Mongol hordes. In 1222 it is punished by Touli, son of Jenghiz Khan, and is said to have been razed to the ground and 1,500,000 of its people slaughtered. Libraries and schools were burned, but the ablest handicraftsmen were spared and carried off to the interior of Asia.

Again Herat is rebuilt. Once again, conquerors and mighty men pass by. As early as 1383 the city has again grown strong enough to be thrown down, once again, by Timur the Lame—Tamerlane the Great. But only a few years later his fourth son, Shah Rukh, has made it his capital. Herat blossoms as never before.

Today, more than half a millennium after the death of Timur the Lame, Herat is still alive. It has seen many rulers and many conquerors ride by, many adventurers and military leaders. It has been burned and ruined and plundered, been broken on the wheel, been hanged, beheaded, and turned into history—but the city has survived. Its streets are still full of people and the samovars are singing in the teahouses of its bazaars. The hookah is passing from man to man. Turkmens in black fur caps, Afghans in white shirts with embroideries from Ghazni, leaders of caravans, peasants come to town, truck drivers from distant cities and petty vendors from the mountain villages—its streets seethe with life, and every tongue mingles with every other.

It is not the Hari Rud which has allowed Herat to grow up again

27

Mausoleum of Gohar Shad, Herat

in the tracks of its plunderers. Nor the trade route. It has been the peoples from many corners of the earth who have gathered beside the Hari Rud and during millennium after millennium slaved and labored and struggled—despite all their plunderers.

IV

Of no work of art, no building, no city can one say: This is the loveliest of them all! Such statements are art-theology, bad idealism, inhuman and therefore anti-human: and an insult to art. What one *can* say about works of art, architecture, buildings or cities, is: This is one of the most beautiful.

A few places, a handful of towns, I always experience as being among the loveliest. Stockholm, the city to which I always return. Clay-brown Cordova. Leningrad—that classical city of the Baltic, with its clean perspectives of streets—in the summer twilight. New York in autumn, with its glittering wet asphalt streets, its red-leaved parks, the mists over the Hudson River, its smell of city and oil. And Herat! Herat whose beauty, every time you come out of the desert into its verdure, among its blue Timurid monuments, gives you a pang at the heart.

India's conqueror, the descendant of the Mongols, the Timurid prince Zahir-ed-din Mohammed, known as Baber, The Tiger, after struggling for many a long decade to recover his throne in his own land of Ferghana, had to be content with the conquest of India and becoming the first Mogul Emperor. He writes in his memoirs: "The whole inhabited world does not possess another city like Herat." Anyone who had once experienced the Herat of the Timurids could never again forget it—not even for all the wealth of India.

The Timurid period in Herat's history is short, it spans just one century. Just as the city had recovered from its destruction at the hands of Timur—Tamerlane the Great—he died, on March 3, 1405. Or, as he puts it in his autobiography:

> The night of the seventeenth of the month of Shaaban, I, calling on God's name, gave up the ghost and handed back my soul spotless to the Almighty and Sacred Creator.

29

A short but violent civil war between his heirs ended with Timur's fourth son, Shah Rukh, governor of Herat, firmly seated in the saddle. His heirs rule from Herat until the year 1506, when Shabyani Khan, at the head of his Uzbeks, captures the city. The Timurid epoch is over. Four years later, in 1509, Shabyani Khan loses his life. Herat is destroyed, and the greater part of its inhabitants massacred. Shah Ismail, the Safavid, establishes his new Persian kingdom.

But during this Timurid century Herat is the center of a cultural renaissance. Between two annihilations the city develops into an abode of arts and sciences. What is created in Herat at this time will be normative from the Ganges to the Euphrates for centuries to come.

The Timurid century in Herat is a counterpart to that of the Medici in Florence. The Timurid rulers' private history of civil wars, imprisonments, patricides, drunken orgies, learned discussions, wars, and intrigues could all have been written by an author of Italian Renaissance *novelle*. Bandello might have been their chronicler. Like the Medici, the Timurids are famous for keeping up a brilliant and cultivated court, whose glory was its artists and scientists, its poets and architects. Timurid intrigues and privy assassinations have acquired a historical patina, become a picturesque frame for artistic creativity and the cultured life. Many, writing of the favors of these mighty dilettanti, have thanked them for taking such an interest in culture. But culture is not measured in lists of regents. Nor is the Timurid legend really framed in court intrigue. Its frame is a frame of camel caravans.

Herat was the hub of Western Asia's mightiest commercial empire. The Mongol storm had blown down cities, exterminated whole peoples; but it had also joined up China, Central Asia, and Western Asia into one economic and commercial unit. Now, after the destruction, the cities were being rebuilt. Once again the peoples were united. A few years before Tamerlane's destruction of Herat, the peasant boy and rebel leader Chu Yüan-chang from Fengyang had driven the Mongols out of China and been proclaimed the Emperor Tsai Tsu. The policy of his new Ming dynasty was one of commercial expansion. Chinese merchant fleets sailed for Indochina, Malaya, the East Indies, India, Persia, Arabia, and East Africa. Chinese caravans crossed the Central Asian deserts, heading for Herat.

This intensive trade between the two great powers of Asia, both heirs of the Mongol Empire, led to political and cultural approaches and exchanges. In their litters the Ming Emperor's ambassadors were carried along the streets of Herat. Craftsmen from the Kingdom of the Middle sat working in Herat's bazaars. Herat's own artists and craftsmen studied Chinese décor, the Chinese way of handling different materials, Chinese technology, and the Chinese tradition in art.

During the Timurid Age the artists of Herat were by and large very much the same as artists at any other time and in any other place. They strove to do their best, within the limits of the possible. That their work was epoch-making, however, was due to the new cultural contacts, the swift transformation of society at that time. For them, too, the boundaries of the possible were extended thanks to the sudden trade boom. And this culture boom they exploited to the utmost. The painter Amir Kahlil, also known as Ghiyath-ad-din, accompanied Shah Rukh's embassy to China. He stayed there for five years studying Chinese art and writing a diary of his travels.

With the next generation of artists, Herat's painting reaches its apogée. Herat's artists were schooled in the Persian tradition, a tradition going back to the times of the Sassanids (and thus connected with French medieval art, with Byzantium, therefore with Moscow to the east and Venice to the west—art is human, not parochial). All the decorative arts of Islam were at their finger-tips. Now new impulses from Chinese culture arrive to fertilize them. They acquire customers who can afford to pay. This synthesis of traditional techniques and new impulses, in a Herat full of money and populated with ambitious barbarians, becomes a vigorous realism. There is a break with all rigid formalism. As in the Italy of the Renaissance, the measure is a human measure.

When Behzad—the leading name in the later Herat school and the man who was to be the teacher of generations—depicts the building of a new mosque, he works with distinct and clear realism. He is living in an age of great building projects. Knows the builder's art. And knows his workers. His workmen are alive. And when Gun and I, almost half a millennium later, come to Herat and see the mosque being rebuilt, then we also experience Behzad's paintings as alive. And we perceive how grey and sterile are all theories of art com-

31

pared with the realities of painting. "In spite of being derivative, his work is based on a purely pictorial synthesis in which no outward feeling, religious or profane, disturbs him. He revels in the pure joy of painting, of the miracle of line and colour for art's own sake," says my art historian. Allah preserve Behzad! But if the gods fight in vain against stupidity, art doesn't. Art outlives its theorists.

The people delineated in Behzad's paintings are strongly individualized. Behzad was close to the people and their work. This is renaissance, realism, the joy of discovery.

Husain Bayqara's empire foundered, and Husain Bayqara himself became a footnote in the history of art. But Behzad lives on.

The Herat of the Timurids saw a boom in every branch of culture, albeit not equally strong in every branch. Nor did it lead to anything comparable with the Italian Renaissance. In Herat, it is true, the first literature in the Turki tongue came into being. Persian poetry developed further. But there was no Boccaccio to write true stories of demotic life in the vernacular, nor (to jump a century) was Timurid Herat's intellectual life marked by the materialism and progressive fervor of a Giordano Bruno. In its place was Jami's mysticism and Koranic exegesis.

Both in Florence and Herat dilettanti and amateurs held sway. In the one city as in the other it was the money from the new commerce which paid for the cultural boom. But there is a basic difference, as great as the difference between the founders of the two dynasties: the sly merchant and art-collecting banker Cosimo de Medici, and the six-foot-tall, lame, redheaded world conqueror, despot, and builder of mausolea, Tamerlane the Great.

Herat was no principality in a commercial republic. It was the hub of an oriental despotism, a crossroads of the trade routes. Here no new thoughts could be developed. All that had flowered in Herat was taken over and developed by other despots, in other despotisms. When Herat fell, Behzad himself was dragged off to Tabriz. When the conqueror Humayun recovered the throne of the Moguls in Delhi, Behzad's pupils had to follow in his baggage train. From Ararat to Bengal the Herat school degenerated into a *mondain* school of court painting. In India the Mogul painters strove to ape Behzad. To rise to the same heights, not to say excel him, became every artist's wildest dream. Behzad's realism stiffened into courtly formalism. After Behzad, the Herat school did not pursue the way of a renaissance; it became aesthetic, and afterwards degenerating into pedantic court painting, died out two centuries later in ham-fisted indifference. The power of the Moguls moldered away. And its art with it.

The Timurids, a foreign, still semi-barbaric ruling caste, were builders of tombs, creators of monuments. It was to the glory of God —or rather, of the Timurid rulers—that architecture and the decorative arts were developed. Calligraphy became refined, monumentalized. Legions of building workers, hosts of craftsmen were set to work on these immense projects. It was in this environment that Behzad got his chance to work and develop. The beauty of Herat arises from the Timurid blue of its mosaic tilework, fired by his workmates, nameless masters, nearly five hundred years ago.

V

The Herat of the Timurids lies in ruins. Where the road to Meshed leads out of Herat, among the conifers, one glimpses a blue Timurid dome and some mosaic-clad minarets, standing at a distance from each other on a yellow scrubland. Far off they rise blue against the remote yellow-parched hills. The closer one approaches, the more impressively they stand up against the sky, the more blindingly white becomes the purity of their white mosaic against the blue tiles. Blue as the deep blue sky. This is architecture. Pure in over-all conception; powerfully astringent in ornamentation; and the details clear, calculated, and deceptively simple.

The yellow earth all about is a carpet of mosaic fragments. Great slabs, whole plaques, tiny details, stick up out of the parched earth. One bends down to pick them up. They crumble to dust between one's fingers. The whole field is one huge grave of architecture and art. In this soil a brilliant colorful beauty is moldering away into dust. Nothing holds the tiles together but their glazing. The minarets lean to one side. In their sides are gaping sores.

Around the mausoleum of Gohar Shad the wind sings in the treetops. Water trickles in the park canals. One tramples on pine-needles and blue tilework; and the cupola, shaped like a peeled mandarin orange, is flaking away. The blue tilework is falling down, and inside the mausoleum beautifully carved stone coffins gape open, heedlessly flung aside. On one, some European tourists have scratched their immortal names. In big figures: 1955. The dome's interior is decorated in blue, yellow, and gold stucco. Here, too, all is ruin and destruction. Yet even in this state the buildings are still lovely. After experiencing Herat, the Taj Mahal is reduced to a faint echo.

Here, during the Timurid epoch, four great buildings, the most beautiful of their time and intended to stand for centuries, were erected. In 1417 Shah Rukh's wife Gohar Shad enabled the architect Qaram ad-din to start building a musallah. Built like a mosque, it was to have been a place of prayer just outside the city. He was also permitted to build a madrasah, a high school. Further, he erected Gohar Shad's own mausoleum, in which eight Timurid princes were afterward buried. The mausoleum stood at one corner of the madrasah. The last of the Timurid rulers, Husain Bayqara, later caused yet another madrasah to be built here, beside Qaram ad-din's great achievement.

An Australian who was passing through Herat remarked to me how typically Afghan it was to allow everything to decay like this. What he meant was: If the British had ruled here everything would have been otherwise. He hadn't the faintest inkling how wrong he was. It is the Afghans who have planted the trees as a wind-break around the mausoleum and built one of the minarets into their new madrasah.

The damage is of recent date. Criminally recent. Best to let the British speak for themselves. Major C. E. Yates, C.S.I., C.M.G., Bombay Staff Corps, F.R.G.S., writes, on July 30, 1885:

> The Musalla consists in reality of the remains of three buildings running north-east and south-west and covering a space of nearly 600 yards from end to end. Of the eastern building—known generally, I believe as the Madrasah or College, nothing but two high arches facing each other and four minarets remain. The arches

Minaret at the Mausoleum of Gohar Shad

must be from 60 to 80 feet in height and are covered with the remains of what was once fine tile or mosaic work of beautiful and artistic designs—now, of course, much defaced. The tiles on the minaret have mostly been worn off by stress of weather, but inside the arches the beautiful mosaic work is still in many places almost perfect—sufficient to give one an idea of the splendour of the building when new. The minarets of this Madrasah appear taller than the rest, and must be between 120 and 150 feet in height. . . . [The Mausoleum] . . . it is faced on the east by another archway and one solitary minaret

To the west of the tomb of Shah Rukh stands the Musalla—A huge massive building of burnt brick, almost entirely faced at one time with tiles and mosaic-work, all the various patterns of which are beautifully fitted together in minute pieces set in gypsum plaster. Musalla means, I believe, a place of prayer; and doubtless on this account the walls were covered with the numerous texts in tilework that now ornament them. The main building consists of a lofty dome some 75 feet in diameter, with a smaller dome behind it, and any number of rooms and buildings around it. The entrance to the dome is through a lofty archway on the east, some 80 feet in height, the face of which is entirely covered with tilework and huge inscriptions in gilt; while above the archway is a lot of curious little rooms and passages, the use of which I cannot tell. To the east of this arch is a large courtyard some 80 yards square surrounded with corridors and rooms several storeys in height—all covered with tilework. The main entrance of all is on the eastern side of this court, through another huge archway, also some 80 feet in height; but though the inside of the arch is all lined with tiles, or rather mosaic work in regular patterns, the outside is bare and looks as if it has never been finished. Four minarets some 120 feet in height, form the four corners of the building: a good deal of the tilework has been worn off by the weather—especially towards the north, the side of the prevailing winds; but when new, they must have been marvelously handsome. It is hoped that they may be preserved from the general demolition. The rooms it is said were built for the accommodation of students, but where they came from is hard to say.

In the autumn of 1885, that is, the plan was to sweep all this away to make room for fortifications. Such were Her Britannic Majesty's express orders, and the men directly responsible for carrying them out were Major Holdich and Captain Peacock. In a thesis on Afghanistan (1950) by Lieutenant-Colonel W. K. Fraser-Tytler, K.B.E.,

36

C.M.G., M.C., this period of Afghan history is called "The Great Game Concluded—." Tsarist Russia and the British Empire were struggling for the hegemony of Asia. Well, of course one can call it a great game. See it as a sort of Russian roulette, with one slight difference: that the barrel of the revolver is not pointed at the players' heads but at the pool. The prize—the Central Asian market.

Major Yates was a military man. He cast a soldier's loving glances on Herat:

> . . . yet this is the hottest month of the year. Certainly no climate that I know of in India can hold a candle to that of Herat, and were the latter a British station with regular houses, etc. it would be one of the healthiest and pleasantest of possessions.

In the same enamoured way he looks at the population. Apropos the Afghan military he writes:

> The material that these regiments are formed of is splendid and under British influence would be fit for anything.

Riding in the mountains above Herat, he notes further in his diary:

> A perfect sanatorium, some will say, for our troops when we garrison Herat. Others, alas! say: Too late! too late! The Russians will have Herat and we cannot prevent them. Not so I trust. Not content with the admission that Herat is beyond the sphere of Russian influence, we shall soon, I hope, lay down the dictum that not only is Afghanistan within the sphere of British influence, but that it is an integral part of the British Indian Empire and that we mean to maintain that Empire in its integrity.

The state of the British administrators' feelings finds expression as early as 1880 by Major G. B. Malleson, C.S.I.:

> People talk without knowledge and without thought of the expense which will be entailed on England by the occupation of Afghanistan. It is true that the occupation of mountainous districts of Afghanistan not including Herat will entail a large expenditure, but the occupation of the whole country inclusive of Herat is a very different matter. The possessions of the valleys Herirud and the Murghab is the possession of a goldmine. In a few years Herat would prove the milch-cow of northern India . . . It is not too much to affirm that a few years of British administration would suffice to place Herat and its districts in the position with respect to Afghanistan which the province of Bengal occupies with respect

to northern India. That is, Herat would pay all the expenses of the occupation of Afghanistan and still yield something more to the treasury. But this is the least of the benefits its occupation would accomplish. The indirect wealth which would accrue to England by the possession of the key to the markets of Central Asia is not to be calculated.

But the British administrators were also obsessed by an altruistic longing to follow in the footsteps of Tamerlane the Great as defenders of culture. Malleson goes on:

The occupation of Herat by England would not only revive the commercial system which, three centuries ago, made of that city and its environs the granary and garden of Central Asia—it would also free from the withering grasp of an inferior race the descendants of the men who cherished learning, art and science when even Europe was but just emerging from the comparative barbarism of the middle ages.

The previous year the publicist Charles Marvin had expressed the British businessman's view of the Afghan question:

> There are hundreds of civil administrators and military officers in England, with their time lying idle on their hands or frittered away in useless political controversies, who would govern Afghan Turkestan for us if the country were taken charge of. There are hundreds of merchants, with capital lying useless in the banks, who would proceed to Herat, Maimene, Saripoll and Balkh, to-morrow, and develop the resources of the country if they could be guaranteed security of life and property. There are thousands of people out of work and starving, who would be benefited directly or indirectly by the establishment of our rule throughout Afghanistan, and the consequent creation of fresh markets for our surplus manufactures.

November 8, 1885, Major Holdich and Captain Peacock can report that the deed is done. The musallah and the madrasah have been blown to pieces and demolished. Major Yates writes:

> There is no doubt but that the money brought into the country by the presence of the Commission, and the expenditure on the fortifications, has given a great stimulus to trade of all sorts: and when so much could be done by the mere presence of a mere Mission, what could not be done with a British occupation?
>
> As we marched out of Herat our road led us through the Musalla. The tall minarets of which are now alone standing. The rest is simply a mass of debris which a perfect army of donkeys is engaged in clearing away.

Thus the blue Herat of the Timurids crumbled into ruins. But Herat never became British. The Russian autocracy and the British Empire fixed their mutual border, and Herat was left lying in a cordon sanitaire between them. Major Yates was never allowed to build his sanatorium for British troops on the slopes of Paropamisus, overlooking Herat. The "great game" went on.

V I

In the yard at Gazergah a lion couchant in white stone rests his heavy head on the ground. Its form merely suggested, massive, mineral, the beast seems just this very moment to have crept out from a pillar; to be resting, hunched there like a butterfly newly emerged from its chrysalis. Behind the lion stand gravestones, row upon row. Their ornamentation is crisp; their inscriptions graceful and ceremonious. Here the stone has been treated as if it were wood. The sculptors have toyed with the forms. But out of his great round saucer-like eye-holes the great animal, his back turned on all these ceremonious gravestones, stares blindly past wandering pilgrims clutching sandals, past holy men, readers of the Koran, blind beggars, toward the Sanctuary gate.

The first time I was in Gazergah that great white beast, where he lay pressed to the ground on the crumbling ledges, letting the grass grow up around his stone body, had escaped my notice. That time all I saw was the splendor of Gazergah. The mosaics, the Chinese inspiration, the clear colors. The trees soughed. Far below us to the southwest lay Herat.

This was where Shah Rukh's builders were at work in 1428. Here are tombs of saints and rulers, tombs of famous men, graves of the less famous. On their coffins, exhilarating stone sculptures. Sovereign craftsmanship, toying and playing with the hard medium, forcing stone to imitate wood, or plaster, or indeed any other material. The Indian craftsman's scorn for his materials. Such sleight of hand is usually tasteless. Stone aping stucco, until one has to lay one's hand on the material to reassure oneself; the trompe l'oeil of sculpture, clever but soulless: but here stylish, so sure of itself as to be almost forgivable in the thoroughness with which the whole conception is carried through; this incredibly fine and meticulous floral ornamentation in black stone.

Here the mosaics which at Herat we had only been able to see in ruins, in patches and shattered fragments, were to be seen grandiose, intact, covering whole walls. Here, too, were mosaic walls of Sino-Mongol inspiration, in which the great rectangular and quadrangular elements made an astonishingly "modern" impression. Here everything our own non-figurative artists were struggling and experimenting with at home in Sweden had already been accomplished. But so much more surely carried through, so infinitely more grandiose, more exquisite—and for patrons who, when they placed their orders for these walls, had not been stingy in supplying the necessary tiles.

That time I had hardly seen the stone lion, out there in the yard. Not until I came back next year did I really notice him. At once the beast became, for me, a problem. Where had he come from? What epoch did he represent? I could not make up my mind. Certainly it was not the same artist who had toyed so superlatively with his materials on the tombstones and coffins. The beast was altogether too clumsy, too stony. But in its very clumsiness clever. The animal was stone. Where it crept out of its pillar, a block of stone, it represented quite a different school of art, with a wholly different mode of thinking, from the other school which had worked at Gazergah. So much was obvious. Questionless the lion must have been sculpted by other artists, having quite other traditions. Artists who thought in stone. But which? And why was it lying in the yard at Gazergah?

Today, almost six months after I last set eyes on him, it is still this stone beast which fascinates me most. I only have to close my eyes to see his heavy immobile visage staring, dead, almost malicious, out of those empty holes for eyes, toward the great sanctuary raised over the poet Abdullah Ansari.

VII

Early one morning we leave Herat. The sun is still so low that even the grains of sand on the road cast violet shadows. We drive out from the oasis. Ahead, the valley widens out as it approaches the mountains. A road leads off to our right and an arrow points to the east: Kabul. The central route via Hazarajat and the high mountains. Just now, we've been told, it's impassable. Its embankments have been washed away by the spring rains, and the bridge across the Hari Rud is perilously rusted. So we continue toward the northeast, and the other road sinks behind the hillocks. To our left a village, still Persian, with cupola-shaped roofs and windbreaks. The road narrows, passes through dried-out river beds, then slowly begins climbing upward. We meet a man on a donkey. He salutes us.

The sun rises in the sky. The contours of the landscape grow softer in the mist and dust-haze; but the hillocks are crowned with bristling thorn bushes, whose firm contours jut up out of the morning mist. We are on our way into the mountains. The colors begin to take on a reddish tinge. We pass a few villages. At one point a heavily laden caravan of donkeys is resting in the shade of trees beside an irrigation canal. We drive through ravines, and the road becomes still narrower, its curves get sharper and the valley ever more deeply enclosed. Now the mist has lifted. The air is clearing. The sky turning a deeper blue. For a long while we follow a stream of clear water. Here and there, grass-grown slopes. We cross a ford; and now the road begins climbing upward in earnest, up toward the high pass. Sheepdogs circle round us, barking as we drive past their flocks; but their shepherds call to them, and the dogs leave us. The landscape is still bare and treeless. The deeply rutted sandy and serpentine road winds onward. Now the stream has disappeared, leaving only a dry thin watercourse following the road up into the mountains. Then, in the distance, we see a solitary juniper tree. We approach. A huge juniper bush, bowing and swaying in the wind, yet tall and green. We reach it. Then the pass. Sabzak. The little green pass. Where at a height of 7,800 feet the road passes over Paropamisus.

To the north the mountains are hard and craggy. Immense juniper bushes cover their slopes. Rock formations reminiscent of the Grand Canyon. Bright sharp reds and whites against this incredibly deep blue sky. It's cold up here, and all about us the wind whistles icily. This is the watershed between the Hari Rud and the Murghab; and now the character of the landscape has changed completely. It's harder now, its colors so clear as almost to beggar belief. And the pass the loveliest we've seen.

As we drive on down toward what used to be called Afghan Turkistan, the road winds dizzily beneath the jagged peaks, runs out onto a white field of drifting sands where hundreds of round tufts of grey-green vegetation come rolling toward us. Their growing period over, their roots have lost all grip on the dry sandy ground. In the strong wind they go rolling past us, upward in the direction of the pass. Ahead, white eroded mountains. And all the while this sweeping wind.

Driving down into the valley we follow a dried-out watercourse. Soon it becomes a rill, grows into a stream. We meet houses, people.

42

Now the villages are no longer built of sun-dried clay. Instead, flat roofs; low houses built of stone and clay. Row on row they line the mountainside. Seem almost to creep into the rock, or melt into the hard ground. Stone of its stone. Along the stream, narrow strips of plowed land. Long stretches of dry desert, grazing land; then a new cluster of low houses. This is a landscape barren of trees, except along the irrigation canals. Yet the houses are not built of sun-dried clay. Their roofs are quite flat. Rest on knotty beams.

We follow the stream in a northeasterly direction, the dust whirling up behind us. It is afternoon. And hot. The hillocks wear such an empty and deserted air, the grey villages are all so sleepy and void of inhabitants. Suddenly, a village. Now cupola-shaped roofs. Sun-dried brick. A wind-break. In the distance, great nomad camps. This is no boundary. It is a transitional region.

Ahead of us, then, between the hills, we see a cloud of dust rising, and hear a thunderous roaring of hoofs, pounding the earth. Rounding a corner we run into hundreds of mounted men and a host of footmen. In the dust swirling all about them they seem at first to be carrying rifles over their shoulders. Yet this is no Turkmen raid—as we see when we get yet closer—of the sort described by travelers in the last century. Nor is it rifles they are carrying on their shoulders. But spades. Sacks of gravel hang from their saddles. We stop. A few of the mounted men are on horseback; most on donkeys. These are the peasantry of the district, on their way to do a job of road maintenance. Twice a year they gather and with spades and sacks of sand ride out to improve those sections of the road for which they are responsible. Laughing and pointing they say, "Over there you won't get on so easily! It's only yesterday we rode out there with the sand. We haven't had time to spread it yet."

In a cloud of dust, amid a roar of hoofs and footfalls, they ride away, spades over their shoulders, sacks of sand at their saddles. Turning, they wave to us. The road deteriorates. Every two yards, between the wheel-ruts, a heap of gravel. If we drive in the ruts, then our radiator runs straight into the gravel heaps. The car staggers; and our right wheels have to clamber over heaps of sand. Skidding in these sandy wheel-ruts, we drive out instead over the rough terrain beside the road, but where it rises into a sandy heathland we are forced back to the road again. Right in the middle of the steep slope,

44

where the wheels spin round and round in the loose gravel and the heaps of sand make it impossible for the engine to keep up any speed, we get a puncture. Swearing, I patch the inner tube. But looking up over her sketch pad, Gun says consolingly, "Well, at least someone's looking after the road. In a country like this, that means a lot."

VIII

We drive toward Maimana. The road is narrow and bad. Winding between sand dunes, it runs along dried-out river beds, dry and brittle now in the summer heat, and clambers over the mountains' last outlying spurs. Along the bottoms of valleys, where water has gathered, are strips of greenery. On the slopes above, black nomad tents. Grazing camels and flocks of sheep. Little clay-yellow villages cluster at the foot of the hills. To the west lies the Turkmen Desert and the Soviet frontier; to the east, Band-i-Turkistan and Hazarajat, in the central mountain massif.

This is a branch of the old Silk Route. One of the ancient roads along which history and culture first came into being. We joined it early this morning on leaving Bala Murghab, a place with a heavy clay castle and winding rows of little whitewashed clay huts. All the doors had just been painted peacock blue. A little place, far from the main routes, it was nevertheless once great and famous. In those days it was called Marvarud: Merv-on-the-River, as distinct from the real Merv, the great oasis out in the western desert. The road led from Merv via Marvarud to Yahudia—the medieval name for Maimana— and thence via Shibarghan and Balkh went on in the direction of China.

Descending from the sand hills and boulders the road emerges onto the irrigated plains. Poplars shading irrigation canals. The road traverses fertile oasis villages; now, in the siesta, silently asleep. At midday the shadows shrink and the village mongrels doze in the irrigation canals, only their noses and eyes showing above the surface of the calmly flowing muddy water. We drive past. Behind our little grey car the dust flies out in an ever widening cone, and the smattering of the engine causes the dogs to leap up, shake the water

46

out of their fur, and run howling and barking after us. We drive away. The dust settles. The noise of our engine dies away. The dogs go back to sleep. Over more sandhills, through new river beds, the road goes on and on. Steep slopes. Sandy gradients. Sharp curves. Disturbed by our wheels the gravel goes rattling away down toward the bottom of the valley. Then the landscape opens out again—and there lies Maimana, greyish white, mud-colored, amid the greenery of its oasis. Now in the afternoon the poplars are casting long shadows. We come down onto the plain, and ahead of us a policeman is standing on traffic duty. Snaps his heels together; waves us on. All alone he stands there on the grey dusty road, his face wearing a serious expression. In the driving mirror, after we have passed him and are on our way into the town, I see how he begins walking after us. All the afternoon he has been standing there, waiting for our car.

Down a brand-new esplanade we drive in toward the city center. Maimana looks as if it has just been bombed. The little grey clay houses, which used to shore each other up, have all been torn down, are vanished. Reconstruction work is going on. A new city is being planned. Esplanades are being laid out, green belts are being planted. This in itself is of no great interest; towns are changing everywhere. But it so happens that this particular transformation is the latest act in a very long urban drama. A drama not merely of roads and all the years of the silk trade, and all who have carried the seeds of culture along this route; but a drama which began when humanity first became human.

Maimana, a little town, far from today's highways. Known, if at all, only for its carpet-weavers and its sheep-breeding; a town with an agricultural upland and newly laid-out esplanades. Maimana has a long history.

The region around the high mountains which bear up Afghanistan is an early land of wheat, peas, and lentils. It is one of the three regions in the world in which rye first grew. Here, between the mountains and the steppes, agriculture started early. And history begins. Man achieving a food surplus. From those first granaries have arisen all our later cultures, all our religions, our classes, our division of labor, our private property, the state and the family—all have their origin in those long-vanished granaries at Maimana. That handful of wheat which in good years the women found they had left over

47

after the family had eaten its fill and enough had been set aside for sowing, was to prove more explosive than any hydrogen bomb.

But it was not up here, in these bleak highlands, that the first great revolution was completed. Maimana itself never became a city. City cultures first grew up down beside the great rivers, and it was there that this surplus showed its power to build states, sprout into religions, and create cities. Labor made fertile the great valleys. The Nile. The Indus. Mesopotamia. The Yellow River. And it was there mankind first divided itself up into social classes, the slaves sinking into misery and abject poverty to enable the favorites of the gods to live in luxury.

Out of that surplus arose all art, all culture, all theology, all science. Mankind had taken a step forward—and for men life became suffering and the earth a vale of tears.

Maimana did not lie in any of these civilized areas. Nor was it a town. Only a village. But Maimana did not lack contacts with these great civilizations—even at that early date the trade route passed through. From here Badakhshan's lapis lazuli was transported down to the urban cultures. Lapis lazuli has been found in first-dynasty graves at Ur, about 3,200 B.C. In Egypt, in fourth-dynasty graves, 2,600 B.C. And there is lapis lazuli at Troy II, on whose ruins, before Homer's heroes laid waste Ilion, four other cities had time to grow up. And all this lapis lazuli passed through Maimana.

The great migration, too, passed this way. Here the Aryans rested before going down to Herat and through the Bolan Pass into India. A thousand years before our era began, Zoroaster was preaching at Balkh, four days' journey northeastward along the lapis lazuli route. And still Maimana wasn't a town. Only a village, its dwellings inhabited by a clan of peasants under a chieftain responsible for their trade. None of which is certain or incontestable, is more than faintly glimpsed in the mists of time.

Under the Achaemenids Maimana falls under the sway of Persia. The roads are extended; trade, no longer being exclusively occupied with luxury goods but dealing also in raw materials and expendable goods, expands. In the seventh and sixth centuries before Christ the price of ore falls. The roads have become safe, and trade is based on narrow profit margins. At Maimana, perhaps, there resides a representative of one or another of the great banks: Murash & Sons of

Nippur; or Egibis Ltd, of Babylon. The village begins to take on a town-like character.

But no matter which kingdom controlled—or regarded itself as controlling—the town, its real rulers were the dikhans, the great landlords. They were closely allied to the great traders, the men of money. This type of society gave the town its character. The heart of the city, the medina or sharistan, belonged to the dikhans. At various times, there was a fortress within this inner town; at others, it stood to one side of it. Outside lay suburbs, gardens inhabited by the artisans, the useful part of the population. Around these suburbs ran an outer town wall. But the inner heart of the city always belonged to the dikhans—the idle and useless part of the population. They owned the soil. Controlled trade. Controlled the city.

To a superficial glance this city-type appears to have remained unchanged for a thousand years. Wars, havoc along the great trade route, swept over it like typhoons. But its character seems to have remained unaffected. Leading families came and went; but not the leading class. Even the Greeks' renowned Kingdom of Bactria wrought no essential changes. One baron gave place to another; but the latter, having no wife, married into his predecessor's family.

With the caravans arrive not only goods, but also craftsmen. The suburban districts, where they live, grow and grow. Chinese goldsmiths and silversmiths set up shop. Chinese ironsmiths move in, take on native apprentices. No longer is it only a few craftsmen's quarters which are to be found spread out among the suburban gardens, overshadowed by the castle and the dikhans' sharistan. Now entire districts of craftsmen are to be found there, with their own factories and caravanserais. The lower-class independent artisans begin to acquire power. But the castle and the inner city—the sharistan —still retain political and economic control; and therewith, too, their status as the city's heart. Finally, during the bloody and violent social conflict preceding the Arab conquest, the power of the dikhans is reduced. But it is not the people who are the beneficiaries. It is the central government bureaucracy.

During the three hundred years which pass between the Arab conquest of Central Asia and the climax of Islamic culture, a great change really does take place. Now it is not the power of the dikhans, but of the central bureaucracy, which is significant. What matters now, the key to power, is not to control the land, but to stand close to the throne, which owns all land. Out of a long struggle between local landowners, the slave population and the bureaucracy, an Asiatic despotism has finally been crystallized. It may be tyrannical, but for Maimana's craftsmen its tyranny is easier to bear than the cumulative weight of all the despotisms of the slave-owning petty despots. Trade flourishes. The town's character changes. The craftsmen's quarters not only grow; they take charge. By the end of those three centuries the suburbs have become the heart of the city, and the old center has been thrust out into the suburbs. A new city-type has come into being.

The commercial city. From its gates the streets, flanked by bazaar stalls and business houses, lead in toward the center to meet in an indoor bazaar under whose vaults buying and selling can go on at all seasons and all hours of the day or night. Where the four main streets cross, the vaulting rises to a tremendous central dome: the charsun. The merchant city has found its form. Its center is neither castle nor mosque, but that richly embellished dome beneath which the great money-changers have their stalls.

Towns develop into municipal republics, ruled by their own commercial aristocracy; a commercial aristocracy which, having first grown out of the craftsmen and petty merchants, at once proceeds to draw up a hard and fast dividing line between them and itself. The craftsmen's guilds close their ranks. Tension between them and the moneyed aristocracy explodes in violent riots.

It is a long while now since the people bore arms, since they were disarmed. Now the army is a Turkish legionary force. The former rulers, the dikhans, have been partly thrust aside, partly assimilated by the central bureaucracy. Now the rulers have their own learned men of religion, out of touch with the people. For their part the oppressed peasants, the poor artisans, porters in the bazaars, follow their own saints, their enthusiasts, their sectarians, their ascetics, their teachers of the one true faith.

This great revolution takes place at the moment which sees the emergence of new city-types in Russia, Bohemia, Poland, and Germany. Over the whole of that vast area, stretching as far as to England and the North Sea, towns undergo a change. Now it is the new world-commerce which is building cities. A change reflected in language: at Maimana the sharistan with its suburb—the Rabad—becomes the heart of a new city. *Detinets* and *Posad* in Russia. *Burg* and *Stadt* in Germany. City and town in England.

But Maimana did not lie outside the perimeter of the earth. Though its transformation had been brought about by the struggles between dikhans, bureaucrats, artisans, and peasants, the change also reflects the tremendous revolution then going on throughout the medieval world. And new wealth attracted new conquerors.

The Mongol Storm. A strange expression! As if it all had something to do with meteorology, or were a natural phenomenon. Popularly it is explained by the drought in Central Asia or some other non-human phenomenon. No one is responsible for a storm. But wars are not storms. They have human causes. And the Mongol invasions of Chorasmia were a struggle for the trade route. It all began with the Shah's attack on Jenghiz Khan's caravans. Jenghiz had written to the Shah:

> Greetings. I know thy power and the great extent of thy kingdom, and I look upon thee as mine own much-beloved son. For thy part, know that I have conquered Cathay and also many nations of the Turks. My land is a mine of silver and a camp of warriors, and I have no need of more countries. We have a common interest, it seems to me, in promoting trade between our subjects.

Yet the Shah had Jenghiz's caravan cut down. At the Shah's orders, hundreds of merchants were executed in the frontier fortress of Otrar. Jenghiz Khan writes:

> Thou hast chosen war. What will be, shall be. Of what sort it will be, we know not. Only God knoweth.

The Mongol wars meant the butchery of entire peoples and a liquidation of cultures only to be compared with the wars of twentieth-century Europe. A whole culture went into its grave. But for certain cities the Mongol wars did not entail destruction. The great merchants were friendly toward the Mongols. The Mongols were promoters of trade and maintainers of roads. As for the craftsmen's guilds and the population at large, in their eyes there was little difference between a Turkish Shah and a Mongol Khan, while in the eyes of Jenghiz Khan and the Shah alike the people were an amor-

phous mass whom God Almighty had himself given into their hands
to labor and pay taxes. The bureaucracy still kept its power—even
the Mongols needed clerks and scribes. The main difference, at
least to begin with, was that the Mongols did not tolerate corruption.
This from the people's point of view was a distinct improvement.
The only element which on the Mongols' arrival vanished from the
urban picture was the dikhans, the last great landowners. They were

no match for the nomads. Land values fell. Those of the landowners who had not become assimilated into the bureaucracy or merchant aristocracy were absorbed into the proletariat and foundered as a ruling caste.

In appearance, however, the town remained unchanged. The form it had assumed in the course of ten centuries was the form in which it was to survive until the beginning of our modern epoch. The streets still led up to the covered bazaar and were united under the central dome. The main streets were still connected by a network of little winding lanes and alleys forking into culs-de-sac and dark corners. For some, the mosques of the official religion; for others, the miracle-working graves of saints, dear to popular faith. For the bureaucracy, the palace; for the legionaries, the castle. As for the tiller of the soil—he whose first mother had once held in her hands that handful of surplus seed out of which all this had emerged—he was as poor and oppressed as ever. Oppressed by nomad hordes, taxed and impoverished, he was far more grievously downtrodden than ever his first mother had been. But the cities were wealthy and powerful. When the Mongols had laid waste the countryside, the rich had become richer than ever.

IX

Medieval Maimana was a powerful and wealthy city. A merchant city, in which a traveler would meet countrymen and hear news from home. Yet Maimana was not the richest nor the most important town on the trade route. Far from it. It was only a minor town, where caravans transferred their loads.

What medieval citizen of Maimana could ever have thought that half a millennium later popular romanticism would style his life-rhythm "calm," his town "picturesque," or himself an "unchanging oriental"? His town seethed with activity. In the stalls along its bazaar streets products from all over the known world were on sale, even skins from the faraway land of dwarfs, by the frozen sea, the countries north of the Arctic Circle. The coins Maimana's money-changers threw down on their counters to test their silver content came from every country. Amid clouds of dust the caravans came tramping into the city, their camel drivers shouting and yelling, and their camel bells tinkling incessantly.

On those streets the medieval citizen of Maimana rubbed shoulders with strangers from every corner of the earth. The day's gossip in the teahouses was as likely to concern the Emperor of China as the King of France or Ali Muhammed, the barber next door. It was a world with wide horizons. To be a citizen of Maimana was to be a citizen of the entire civilized world.

That the religious way of seeing things held sway over men's minds, or that fanaticism was only with difficulty restrained by the businessman's monetary interests, was no circumstance peculiar to Asia.

How did it come about, then, that within a few centuries these rich and living cities had declined into nothing more than dusty oasis villages? Usually the blame is laid on the "discovery" of the sea route to India. This new route is alleged to have out-competed the caravan route—whose cities consequently declined. Once again, a thumping oversimplification.

For nearly two thousand years the trade route between Europe, China, and India had provided both the occasion and the theater of wars. Though these wars had interrupted the trade, they had never been able to destroy it. Even when the Crusaders razed Byzantium to the ground—the greatest market town in Europe—the situation had not changed. The Turks had taken over; and the trade had gone on.

Neither was the sea route to India new or unknown. That Europe after a long period of barbarism and decay should have reopened this route seemed no more than a revival of the policies of Imperial Rome. During the struggle between Rome and the Kingdom of the Parthians most of Rome's oriental trade had gone by sea. The Periplus gives detailed sailing instructions for Roman ships bound for India. Roman factories lay dotted all along India's coasts right into the Bay of Bengal. The Periplus describes how Chinese commodities came down from Balkh over the Hindu Kush to Barygaza, Northern India's great export harbor. Right up to the beginning of the eighteenth century the volume of Europe's Indian trade was hardly in excess of what it had been in Roman times.

But this time the opening of the sea route meant decline and poverty for the trading cities along the Silk Route. During the Parthian wars those towns had still been small, with a hinterland adequate to their support. Though significant, their trade had been mostly local. They had been small compact fortress towns, in the hands of a landowning aristocracy. But now the situation had changed. Local trade had declined. The hinterland was no longer wealthy. The Mongols had not destroyed the trading cities—on the contrary, they had made possible their further development by providing a new network of roads and greater safety for those who traveled along them. But they changed the cities' circumstances. Agriculture had been transformed into grazing. Great areas had been laid waste, never again to recover. Travelers at the end of the fourteenth century describe how the little towns had been wiped out and laid waste, how where there had once been farming districts were now grazing lands. Maimana itself had grown richer and more powerful, but at the expense of the smaller towns. Its hinterland was poorer, its local trade without much importance, its entire economy based on the taxes gathered by its administrators and on world trade. The merchant cities, which had become isolated cultural units in the midst of the grazing lands, were wholly dependent on the roads being kept open. When they were strangled and trade passed to the sea routes, Maimana began to decline; until not even the heaviest-handed tax-gatherer could squeeze enough money out of that exhausted region to keep the town's life going in all its former splendor.

Simultaneously, a great change had been occurring in Europe. Its society had been transformed. The gold of the Americas had been brought across the ocean. Its states, too, had altered. And when, in the eighteenth century, the British begin to force their way up through India, it is soon apparent that their interests are not going to be restricted to establishing factories and trading stations. After exploiting the country to the utmost and carrying off its wealth to Britain, they establish their own tax-gathering system. Later they turn the entire Indian subcontinent into a preserve for British trade and British goods. And now the decline becomes precipitous. In India it can be seen clearly in the vast slum areas; and finally, in

55

the nineteenth century, after the British had established their upper-class school system, in the whole crushing spiritual castration which has contributed to the enormous poverty of modern India.

From India that decay is spreading. Mass poverty is eating up Asia like a cancer. The living city has become the picturesque city, the type of city popularized by travelers and romantics as "typically oriental." Walls bulge and collapse, the mighty vaults fall in, the ground is strewn with fragments of mosaic. With vanishing prosperity the whole urban organism begins to die. Plundered of their lead linings, the irrigation canals which used to bring the city its clear drinking water begin to leak, crack, and dry up. Wherever water still trickles, the canal's course, for lack of anyone to clean it, becomes blocked with slime. Drinking water has to be fetched from home-made wells in backyards. The street kennels (open gutters) turn into ditches, stinking with filth. Disease and poverty set their stamp on the town. Of a clean white city nothing is left but fly-blown romanticism and epidemics.

The decay of Maimana was of such sort that not even any remains or ruins of its former greatness are now to be seen. With poverty and the decay of the trade comes banditry. The nomads turn to plunder. With no caravans left for them to lead the caravan drivers become roving robbers. Out of sheer poverty and misery even the Turkmens, who in adventure stories are made to seem so thrillingly powerful and virile, give themselves up to plunder. One of the leaders of the raids against the Maimana region, a Turkmen from Yulatan, gave evidence in the nineteenth century:

> Thus the entire result of our plunder was 140 krans, which we got from the sale of cows, horses, etc. Of this I got 40 krans and each of my men 10 krans. This was all we got out of sixteen days' hard and dangerous work. Plunder is certainly most unprofitable work. I was engaged in it for many years, and when I gave it up I was indebted to the extent of 150 tillahs (1 tillah = 13.5 krans). Whereas in the days when I was still a shepherd and before I was forced to turn to plundering I had saved up enough to buy myself a wife. I never managed to do that when I was plundering.

Everything combined to annihilate the urban culture—the British campaigns in Afghanistan which demanded the last ounce of effort from the population if they were to keep their independence;

British policy, which blocked their trade and strangled the whole country; the incessant plunder raids of the Turkmens; all the interior strife in a poor and ravaged land. Within a period of less than thirty years Maimana was captured no less than eight times:

1855	(1868–70 famine)
1858	1875
1859	1876
1860	1882
1868	

While all this is going on the surrounding nomads, poverty-stricken and starving plunderers, make incessant raids. In the oasis of Maimana agriculture shrinks steadily. When no one any longer dares go there for fear of being attacked the outlying fields have to be abandoned. Vámbéry, visiting Maimana in the 1860's, describes the town as being in the dirtiest, poorest state of decay he has ever set eyes on. The final act. The end of trade and industry. Of that once proud merchant city nothing now remained. Of its civic culture, hardly so much as a memory. A filthy little village of clay huts among the sand dunes. The state of its peasants was indescribable. A few centuries had sufficed for a whole culture to be wiped out.

This was also the period when in Europe the ascendant bourgeoisie's romantic orientalism stood in fullest flower. Asia's annihilated culture was imported as knickknacks for gentlemens' smoking rooms. Smoking sets were called "Moroccan tables." On the walls of those smoking rooms hung steel engravings showing an "unchanging oriental" smoking his hookah in a picturesquely decaying city.

X

When in the first days of November, 1885, Major Holdich and Captain Peacock were at last able to send messengers to the telegraph station at Meshed, to report to the Viceroy in Calcutta and Her Britannic Majesty in London that their work had been accomplished and that Herat's monuments had been blown sky-high, they thought

they were witnessing the beginning of a new era. As the Timurid vaultings caved in, the Central Asian market would at last open up to the British Empire. To the sound of salutes from the demolition squads' explosives a new age was being born.

But those explosions were to mark the end of the period of decline. The Tsarist autocracy and the British Empire reached an amicable settlement over the markets. Afghanistan became neutral

—but without the right to manage her own foreign affairs. Nevertheless, the great Amir, Abd-er-Rahman, succeeded in restricting British influence, which required that Afghanistan should not have relations with any other power. To save his country's independence he cut it off from all relations whatsoever. The British Empire never reached Herat. Its military mission had to withdraw across the deserts to the south, and return to British India. Thereafter the frontier commission's work began. The frontier was fixed. But Afghanistan remained free.

Now Maimana's Turkmen frontier was marked and blocked by Cossacks. And the raids ceased. With an iron hand Abd-er-Rahman united the country. The day of the petty kings and robber chieftains was over. Where necessary, he had the robbers' heads built into the masonry of his watchtowers. The roads again became passable. Governors, sub-governors, village elders were all made responsible with their own necks for travelers' safety. Slowly, Maimana begins to recover.

To say recovery led to prosperity would be an exaggeration. The terrible wars of liberation from the British had been too costly. Long years of chaos had ruined the country. The British Empire held it in a strangle-hold; and no longer was there any question of world trade. Even so, as the nineteenth century ended and the twentieth began, the country began to recover under the sign of a strict and astringent life-style.

Maimana was rebuilt as a town around the governor's castle. In a manner of speaking, the city plan again resembled what it had been before the Middle Ages and its development into a great city. Again Maimana became the center of an agricultural district, a town of carpet-weavers and dealers in hides. Its center was the earth-brown fortress. It was a town for local commerce, a provincial capital in the remote outskirts of the realm. Gone were the great transcontinental caravans. Instead, its roads were traveled by the nomad merchants' solitary camel caravans and the donkey caravans of its local commerce. In comparison with the first half of the nineteenth century, however, or with the preceding period, trade flourished. Every third mile stood a robat—a fortified caravanserai, with guards and accommodation for travelers and beasts. Trade from Afghan Turkistan down to the Hari Rud Valley passed through Maimana.

Gone are the bazaars and merchants' palaces. The muddy winding alleys push their way between the river bank and the main highway. The bazaars are thatched over with minimal straw roofs. There is almost no artistic embellishment. The art of vaulting is dying out. A poverty-stricken cluster of architecturally meager shacks in sun-dried brick grows up. A poor country can no longer afford the style which even a poor man can achieve in a prosperous one. Maimana is a town without a city plan. But a town whose inhabitants can at least be sure of life and limb. Through their relatives in Bukhara and Meshed a handful of Jewish businessmen manage the minimal long-distance commerce. A visitor from distant parts is a rare phenomenon.

Slowly, planlessly, the town continues to develop, its level of prosperity rising slowly, up to the thirties. Robert Byron, who visits it at that time, describes it as a minor trading town. A town where all the peoples of Afghanistan (no longer of all Asia) jostle each other in the bazaars. He stresses its lack of architectonic character. But even when he arrives, its castle is already in ruins. The commander is living in a villa in the suburbs.

We arrive in Maimana for the first time just as its governor has begun to demolish it. The second time, just as the new town is beginning to take shape. Since Byron's visit a whole generation has passed away. The old caravan routes have become motor roads—none too good driving, admittedly. As early as the beginning of the thirties, the road from Herat to Mazar-i-Sharif was opened for motor traffic. During the subsequent generation motor traffic has gradually become a serious competitor to the caravans. A car carries more than a camel. It travels further in a day. And, if properly looked after, lasts as long. Most long-distance goods and all passengers now travel by the overladen trucks. The old caravanserai, the only building in town of architectural interest, is abandoned. Pulled down, it gives place to the new hotel and its parking lots. The truck driver, his mate, and his brakeman have supplanted the camel driver.

Trade has grown. The world market is wide open to sheepskin furs. The karakul must be got out to the markets. Schools have been opened. Doctors have been commandeered to Maimana. The governor's order to demolish the town has begun to be implemented.

Great wide streets, provided with pavements and electric light (even if it doesn't always function), have been cut right through the jumble of muddy lanes and clay huts. It is hoped that in a few years the streets will be asphalted. At the street corners traffic police have been stationed. There they stand stiffly at attention, directing the traffic of the future; a traffic which as yet hardly exists. But when it does, it will not lack controls.

The bazaars have been cleared away, their old streets opened up and aired. There they lie, now, in their whitewashed hygienic rows, along streets which run parallel to the main road. Block by block, the little narrow winding alleys are vanishing, and their place is being taken by straight residential streets, with rectangular blocks, and streets crossing them at right-angles. No one stops to consider what may be picturesque.

The perspective of the new streets leads up to the central square of the town, the hill where the authorities formerly ordered the governor's fortress to be raised in sun-dried clay. Today a new palatial cinema stands there instead, with white pillars and pink walls. The film posters provide a splash of color against the houses' whitewashed walls. Only a decade ago films were banned by the mullahs. Films were immorality, were anti-religious. Now it is the cinema, the temple of the new enlightenment, not the mosque, not the castle, not the charsun, which is the new city center, and the police are ready.

What is vanishing is not the monuments. The monuments have either been destroyed already, as at Herat, or else are not yet excavated. What is disappearing is slums. The decayed city.

Just as I am writing this, a Dutch merchant arrives here in Kabul on a visit. He laughs at the Afghans. Says they're out of their wits. Here at Kabul the authorities have had all the façades of houses on the main streets repainted in one color—and sent the bill to their proprietors. The authorities have also decided to allow only one sort of marquee sunshade. The Dutchman has a good laugh at such vain lunacy. I remember one night, a year ago, all the wooden balconies were suddenly torn off the façades of the houses. The wooden balconies represented a dangerous fire risk; they were also unaesthetic. That time, too, the demolition bills were sent to the proprietors. And now, when I take a walk in the city, I see it is more beautiful.

XI

It is hot. And the air heavy. It's very hot, and we can't sleep. The doors stand open onto the loggia. We go outside, and all around us the heat is like black velvet. We're at Andkhui. The rest-house stands on an artificial hill rising out of the great steppe; but over the steppe, the house, and ourselves the breathless July heat lies like a bolster. Even the hill cannot pierce this all-embracing blanket of heat. An old trading town and sheep-breeding center, with a network of caravan routes stretching far and wide all around it, Andkhui lies in the northwest corner of Afghanistan. We have come out into the plains, up in the Amu Darya region.

Just now, in July, there is a water shortage. As we passed it the river was all dried up and in the canals only a slowly drifting driblet of liquid clay. The subsoil water, they tell me, lies at a depth of two hundred feet. The tea had a salty taste to it. For our washing we were only allowed small jugs of water, fetched from a distance. Despite the drought, the heat is heavy and humid. For lack of proper washing facilities one's skin feels sore and dusty, every pore blocked with dust. Though we are out of the highlands now, and only a thousand feet above sea level, we are in the great plain of Central Asia, the heart of a continent, far from any sea. I sit smoking with my back against one of the pillars of the loggia. Beneath us the town, with its cupola roofs, its tanneries, its bazaars, caravanserais, and teahouses. Here and there an occasional yellowish red light glimmers, faint in the dusty air. We are on the fringes of the Kara Kum Desert. From its black sands great waves of heat come rolling toward us through the night.

Beneath us passes a caravan. Then another. The caravans are traveling at night now, to avoid the burning midday heat. And all the while the song-like sound of camel bells, from far and near. The bells' monotonous jingling is pierced by men's voices calling to their beasts. Through the soft sound-patterns woven by the camel-bells the voices strike us like blows.

Just after the liberation of Norway in 1945, when I was eighteen, and living in Oslo beside the West Station, I used to sit all night long at my window listening to the sound of wagon wheels passing over the joints in the line and the whistling of the locomotives, and after following the track-workers' lanterns returned again to my heaps of books and my studies. This was the romance of reality. Anyone who calls camels romantic can only do so on the same grounds. This land's entire culture has been based on camel transport. All along the routes the caravanserais and robats are found every eight or nine miles. The geographical unit of measurement is the distance a camel can go in a day. A camel is an item of transport equipment. Its maximum load is limited. Its rate of march slow. But it gets there. The camel suits the climate and the landscape.

Driving over the Sabzak Pass we had also crossed the "camel line." Everything south of that line and south of the Hindu Kush is dromedary territory, reaching as far as to Arabia and North Africa. The two-humped camel's homeland is far away, by the Gobi Desert. But all along the caravan routes of inner Asia walk the long-haired, two-humped, unflagging, hard-working beasts.

In my youth I owned a children's encyclopedia. It described these beasts as slow-witted, stupid, obstinate, and cowardly. Their only redeeming feature, it seemed, was their toughness and capacity for hard work, typical of the beast of burden. These words, however, were written in the days of European greatness—the days when Teutonic dust was being blown all over our countries and into our eyes. When even animals could be condemned for cowardice.

Now I have made their acquaintance. And I find them wise, well adapted. They prefer flight to a fight for which they are not suited. They decline any burden beyond their capacity. They know their own nature, and their climate. A baby camel has the touching helplessness of all young mammals. But a lead camel is a wise and experienced beast. The caravan bells tinkle as they pass through the night, and I wonder why the author of that article should have called a whole species of animal stupid. It is a breach of the language. A solecism. Yet intentional. The camel has adapted itself and survived. Domesticated, he has lived in symbiosis with man.

Now he is being thrust aside. Internal combustion engines, caterpillar treads, heavy trucks are replacing him. But for many years yet awhile he will be carrying goods and men across steppes and deserts.

However pretty they sound, then, and no matter how dark and hot the night, camel bells are not romantic. Driving trucks across deserts isn't romantic, either. But it certainly is romantic—in the sense of unreal and unworldly—to drive about in these parts with 12½ horsepower and 550 pounds of baggage on worn-out tires. Romantic because impractical.

Driving northward from Maimana one traverses a well-cultivated countryside. The road crosses fields, passes through villages, between avenues of trees, and past teahouses. Then, climbing over some hills, all this is left behind; the vegetation becomes sparser and ahead of us the sky hangs down, hot, heavy, lead-colored. We drive out onto the plain, into the desert. And now the landscape changes completely. To the west, low cliff formations. The parched sandy ground keeps causing the car to skid. As we drive toward Andkhui the heat is stifling. Terrified desert rats run out ahead of us. Chased by the car, they suddenly put on their brakes; the dust flies all around them; they leap to one side. Our wheels thunder over their holes which perforate the middle of the road.

At long last Andkhui meets us, in the form of dry irrigation canals. Then of walled gardens. And finally, in the dusk, houses and bazaars. Heavy. And hot.

The stretch between Andkhui and Shibarghan illustrates the romanticism of traveling in a small car with a heavy load. Sand dunes drift across the road. The heat is insufferable. Hour after hour we struggle on. Halfway across the desert we stop at a robat. Running our front wheels up onto some firm tussocks, we walk over to a bus standing parked outside. Its passengers are resting in its shade. The driver comes to meet me. He is worried on our behalf. Wonders if we have water. Though his bus is new, the merciless heat has already patterned its paintwork with cobwebs. The air is hazy and on the other side of the robat the road splits up into numerous wheel-tracks, all in the direction of Shibarghan. Where they disappear behind sand dunes they leave a belt of road a half-mile wide. The sand is loose. I wonder which track is best.

"One's as good as another," he says.

I wonder whether the road gets better further on.

"It's good," he says. "Very good. If you've got as far as this, you'll get to Shibarghan. The road is very good."

He takes a look at our car, thinks it on the small side. Asks if we are hungry. At least we must accept bread and tea. It is bad to get hungry. And we are guests.

When we drive on again, out into the desert, everyone waves. Reposing in the shadow of the gaily painted bus, waiting for dusk, they too had urged us to wait for nightfall. I had replied that we didn't know the road and were afraid of losing our way. At night it is all too easy to get lost among so many wheel-tracks, all these different paths. It has happened to us before.

"It's hot now," was all they said.

The going is heavy and wearisome; sand and newly dug ditches. The wilderness is to be made fertile. Far away, like a mirage above the horizon, we glimpse a green oasis. A green plate, borne up on quivering grey air. Gradually it comes closer. And closer. But often we get stuck; and often I have to dig us out; and all the time this merciless sun; and then again, in the distance, the greenery seems so remote. Shoveling sand on the fringes of the Kara Kum Desert, I realize suddenly how realistic, how wise a beast the camel is.

Major G. B. Malleson, C.S.I., writes in 1880:

> From Andkhui to Shibarghan the distance is about twenty miles. The road crosses an extremely rich and fertile country, resembling an immense garden.

But then, he had never been here. And he had his own reasons for praising the country's fertility. He wanted to rouse public opinion at home into incorporating this land, too, into the British Empire. Certainly it could be made fertile here. With irrigation canals. Capital investment. Hard work. As yet there is only the desert. And a few odd tufts of camel grass.

Next year we do not go by Andkhui. Instead, where we emerge into the plain, I turn off from the main route, and drive from Daulatabad straight across the desert to Shibarghan. Around Daulatabad, the carpet town, are still some irrigated fields and cultivated lands. Then the route crosses small salt marshes with a white salty crust, hard and brittle. There is a sharp boundary between the brown sand and the white surface of the salt. A sound like driving over crisp snow.

The route leads up to some sandhills. This is no road for cars. We drive along the bridle path. The path gets narrower and narrower. Now it becomes a steep sandy-sided ravine. Where it winds up among the hillocks we can no longer drive on it: the four wheels spin round on the walls of the ravine, with the path itself directly below us. Now it is no more than two or three feet wide and the distance between its surface and the bottom of the car is more than a yard. The walls are sheer. If anything happens, now, we won't be able to open the doors. The car lurches forward in first gear, its whole weight supported on the outer rims of its tires—tires which are already in none too good a condition. Even before entering this ravine we've already had two punctures. For half an hour we've been driving up this twisting, lurching path.

A long while we drive on across the steppe. The ground is hard now, and our wheels get a good grip. In the remote distance, a solitary gazelle. The sky is a leaden blue-grey, and the steppe a greyish yellow. Beside the route lie white bones. Skulls of asses, camels.

One map of Afghanistan shows this route as a main road. The distance must be about sixty miles. The hours pass. The car drives on and on across the steppe.

In the middle of the steppe we stop and eat melons. A car gives you a feeling of safety. Even out here, where the horizon stretches without a break, a car is security, protection. A caravan crosses our route, coming from the southwest. Far ahead, at the bottom of a gentle slope, we can see the well. Three tents, a few dogs, sheep grazing off the sparse thin grasses.

Then we run into sand. Last year it would not have been lying across the road; but now it has driven in from the north. Deep loose sand. At regular intervals we stick fast. Get another puncture. The landscape turns into low sandy hills; and again the route is a clearly marked trail. Now Gun, who weighs least, is driving our little grey car. I am ready to jump out and shove whenever she gets stuck. Our car dances and skids along among the sand dunes, its front wheels skidding and slithering. Yet it keeps going, and Gun flings it from tussock to tussock. Each time its front wheels get a grip on firm ground, on limestone fragments or grass tussocks, the car is flung

Sultan Mahmud ordered a residence to be built at Lashkari bazaar.

forward, then slithers on again slowly through the sand. Every now and again it sticks fast in the dunes. But again we get going, and drive on toward Shibarghan.

In 1878 Major N. Grodekoff, of the Imperial Russian Staff, rode this way. In his report he describes the road:

> From Shibarghan to Maimana are two routes. One of these traverses a plain as far as to Khairabad and then proceeds along the Sangalak River. The other runs direct to Sar-i-Pul, and afterwards across the mountains.
>
> Formerly, when numerous robats with cisterns of water existed along the Khairabad route, it was the principal highway of traffic; but today the robats are in ruins, the cisterns are choked up, and there exists between Shibarghan and Khairabad a stretch of sixty

miles of waterless country, unfit for traveling. Nowadays the caravans use the Sar-i-Pul road . . .

A report which is by and large correct, even today. But then, Major Grodekoff had actually been here; and he had every reason to hand in a correct report. Tsarist Russia was expanding and wished to know whether it would be worth the trouble to expand across the Oxus.

XII

The plains roll wide and free. Far away to the northward a glimpse of the spurs of great mountains. In the distance the yellow clay walls of a village, occasional green trees, clusters of white flat-roofed houses. The earth is sun-scorched, the sky a dome of steely blue. A flock of sheep is spreading out over the hills, grazing on its parched vegetation. The great shaggy-furred dogs keep it together. The dogs' tails and ears have been cropped. Without themselves offering a hold for their enemies' fangs, they must be capable of tearing wolves to pieces. Heavy-jawed, they lope along on powerful legs. Against the grey sky, the silhouette of a man. He calls to the dogs—they gather the flock together and drive it after him over the brow of the hill.

When I was young I used to call it "Persian lamb," associating it with the black-marketeer's fur cap and coat, with film stars and society wives. Now I own a "Persian" fur cap myself. It is Afgan; straight, clean. Nor do I call it "Persian" any longer. I give its material its right name: karakul. Instead of the appellation Persian lamb, it has resumed its original name: sheepskin from the "Black Lake." A change of name which comprises a whole chapter of social history. When the century was young, karakul came to be known in Europe as Persian lamb, because the merchants offering it for sale were Persians. They put this fur on the world market, gave it a name. They took the profits, and the wearers of Persian sheepskin caps, collars, and furs had not the faintest inkling of the whereabouts of the shepherds or where the sheep had been skinned. Nor did they much care.

In Afghanistan, allowing for a very wide margin of error, there are some five million karakul sheep. The great majority in the northern parts of the country. Asiatic karakul is superior to the African, and the best Afghan skins are regarded as being in the very highest class, though internationally speaking the Afghan quality is uneven.

The romantic sees the shepherd with his sheep; sees the sheepdogs; and dreams of peace and quiet and freedom from stress. In doing this the romantic lies. And is ignorant. In practice this amounts to the same thing; leads to the same result, and is therefore equally immoral.

The shepherd just now vanishing with his sheep behind the slope of the hills is intimately related to life in the big cities. Karakul is one of Afghanistan's major export items, its prime dollar-earner. Now the karakul fleeces are to pay for the new irrigation schemes in the south. This shepherd is responsible for dam constructions and hydroelectric power stations, roads, factories, and schools. And his peacefully grazing sheep are to be transformed into pumping stations and water regulation plants.

A bad winter, causing many ewes to perish in the snowdrifts, thus costs the country generators and power-transmission lines.

Now the sheep are on the slopes of the next hill; they seem as small as ants, and the barking of the dogs has grown faint. As for the shepherd, now scarcely visible, his whole existence depends upon changes in taste and fashion among the fur-wearing foreign women.

After the Second World War, the moneyed fur-buying public in the USA had more money to spend, and the fashion switched from the beautiful and durable karakul to the beautiful but less durable mink. Then the karakul prices came tumbling down on the New York market. While the real value of the dollar was year by year being undermined and ever smaller power stations could be bought with that currency, the average price per sheepskin fell from $11.60, in 1945, to $8.17 ten years later. At the same time the number of fleeces sold fell from 2,739,000 to 1,368,000. To Afghan economic planning and the lives of nomad Afghan shepherds the changing status of rich American women was a catastrophe.

In the early fifties, however, the West German "economic miracle" led to a relative improvement in the market. The upper-middle-class German housewife began to appear in karakul sheepskin. But no joy lasts forever. Success breeds success, and housewives wearing Persian lamb begin to dream of mink. Although Afghanistan sold 2,900,000 sheepskins in 1958, there was a relative fall in exports. During that year the karakul sheepskin's share of Afghan exports fell from 25 per cent to 23 per cent.

But changes in the world market, new fashions, social regroupings, and the transmutations of status symbols in remote parts of the world have other effects than on over-all Afghan economic planning. Nor is it merely a question of the family budget of North Afghan shepherds and their living conditions.

They also have a decisive influence on meat prices, on carpet qualities, and on the vegetation up here in the great plains beneath the Amu Darya. The karakul skin is lambskin. It is to be had in many grades and colors. But the finest skins are flayed off unborn lambs. The ewes are brought to miscarry. Lisak, the skin of an unborn lamb six weeks before birth, Tikir, the skin of an unborn lamb four weeks before birth, and Nazukcha, the skin of an unborn lamb ten days before birth, have such lustrous beauty they can be counted on to raise any woman's sexual market price.

But if suddenly that woman goes over to mink and the price of karakul lambskins drops, then it will become profitable to let the lambs be born and grow up as sheep. To rear them, that is, for their mutton and wool. The wool of the karakul sheep is fine, and highly characteristic. And it is this wool which gives genuine carpets their durable beauty. A carpet woven of karakul becomes only more beautiful and more brilliant the more it is worn.

But a falling price for karakul fleeces on the world market is not only discernible in the form of more meat for sale in the bazaars or a more plentiful supply of high-grade wool for carpet wool. It also leaves its mark on the landscape. When women who wear furs insist on their husbands buying them mink, then the deserts of Northern Afghanistan grow larger.

For a region which provides enough grazing as long as the lambs are killed before or at birth is quite unable to support the increased herds which result from all these lambs growing to maturity. When the lambskin market shrinks, the nomads are forced to speculate in wool and mutton.

The flocks increase, clamber all over the hillsides, chewing and trampling. In spots the earth becomes quite bare, and the wind carries away the soil. Barren patches of sand appear. The flocks increase. The price of karakul drops. And the barren patches become more numerous until the hills again become sandy dunes. In a gusty wind one sees the crests of the dunes being blown away like smoke. The further the price falls, the greater become the dust-blown areas; the smaller the grazing grounds; and the harder they have to be worked; and the more fiercely the wind snatches at the dunes.

In irrigated districts farmers notice how the sand is collecting in strings behind bushes and plants. They grow with the wind, turn into miniature dunes which, gathering and collecting and joining up, grow into big dunes and come rolling in across the arable land. The field crops shrink; and the little dunes turn into wandering barkhans. Creeping into the orchards, they block up the irrigation canals with sand. Ramparts of sand build up against the houses and the village succumbs in a torrent of dust and sand.

The flocks grow and grow. The nomads become poorer. No longer can their children eat rice with roghan and meat. Now they are on bread and water. All over the hills the sound of trampling and chewing makes itself heard, and their crests are being visibly blown away. In the metropolitan countries the fur-wearing women have a new fashion. And over the steppes the black sand drifts in from the west.

XIII

The children at Akcha are throwing stones at a mangy yellow-brown bitch. She slinks away and flees whining, her tail between her legs. Howls as the stones hit her. She has just had puppies. Her swollen dugs dangle beneath her starved body, and as she runs out of the bazaar—an unclean animal—all the children scream and throw stones at her. Without knowing what her sin is, or the stone-throwing children knowing it either, the whining bitch is being punished for her ancestors. Once, long ago, they were the sacred animals of a long since fallen religion.

Which is the usual fate of religions. The Brahmins, to arrogate to themselves the right to eat cow's flesh, declare the cow sacred. In the end she becomes so sacred that no one is allowed to kill her at all; until today staggering cows with dried-up udders are dying of starvation all over the plains of Northern India. At the sacred mounds outside Uppsala my own forefathers sacrificed horses. It has taken nine hundred years before we Swedes again dare to eat horse-flesh. The priest of the sacrifice becomes a knacker.

About four thousand years ago the steppe lands which stretch from Poland to Central Asia were populated by semi-nomadic barbarians. They had tamed the horse. They owned two-wheeled wagons with spoked wheels. Their patriarchally organized clans showed the beginnings of an embryonic class-system. They had father gods in the sky, and axes with holes for shafts; and in their tribes and their clans they migrated in a southwesterly, westerly and northeasterly direction. All nomads are wandering peoples; and when these nomads came up against wealthier cultures they conquered and pillaged them.

The natives, even the more civilized, could not resist the chariots. Their footmen were defenseless against the horses. The conquerors established themselves as warlords, and in the conquered countries as receivers of tribute. They married into the original populations and were absorbed. All that remains of these wars of conquest is a family of languages: the Indo-European. In India they called themselves the Aryans: the noblemen, the well-born.

Up here by the Amu Darya these barbarians built their first town. Balkh, the mother of cities, as it was called all over Asia.

According both to the *Avesta* and the *Rig-Veda,* they also acquired their first dynasties of kings. The city began to assume its shape. They had conquered a people of horseless farmers. Now they were knights. In their fortified houses, they sat surrounded by their families and slaves, ruling the inhabitants of the country. To Balkh they had brought their heavenly father-gods, and also the mythology later to be codified down in India as the *Rig-Veda.*

The mother goddess of the matriarchate, the little old woman who appears in the clay amulets of the sedentary farming peoples, was thrust aside. The old thunderer of the patriarchal shepherd peoples had ousted her.

Zoroaster, it seems probable, was active at Balkh some time after the first millennium before our epoch. His great reform was not merely a monotheistic reform in the tradition of the patriarchal shepherd peoples. His teaching reveals the opposition between the settled cattle-breeders' belief in their gods and the nomads' belief in theirs. "On earth as it is in heaven."

Zoroaster's activities, like those of all founders of religions, are swathed in darkness and legend. But his great religious crisis was precipitated in the course of a struggle with a hostile sect, a sect which slaughtered bulls and ate them ritually. The most important thing about Zoroaster's religion, however, is neither its dualism, nor the Ahura Mazda. It is his solicitude for the cow and the irrigation systems. No longer did the sacredness of the dog lie in the comradeship and respect it could offer a hunter. Now it is the watchdog of the settled cattle-breeding folk which is apotheosized; the chained dog of the villager, the protector of his property; a scavenger, necessary to any permanent abode. The huntsman's comradeship with his dog, like the slaughter of horses, belonged to an earlier epoch, and only lived on in half-forgotten ceremonies.

It was here at Balkh that large portions of the theology which later exerted such influence on Indian cultures, which influenced the Sassanid and therefore also the Jewish-Christian environment, were worked out. Balkh is the link between them. But Balkh was certainly not wealthy in the same sense as the cities of Egypt, of the Fertile Crescent or of the Indus Basin, were wealthy. Balkh was quite a small town. The district was still poor, as can be seen from such things as taxation rolls kept by the Achaemenids. After Balkh had fallen to the Achaemenids and Cyrus had marched through it on his way to Kapisa, Balkh, the twelfth satrapy of the realm, was only paying 360 talents a year, a low figure compared with the 1,000 talents paid by the Assyrian satrapy.

But when the day comes on which the people can afford to make serious excavations at Balkh, world history will have to be rewritten. Instead of mere guesswork and loose assumptions, we shall have firm archaeological evidence. Until that day comes, we can only surmise Balkh's greatness: in its religions, and in the stones which the children at Akcha are throwing at that poor whining bitch.

XIV

The mountains have vanished behind mist. A hot afternoon wind is causing the dust of the little hills to fly like smoke. The world is hot, grey, yellow, horizonless. At the limits of vision sky, hills and the steppe all blend into one dusty mist. The wind is coming off the great deserts, and the Kara Kum is being swept clean. Behind each plant, each stone, a little barkhan is growing. You can see how the dust is settling behind the obstacle. But if you bend down you can also see how each miniature dune trails behind it a pennant of flying dust. The loose soil is drifting eastward. Day by day, wind and sun are crumbling the stones of the desert into sand, and the sand of the desert into dust, which is swept whistling away out toward the steppes and the plains.

The air is compact, the dust so fine you can't even grind it between your teeth. We have just finished washing in the irrigation canal, in which this same dust which has been blowing across the plain turns into a sticky yellowish brown viscous mud. It is like a living substance underfoot, forcing itself up between our toes, clutching at our legs. Evaporating, the warm water cools our bodies. The boundary between rolling plain and cultivated lands is sharp as if cut with a knife. And cut it has been—albeit with a spade. Excavated for irrigation, and built into a clay wall. Now the clay wall vanishes into the remote distance and the horizon haze. On one side all is green, a clear sharp green. On the other, all is grey as dust and smoking hillocks. The irrigation canal leads in toward the oasis. Its banks and humps and the soil of the oasis, like all firm ground here, are built of loose soil. And the air, too, on its journey eastward, is grey and heavy with loose soil. The mud between our toes, the grey air, the smoky hillocks, the muddy water, the green fields, and the wall of clay—one and all are loose soil.

This, the most fertile of soils, is as loose as can be. A product of nothing but crumbling decay. Rich in minerals, in salts, in calcium. Loose soil and water yield good crops. Year after year the soil builds up. The dusty air is filled with wealth. A millimeter this year; half a millimeter last; and two millimeters next year. The wind and the winter rains beat the dust to the ground and bind it, allowing the soil to grow and become steadily more fertile. The farther from the desert fringe, the richer the dust.

The desert scares the naïve. He sees in it nothing but death, an enemy. The world to him is all black and white. The desert is evil; the oasis good. What he does not perceive is that the one is the condition of the other. Just because the desert is dead and barren it spreads its wealth all about. Like a mighty broom the centrifugal desert winds sweep clean the stones and the sand. The sand, it is true, drifts out in belts around the desert. And man, it is true, fights the sand to rule the desert fringes. A struggle between man's and the vegetation's power to bind and control, and the sand's power to destroy. But the more furiously the desert crumbles away and the more bare and dead its heart, the more fruitful becomes the great belt of steppe outside it. To the surrounding lands the very curse of the desert is a blessing. Our agrarian culture has been built up out of the crumbling of long-vanished deserts. The naïve man does not perceive this. All he sees is sand and crumbling cliffs, hot hard lands, and violent storms of dust. That destruction, annihilation and death are only the necessary condition of new creation, growth, and life, is something he does not perceive. The deserts are mills grinding wealth out of barren cliffs. The dust-storm is a gift from heaven.

Again I am pouring water over my body, first warming it, then cooling it in the wind. Through the grey air we walk up to the teahouse. It stands on the very borderline between the cultivated oasis and the barren lands. The closer we approach the greenery, the denser it becomes. A wall of greenery behind the clay rampart. This greenery, this vegetation, would be impossible without the water just evaporating from my body, and without all this dust flying through the air. Both are its necessary conditions. Yet there is a third factor, too. A factor which has governed all developments in this part of the world, linked together the destinies of its peoples and exerted on their history a far more massive and decisive influence than all the military commanders, all the rulers and all the much-sung heroes put together.

In this climate, in such a landscape, a man can do nothing on his own. A man on his own cannot build. His plantations become inundated by sand. His crop will be nothing but tangled straws. His wheat turns yellow, dries up and is blown away before even it has time to bear sheaves. Here all work is—always has been—collective. A solitary tiller of the soil has always been an absurdity here. Out here, on the fertile steppes, crops will only grow after many people have made a joint effort. The irrigation systems, alone, demand thousands and thousands of hours of work. Irrigation, plantations to bind the soil, and a common harvest have shaped history differently from its course in Europe. Asiatic despotism has rested on the immobility of communal villages. Since no man could own his land individually, one man, owning all land, all power, and all glory, has been able to rule unrestricted by rights, laws, or other men. Irrigation has been crucial. And irrigation was the property of the central power.

Out of the surplus of the villages, kingdoms, empires, armies, bureaucracies, cities have all been built up. Kingdom has risen against kingdom, empires have been overthrown and crashed, and history has been shaken to its foundations. But the villages have gone on. Good governments with good irrigation systems have given the villagers good harvests; and bad governments with decaying irrigation systems, or through the havoc wrought by their warlords, have allowed the deserts to encroach on the fertile land. Good governments gave good years with good surpluses, used them to enrich their bureaucracies and made more powerful their armies, and thus sowed the seed of new wars which laid waste the irrigation systems and allowed the fields to sand up. But notwithstanding all their conquerors the villages have always been the same. The wheel of existence. Eternally the same. For fifteen hundred years, even from the days of the tremendous conflict preceding the Arab conquest, there has seemingly been no way out of this cycle of building up and throwing down. Conquerors have come and gone. But one conqueror has been his fellow like.

Behind this green wall of vegetation lies Balkh. The remains of Balkh. We enter the shade of the teahouse. The copper samovar is singing. A Russian samovar. The teacups are Japanese. The host is a Hazar. And the men who are sitting beside us in the shade are Uzbeks. They are wearing long striped caftans—chapans—and their faces are Mongoloid. Northern Afghanistan is Turk country. This is where the Turkish languages' southeastern frontier runs through Eurasia. Yet even today, despite all wars of conquest, all linguistic transformations, administration is still on the lines which emerged after bloody class struggles in late Sassanid times. Since then, bureaucratic, fiscal, and governmental methods, by and large, have not changed.

Two men ride by. They sit elegantly on their horses, the greyish yellow dust squirting from their hoofs. It's strange that just this region,—Balkh of the spoked wheels, Balkh of the war chariots— should have become a land of horsemen and pack horses. The chariots of the barons and the great slave-owning landowners vanished with their masters; in their stead came the mounted troops and foot soldiers of the central power. For long periods, up here in these plains which might have been made for wheeled vehicles and which once saw the onrush of the war chariots, wheel and wagon fell into total disuse.

Not until the end of the 1870's were wheeled vehicles reintroduced, by order of the Governor General of Mazar-i-Sharif. Four battalions, quartered in Mazar-i-Sharif, were each provided with a cart of the type formerly used north of the Amu Darya: the arba. But the arba is a primitive sort of wagon. It has two wheels. Its driver sits on horseback. Its massive wheels are a yard and a half in diameter, and heavy. True, its tall wheels enable it to move over the rough and pot-holed steppe terrain; but the very weight of the wheels is so great there is a limit to its load. The arba never became popular. Not until half a century later, with the coming of the first motor trucks, did wheels again arrive in Balkh. When the first truck drove up toward Balkh after the First World War, history had come full cycle.

After drinking our tea we take a closer look at the cups. Unlike all the cups we have seen hitherto, they are not Japanese. They have come from the porcelain factory at Kunduz. If they look Japanese and the decoration is of the Japanese type found in every teahouse, it is because production at Kunduz is in the hands of Japanese technicians. In point of fact, however, this decoration is nothing but an imitation of the Bukhara pattern. When the Japanese began selling utility china to the Central Asian market, they adapted their design to an existing tradition. But the Bukhara pattern is in turn based on the Turkish, Mongolian, and Chinese patterns. Once again, culture goes in circles; and in its decoration the simplest utility article, the cheapest teacup with edge chipped and cracked glaze, subsumes all history in its own.

The deserts give the steppes their fertility. But the fertility of the steppes calls for collective labor. When the great landowners met their end and there were no longer any slaves to keep up the irrigation canals, the primitive village collective was forced into existence. And on its back the despotism arose. But this village, of its own strength, cannot break the wheel of existence. Nevertheless— the spoked wheel returns to one of its homelands; propelled, this time, by an internal combustion engine.

Japanese mass production has ruined the Afghan potters. In every teahouse, nothing but Japanese cups. The local craftsmen have vanished. But at the same time a market has been created for an indigenous porcelain industry.

In the metropolitan countries the karakul becomes valuable. Foreign merchants reap the profits and give the product its name. But as early as 1914 production is forced over into Afghan hands; and in 1933 the trade is regulated. Five years later, a state karakul company is formed. Now the sheepskins are to yield much-needed currency with which to import machinery, increase irrigation, and raise agricultural output. The northern plains become integrated in the world market, their life becomes dependent upon Wall Street fluctuations. When prices fall, ruin stares the country in the face. When the countryside is overexploited, its hills are laid waste. To all appearances everything is going in the direction of an ever more vicious circle of land erosion, increased poverty and starvation in nomad tent and sandy bazaar. Thus the foundation of a future is laid.

XV

From the plain we drive into Mazar-i-Sharif. It is the country's northern city, just as Herat is its western. Buildings close in on us. Blind clay walls and a main road which narrows down into an alley twisting along between the shady tree-lined canal and the yellow walls. We pass a man driving a team of donkeys; he yells at his animals, hits them with a heavy club, but even these yells and these blows have a mild sleepy rhythm. Two children are playing quietly under a tree. Some water-carriers are filling their water-skins, and their donkeys have taken refuge in the shade. Cupolas of houses rise out of the gardens' walled greenery and the dust of the road dances in the sunlight.

But this impression clashes with its opposite. The alley straightens out, turns into a street. The houses change character. Now they have shaken off their clay walls; are built of burnt brick in turn-of-the-century style. Their gardens are strictly designed parks. We feel as if we are driving through the center of a provincial town in Russia, fifty years ago. The police station here; the governor's residence there; the school, the bank, the hotel.

But now this image, too, is erased. Among these small burnt-brick palaces of a provincial bureaucracy an echo of automobile horns. Big trucks drive by. Now we're coming down into the bazaar quarter. The streets swarm and jostle with people, cars and donkeys loading and unloading. The vehicles are being filled from the store sheds. All the goods of the northern district pass through Mazar-i-Sharif's storehouses. Businessmen are making deals over teacups. Everywhere people are shopping, talking, quarreling. All is life and movement. Mazar-i-Sharif is the big trading city.

But, unlike Herat, it is not stamped with the character of its own province. Not merely does one meet many Afghans and Tadzhiks in its streets, and a comparatively few Uzbeks. The town's whole atmosphere, its architecture and street life are not provincial. Mazar-i-Sharif is quite another sort of city from Herat. More splintered and fumbling. Even the ramshackle old buildings, currently being pulled down, lack character. Have no traditions. Pioneer buildings.

For they *are* being pulled down. New streets, meeting at right angles, are forming a new city plan. New buildings, strict in form, schools, workshops, administrative offices for the city's trade organ and the new state oil company. The new houses are rising on deserted plots. To acquire offices for state monopolies and banks the city is shaking off its bazaar stands. The broad streets are properly lit. Yet this town, as a town, is no older than the Middle West cities of the USA.

This splintered city, without any over-all style, is the capital of the northern districts. And the building which has lent Mazar-i-Sharif its name—and which might have created a style for it, and could have remained its center—is also hesitant, unclear; has no thoroughgoing architectonic form. Ali's Tomb. The great green sanctuary, the great center of pilgrimage, the noble tomb. But even this is dubious.

For here a miracle occurred. One of the greatest. In principle it is assumed that Ali, the Prophet's son-in-law, the fourth Caliph, lies buried at An Najaf, in Iraq. That's where the Shiite pilgrims go. In their opinion, the Caliph Harun-al-Rashid had the first mausoleum built there after the discovery of Ali's grave in 791. It seems more probable, however, that the grave did not come into being until two centuries later, in 977.

The exception to this main tradition is that Ali is also buried here at Mazar-i-Sharif. Which makes this city, too, one of the holiest. For, even allowing for all schismatics and their deifications, Ali ibn abi Talib is without question Islam's great popular hero; of whom it is said that there is no sword like unto al-Fakar and no young warrior like Ali.

Now, during the twelfth century, they say, a man came up to Balkh from India, announcing he had discovered in old books that the true grave of Ali was to be found by the Khairan Fort, just outside Balkh. Some of the Prophet's descendants in Balkh swore on oath that they had dreamed dreams in which the same thing had been revealed to them. Appeal was made to the authorities. But the chief scholar of the city denied emphatically that any such thing could be true. Was it not common knowledge that Ali lay buried near Najaf?

That same night Ali himself appeared to the learned man and taught him a lesson. Instantly he mended his ways, and putting himself at the head of all persons in authority in the city, walked in procession out to the place which had now been pointed out to him in his dream. And when they began to dig, they found Ali's uncorrupted body. Upon which the Sultan Sanjar himself is said to have had a mosque built over the grave. Allegedly destroyed by

Jenghiz Khan, the very site is said to have long lain in oblivion. Once again Ali's grave had been forgotten. Marco Polo silently ignores the whole matter. Ibn Battuta, who passes through Balkh in the fourteenth century, hasn't a word to say about any grave of Ali in its environs. By contrast, he has earlier spoken of Mashad Ali at Najaf "where there is a grave they say is Ali's." He is a cautious fellow and a skeptical traveler, and when he describes the mausoleum he does so in the words: "Therein are three graves which they state to be the graves of Adam, Noah and Ali."

But during the reign of Husain Bayqara this grave was once again discovered, and the mosque was built which stands there to this day.

But the mosque is not one of the most beautiful Timurid monuments. Green and newly restored, it stands in the midst of a field of deserted ruins. The city planners have swept away the bazaar stands from its immediate neighborhood, converting the space around it into a park. White doves strut about in its yard, and in front of its main entrance a new traffic circle has been laid out. The pilgrim industry needs space.

This miracle, so disputed and doubtful, is in some way quite typical of Mazar-i-Sharif. The town is deeply split. It is a town whose development has been uneven and interrupted and whose social and political conflicts have found expression in brick and clay and burnt tilework.

And on closer examination this dissentience turns out to be something considerably more crucial, a good deal more serious, than a mere confusion of styles and an old controversy over the graves of saints. The history of Ali's grave and Ali's importance illustrate the part played by religion and the religiosity of politics. Or again, to express the point more exactly, they illustrate the way in which in this part of the world, as in Europe during the Middle Ages and the early Reformation, every social and political movement took on a religious form.

The story begins with the death of the Prophet. On Friday the tenth day of the month of Rabial Awwal in the eleventh year after the Hegira, the Prophet falls sick and is unable to lead prayers. During Saturday and Sunday his sickness grows worse, he becomes delirious. On Monday he seems to be better, and gets up to say morning prayers. Shortly after, he dies. This happened in the year 632 of our epoch.

From the struggle of factions between his closest friends and relations, notably between the Prophet's father-in-law and friend Abu Bakr and the Prophet's son-in-law, Ali, married to Fatima, the former emerges victorious. He becomes the first Caliph. The Leader of the Faithful. During the following years the Moslem armies sweep forward and Islam is everywhere victorious. After their long conflicts and fierce civil wars, Byzantium and Sassanid Persia were both weak and rotten. In Syria the Christian rank and file greet the Arabs as the restorers of the true faith and the people's liberators from Byzantine oppression. In Persia the tremendous social struggle had just closed with the downfall of the great slave-owning landlords and the rebellious masses had been tamed by a new noble caste of bureaucrats, tied to the throne and the despotism. In the struggle with Christian Byzantium the Christian and Jewish minorities which, in brotherly alliance with the state power, had recently acted as the people's executioners, were thereafter regarded as potentially disloyal and were wiped out in pogroms. Everywhere the Arabs were welcomed as liberators from an intolerable oppression.

Islam's armies conquered because everywhere the powers opposed to them were so rotten. It was a social, not a theological, conflict. Islam triumphed as a religion, and the Arabs as a ruling caste. They turned liberation into its opposite. The Arab garrison towns became the centers of power. The local population were allowed to resort to them to sell their products, and it was from there the country was ruled. Islam was broad-minded—but the unbelievers had to pay higher taxes. But the converts did not become Arabs; only second-class Moslems.

The Arab tribes had good commanders but few administrators. So the old administration remained by and large intact. No social transformation followed in the wake of the religious conversion. The victory of Islam was the victory of the Arab rulers, and under the second Caliph, Omar, the entire empire was declared to be the property of the Moslems. This made the situation more acute. What up to then had been a factional struggle between various individuals and families in the entourage of the Prophet—a private family quarrel based on individual whims and personal desire for power—was turned into a great disruptive struggle between the Arabs and their new converts, the latter, under Islam's doctrine of equality, demanding their fraternal rights.

Ali himself, the last of the four legitimate Caliphs, can hardly have been aware of the role he was playing. Few people are. For him it was still no more than a question of persons and power within the little group. But by his opposition and the factional struggle he became the point of focus for all the dissatisfied. He stands in the unique position of being at once the orthodox Sunnites' ideal and the heretical Shiites' apotheosized hero.

The factional struggle became religion and theology. Transformed into a political movement, it grows into a mighty religion which even today controls the whole of Iran and large parts of Iraq and Afghanistan. Out of this conflict arise various later politico-religious movements. The Ismailis secede from the Shiites. They carry the Shiite opposition a step further. They pick up the thread of tendencies from the recently concluded but still simmering civil war, and stake a religious-communistic claim to equality. Under the Old Man of the Mountain they become the assassins, famous in medieval European history, execrated and slandered; a steely political movement which through intrigues, assassinations, and open warfare first plays its part in the great struggle for power, but afterward degenerates and becomes an end in itself. The condottieri of the *attentat*.

Once in my youth I saw pictures of the Aga Khan, faithful ally of British imperialism, playboy and night-club habitué of the Riviera, being acclaimed the one true teacher, inspired of God. Him-for-whom-all-things-are-made-clean. Who may drink wine, since as soon as it touches his lips wine is turned into water. Who may sin, because in him all sin is purified. And I saw other pictures, in which he was being weighed on a pair of scales against all that collected gold; and I felt I was witnessing the transmutation of the sublime into the ridiculous. A movement originating in a fight against poverty, injustice and oppression had been turned into a safe income for an Aga Khan. But years afterwards, talking to a young Hazara in Kabul, one of the poorest and most oppressed of men, a water-carrier, a hewer of wood and a drawer of water, and hearing him speak of his God—for to him this fellow was a god—and tell how he, too, subscribed out of his miserable penury, and seeing poverty skinned to the bone to send this god to a white, Western, and Anglo-Saxon university and enable him to wallow in night-clubs and thereafter in the fullness of time copulate with strip-teasers—then I realized how deeply tragic the ridiculous can become.

Ali's grave has always been a powerful weapon. When the Ilkhan Oljaitu found it convenient to forswear his forefathers' heathendom and go over to Islam, he weighed the power of one sect against another. From being a Hanefi he became a Shia, and in 1306 at Sultaniya, west of Qazvin, in Iran, ordered the erection of the most beautiful of mausolea; planning to remove thither the corpse of Ali. Under the protection of Ali he would be able to rest safely in his grave, for Ali was always a sharp sword in the hands of anyone who could secure the services of those who believed in him. But things never came to the point where there were three mausolea raised over Ali. Oljaitu died as Mohammed Khodabanda and a Sunni.

The mosque over the grave of Ali at Mazar-i-Sharif is no monument to a naïve faith. It is a monument to political speculation in religious guise. Yet thousands of honest believers flock to it. That is the great religious conflict under Ali's green dome.

But it isn't only the religious conflict which has sundered Mazar-i-Sharif. Four great cities, each in its own quarter of the compass, stand around the mountains which bear up Afghanistan. Kabul to the east, Kandahar to the south, Herat to the west, and Mazar-i-Sharif to the north. Each of these is the capital of an old cultural region. Three have long histories, stretching back over a thousand years. But not the fourth.

Cities may change their names, cities can be razed to the ground and be rebuilt, cities can move a few miles in either direction and still keep their identity. Despite all catastrophes, devastations, and changes of name, Kabul, Kandahar, and Herat have continuously been cities. With Mazar-i-Sharif it is otherwise. It is a new town. For several thousands of years the capital of this district was Balkh. Balkh was destroyed, rebuilt, razed, changed rulers and the language of its rulers, yet it retained its continuity. Only suffered a "break" in urban development. Mazar-i-Sharif is a new town. A new center for the north provinces.

There is no geographical or economic reason why the center of the northern plainlands should have been moved from Balkh to

Mazar-i-Sharif. The distance between the two towns is insignificant, hardly as much as between one robat and another. A day's march for a camel caravan. Nor is it a question of Balkh having ceased to be a city and Mazar-i-Sharif taking over. The decline of Balkh is a result of a shift in the center of gravity in the north; not its cause. The key to what has happened lies in history. Modern history, relating to the consolidation of the State of Afghanistan.

In 1736 Nadir Kuli, a man of the Afshar clan, a camel driver born at Meshed, who became a brigand chieftain and thereafter a warrior, rose to the throne of Persia as Nadir Shah. He was a great warrior, a clever strategist and supreme commander, conquered many countries and plundered many a city. In North India a bloodthirsty massacre is still known as a Nadirshah. His might lay in his army. His military headquarters were his capital and the support of his army the state's only function and the administration's sole *raison d'être*. He was a typical oriental despot. He extended the boundaries of his kingdom, he conquered cities from Delhi in the east to Bukhara in the north, from Mossul in the west to Barein in the south. In 1747 he was assassinated.

The northern plains went to Ahmad Khan, chief of the Saddozai clan of the tribe of Abdali, who was crowned the first Shah of Afghanistan. He was quite another type of monarch. He laid the foundations of a unified Afghanistan, a new state. At once the last great chieftain and the first modern monarch, he built his state on barbarian tribal democracy.

But it was a shaky inheritance. There was a huge difference between the northern and southern regions of his realm. To south and east lay the tribesmen's countries, with their still-functioning military democracy, their jirgahs—equivalent to the Anglo-Saxon *thing* —the free man's right to carry weapons, and the equality of all males. The northern districts were different. Certainly they were subordinate to Afghan power. But they did not form part of Afghanistan, the land of the Afghans. A region of little emirates and petty principalities, torn by their internecine strife, wretchedly poor and ravished by plunderers, according to the changing political situation it alternately recognized and defied the authority of cities and sovereigns. There society had another structure from what it had south of the mountains. The people were poorer and more oppressed. It was a decadent society. These were slave states, states of petty rulers. There was no male equality. Nor were there any barbarian democratic traditions. Its people were oppressed to the uttermost. Decade after decade they had become more and more backward. No atrocity was lacking in that society. The Uzbek slave markets were notorious. The petty tyrants—something otherwise unthinkable—even sold Moslems into slavery.

During incessant civil wars and raids the annual income of the Afghan State from these provinces, so loosely united with Kabul, fell from 1,800,000 rupees at the beginning of the eighteenth century to a mere 200,000 rupees at its middle. Maimana recognized (in a shadowy way) the higher authority of Herat, and all the petty emirs recognized (in principle) the Lord of Balkh's right to the title of Supreme Lord of the Uzbek States. But the title, for want of any means to implement its powers, remained null. Now these petty emirates seemed on the verge of seceding from Kabul altogether. During the first half of the eighteenth century great parts of the region fell under the rule of the Emir of Bukhara. Andkhui, Shibarghan, and Balkh all became subordinate to Bukhara. And this made the Emir of Bukhara the country's official overlord. The Emir of Kabul had lost that right.

But when, during the first British Afghan war, the Emir Dost Mohammed was forced to flee to the north from Kabul, then he was obliged to throw himself on the hospitality of the princes of the northern emirate (against whom he had just been sending punitive expeditions). Whereon the Emir of Bukhara gave the city of Balkh and its income to Dost Mohammed as a personal appanage. This made Dost Mohammed, in theory if not in practice, Supreme Lord of the Uzbek States, even though he was simultaneously a vassal of the Emir of Bukhara. On his return to Kabul he retained Balkh. But even if he held the rest of the country as emir, the northern part remained under the suzerainty of Bukhara. The situation had hardly become clearer.

The period immediately following is one of confused strife and dynastic civil wars. But out of what seemed mere struggling chaos, bereft of any principle, of fraternal strife, swiftly changing coalitions and petty khan politics, a pattern even so emerges. During the ten years which preceded the Second Afghan War, nine of the ten Uzbek

states disappear. As for the tenth, it is only permitted to exist on sufferance. The lord of Andkhui backs the right horse, is rewarded with rights of life and death over the town's inhabitants, but loses his own independence. During the fraternal strife, the civil wars, the conflict between the slave society of the petty principalities and the tribal traditions of the Afghan lands, Afghanistan becomes a united state. During the civil war, as a symbol of this fact, the Governor General is removed from Balkh to Mazar-i-Sharif. And therewith the juridical fiction is shattered. No longer does the Emir of Kabul hold the northern provinces as Bukhara's vassal. Now he rules in his own right. This series of events is one of the most crucial in the entire history of Afghanistan. Twenty years before the British Empire and the Russian Autocracy reach their agreement on the Afghan frontiers, Afghanistan has welded itself into a state.

Which means that all ideas of Afghanistan being a "buffer state," set up by the great powers, are empty talk. Talk to justify eventual conquest.

Mazar-i-Sharif is a historical conflict, and its solution, in brick and clay: the conflict between feudalism and the central power of the state, between a slave society and tribal democracy. It is a monument to Afghanistan's struggle for unity. But the town also has a personality of its own. In its business quarters the winds of life and commerce are blowing strongly. The new suburbs are substantial artifacts of the oil monopoly and of the new age. Only within the context of that age can Mazar-i-Sharif find its own style. Grow into a great city, south of the Amu Darya. As yet it is still struggling in its own birth pangs. In every one of its quarters it is contradicting itself, denying itself, tearing itself to pieces. For the revolution, and the union of which it is a monument, are still unfinished. Still incomplete. Not yet finally decided. The great upheaval is in the future.

XVI

At Tashkurgan we leave the leaden grey steppe, scorched by the July heat, and drive toward the cliffs. Like a great wall they rise up ahead of us. Beside the stream running at their foot the vegetation is dense. Suddenly a cleft appears in the wall; the stream has cut a deep ravine through the rocks. We drive out of the plains country into the darkness of this hollow road.

Green valleys, rolling reddish mountains. Haibak, a green valley among red hills. The great trees shade its main street. Flies buzz around its bazaar stands. In its teahouses the samovars sing their beckoning song. Haibak is a town which has given hostages to world history. A center of Buddhism, it was the northernmost town in Afghanistan ever to be seized by British troops.

The visit of those British troops of Captain Hopkins' regiment, who were billeted in Haibak a few months more than a century ago, has left no trace. But the process which flung them hither, scattered them among the red hills and drove them away again is still by no means at an end.

Up to 1840 Russia had a monopoly of all trade as far south as the Indus. Planned with miserable inefficiency and clumsily executed, the British made a thorough mess of their First Afghan War. Britain lost her armies and her honor, but acquired the trade as far as the Hindu Kush. From 1840 on, from Trebizond to Pamir, London and St. Petersburg were at daggers drawn. The prize: the Asian market.

When America had been conquered and the Indian civilizations had been crushed to give Europe new room for development, plunder had followed the flag. The fresh flood of gold gave birth to the revolutions of the Renaissance and the Reformation. In Northwest Europe new nations grew up. Societies came into being which, no longer satisfied with their own province, required the entire world for a market. As the British force their way up through India, trade follows the flag. The Honourable Company pays high dividends. Plunder builds industries, which demand wider markets; and now the whole continent is opened up for British textiles, until in 1843–1845 the Governor General declares: "The bones of the cotton weavers are whitening the plains of India." In 1850 British exports of cotton to India have reached a value of £5,220,000 sterling. Britain's economic world empire is being built on India's poverty. So the Indian civilization is liquidated. The expansion must go on. And Afghanistan lies in the way of trade.

The Russian trade is thrust aside. Russia, herself a semi-Asiatic country, thrall of a corrupt and bureaucratic despotism, proving no match for the modern commercial empire, is forced to yield, and begins to undergo transformation. Her trading stations become provincial capitals, and her armies approach the Hindu Kush mountains. The British statesmen hatch their diplomacies, their negotiations, their great speeches and their parliamentary debates on such elevated matters as freedom and culture. And in that guise their troops are forcing their way into Afghanistan.

It is a play for very high stakes. A world empire, based on so much poverty, cannot rest without collapsing. Its markets must steadily expand. Crises and wars shake the new society; but expansion must never come to an end. Armies may be annihilated in the valleys of Afghanistan; but at once it is declared that the trade of Central Asia is worth whatever price has to be paid for it; and Major Malleson writes:

> The Hindu Kush with a line of fortresses from Herat to the capital of Badakshan would be a perfect frontier. Strong in every essential demanded by military strategy. The number of troops required would not be large—less than those needed to defend the Hindu Kush alone. Fifteen thousand men at Herat, five thousand at Faizabad, and two thousand at Maimana, Shibarghan and Takhtapul—not Balkh—and Khulm, would be all that would be needed and only a third of these men need be British.

Expansion goes in a vicious circle, and the stability of the home countries, their quiet democracy, their respectable trades union movement, their Fabian revolutionaries who are such loyal subjects of Her Majesty, their philosophers, their men of letters, their painters, and their music-hall artistes—one and all are dependent upon, and rewarded with, the profits from this steady expansion. And seventy-five years after the men of Captain Hopkins's regiment have marched away out of Haibak through the red mountains the world catastrophe is a fact. No civilization ever had a bloodier genesis.

And it is during this dark and bloody epoch that Afghanistan is forged by invasions and wars into one nation. It was in the struggle with Captain Hopkins's soldiers, the armed agents of the cotton industry, that Afghanistan became united.

As for Lord Curzon, Marquess of Kedleston, who declared that Afghanistan, the Transcaspian Region, and Persia were nothing but pawns on the chessboard on which was being played the game for the empire of the world, he lived long enough to see the whole board flung upside down. The great game was over; but no one applauded, and the actors did not voluntarily leave the stage. Twenty years after his time the cremation ovens were belching their black smoke across Europe, and on the plains of India people were dying like flies. The civilization which had had such a bloody birth was itself on its way to foundering in an orgy of blood and poverty.

Now the great green trees are shading the street through Haibak. The soldiers of Captain Hopkins's regiment have long ago moldered away in their foreign graves, and the road leads on toward the Hindu Kush. Graveled empty passes; deserts of stone, grey and unfertile. Cliffs, hills, water, and strips of greenery. The landscape opens out. Everything becomes green; and now yet another valley. Another sort of valley. A valley not merely of harvest, crops, and vegetation. But a valley with a hydroelectric station, white factory buildings, and little workers' houses in neat rows among kitchen gardens and orchards. Pul-i-Khumri. One of the new industrial towns.

This is the first sign of industry we have seen in the country. No beauty is to be compared with that of the white lines of these factory buildings, and no architectural form is so good and rich as the power dam. They are the guarantors of a possible freedom and independence.

And then on again and upward. The mountains, turning chalky white, stand up clear against the sky. The air is different and the green valleys are still fertile; but narrower now and more confined. Water is rushing over their stones. And then massive mountains under a clear blue sky becoming ever darker and deeper; and we are driving through a deep cleft in the mountains, an eroded ravine, up to the heights.

On the heights, ruined castles, robbers' lairs, caravanserais; and then ever more deeply into the rocks and narrower ravines with water foaming between high vertical rock faces and the road nothing but a thin strip of cemented stone, clinging to the cliff face. This road is a triumph of engineering. It leads through the huntsman's gorge, right up onto the backbone of Eurasia. According to his own claim, the first European ever to penetrate this pass was the geologist Trinkler, in the autumn of 1924. Nine years later, a motor road had been constructed. Now it climbs, serpentine, to the roar of our engine, higher and ever higher; and above our heads we glimpse the

Ghorid decorations (twelfth century), Friday Mosque, Herat

deep sky whose color is ever darker and clearer, intimating clear air and the freedom of great heights above sea level. From the right we are joined by the route from Bamian. The road, older than the memory of man, goes on; and now, once again we are on the Silk Route, and climbing with it up toward the rocky mountains. The caravanserais are greyer, more antique. Then stony slopes, mounting ever upwards, red mountains with white sides, hard violent inclines; and now the altimeter jerks violently as the engine goes slowly in second to rise singing to first again, and then the last white rising slopes among rolling perspectives, the engine gasping for oxygen. Open mountainsides, with sheep grazing under the violet sky. And at last, at long last, the pass.

With its long wide lines and ever-receding horizons of mountain tops and distant valleys it comes like a deep breath, a calm liberation. This is the boundary between Central Asia and the Indian subcontinent. Here the rivulets trickle down toward the Indian Ocean on one side, and in the direction of Aralskoe More on the other. Beneath, the road pitches downward into the vegetation of the Ghorband Valley.

Each time we have gone through the Shibar Pass we have stopped. Not because the pass is beautiful, like the Sabzak Pass. Or as attractive as an Alpine pass. But the Shibar Pass, ten thousand feet above the sea, is grandiose in its breadth, stupendous in its lack of beauty, its lack of all prettiness. It is a much-used pass, of great human dimensions. We arrive at it one evening when the valley beneath us, the green fertile valley which leads down to Kohistan and Kabul, is already deep in the shadow of the mountains, but the mountains themselves and the hills all around are blushing red in the sunset. As always, the Shibar is freedom, relief and a great happiness. Here we cross the Hindu Kush. If not on the roof of the world, at least we are standing in its porch.

XVII

In October, 1872, a seventy-two-year-old quack, an unlicensed doctor, a gentleman who had seen better days, was buried in San Francisco. People had known him as "The General," but no one had

94

taken his exalted rank very seriously. In those days, after the Civil War, there was no shortage of resounding titles. For which reason neither the clergymen nor the mourners had any interest in—even if they were conscious of—the fact that the Josiah Harlan they had just laid in his grave was none other than The Lord of Jesraotam, Norpore, and Guzerat, the King's closest friend, the Equerry of the Imperial Stirrup, Lord of Kurram, General-in-Chief of the Army of the North, supreme commander of the armed forces of the Emir of Kabul, the Prince of Ghor and the ruler of Hazarjat. A man who had once thought he had a chance of becoming a new Tamerlane, a scourge of God, a ruler of the world.

And the State Department in Washington—or at least its representatives at Kabul—are also blissfully ignorant that in 1838 this man, up in the Kharzara Pass, just north of Shibar, to a salute of twenty-six guns, had the star-spangled banner hoisted over the Hindu Kush. All things considered, notably the minimal wisdom with which the world is ruled and the fates of nations decided, we should be grateful for their peaceable ignorance.

Josiah Harlan, ninth child of the Quaker couple Joshua Harlan and Sarah Hinchman Harlan, was born in Newlin Township, Chester County, Pennsylvania, on June 12, 1799. At the age of twenty-four he sailed for the East Indies. There he found employment with the Honourable East India Company and, during the First Burmese War, without ever having studied medicine, was appointed assistant surgeon in Colonel George Pollock's Bengal Artillery. To set fire to pagodas and rape Burmese women in the interests of the great trading company not seeming to him a sufficiently glorious occupation, and the Burmese War coming to an end, he leaves the Honourable Company, sets out westward, and turns up in Ludhiana, where the exiled Afghan monarch Shah Shuja is living on British money, awaiting his chance to recover the throne at Kabul.

Josiah Harlan enters Shah Shuja's service. Disguised as a dervish, he goes to Kabul as a secret agent to bring about a revolution in favor of Shah Shuja. He has some success, but the revolution fails, and he returns to the court at Ludhiana. There his services win him the highest decorations, and he leaves Shah Shuja—that everlasting exile, that chronic failure, that victim of constant bad luck who contaminates those around him with his bad luck, who, later, stripped of all

95

his dignity, sinks to the level of a British and Sikh tool, and finally, as a puppet monarch for the British, after attaining the semblance of power in Kabul, is murdered by his own unwilling subjects. Harlan, meanwhile, enters the service of the Sikh prince Ranjit Singh, just then carving out a Sikh kingdom for himself in Northern India. Harlan rises in the ranks; becomes governor; is honored. When, in 1835, Dost Mohammed and the Afghans try to recapture Peshawar from the Sikhs, it is Harlan who defeats him. Not by force or arms, but by means of intrigue and gold. Arriving in Dost Mohammed's camp as an ambassador, by bribes, intrigue, half-promises, and holding out the prospect of honors and the throne, he brings Dost Mohammed's army to the point of dissolution. Dost Mohammed himself has to return to Kabul, having lost his army, though not a single battle. And now in the background the British are playing off the Sikhs against Afghans, and the Afghan countries between the Indus and the Khyber are ravaged by war and suffering, and no power remains capable of resisting them. In war after war the Sikhs are played off against the Afghans, become Britain's henchmen, their job being to crush the Afghans; and when the First Afghan War is over and the power of the Afghans has been reduced, the Sikhs realize their allies the British are now marching against them. Too late they understand the British game. They turn to the Afghans for help, and in the last decisive battle five thousand Afghan horsemen fight on the Sikh side. But the power of the British has grown too great. The Sikhs, notwithstanding the aid they get from Afghanistan, are crushed, and at the last moment Dost Mohammed is forced to flee.

But all this is still in the future. The Sikhs, trusting their British friends, are carving out their Sikhistan from Afghan territory. Harlan breaks with Ranjit Singh and goes over to Dost Mohammed. Becomes a general, trains troops, and when at the battle of Jamrud, in 1837, the Afghan troops defeat the Sikh army and kill Ranjit Singh's commander-in-chief Hari Singh, Harlan writes:

> The proud King of Lahore quailed upon his threatened throne as he exclaimed with terror and approaching despair: Harlan has avenged himself. This is all his work.

Harlan leads the Emir of Kabul's forces northward across the Hindu Kush. In the northern principalities he fights and intrigues to assert Kabul's sovereignty. He recrosses the Hindu Kush, meets the Princes of Hazarajat, is elected Prince of Ghor and supreme among them. They promise to follow him if he will take up arms against the outside world. But the British are already in the country. Harlan becomes commander-in-chief of the Afghan forces. Is forced to flee. And his oriental adventure is over. At the age of forty-two he returns to Philadelphia.

The Tom Sawyer who five or ten years later sits beside the Mississippi dreaming of becoming a pirate, the terror of the high seas, and of returning to his home town clothed in honors; of walking down the street in his great sea boots, casting black glances at the shrinking crowds who whisper, "There goes the Terror of the Seven Seas"—Tom Sawyer would certainly have been disappointed had he known how little attention was the lot of the Equerry of the Imperial Stirrup among Philadelphia's Quakers.

He was not as rich as he believed. All the money he had sent home had melted away in speculative investments. He married, could not get along with his wife's family, and was frozen out. No one had the patience to listen to his tales of adventures and wars in distant lands. For ten months at the beginning of the Civil War he was Colonel of Harlan's Light Cavalry in the Army of the Potomac. Then for a while he lived in retirement at Philadelphia; emigrated to California; and settled down as a doctor in San Francisco, where no medical certificates were required. Died, and was buried. In Afghan history, he has one line devoted to him: ". . . a notorious American adventurer, by name Harlan . . . " His fate, too, seems to be an adventurer's. His tragedy the tragedy of a TV serial. But that is an optical illusion. His was no dream of adolescent adventure. He did not come home in sea boots, clothed in blood and honor. True, he notes with a certain pride that he had been Prince of Ghor —it is a trait of normal human vanity. But what interests him most is his description of Hazarajat, its people, its mountains, and its passes. He was a Pennsylvania Yankee at the Emir's court.

He was a different sort of adventurer from that found in boys' stories. He has written the best military topography so far of Northern Afghanistan. He was obsessed with an objective passion for facts. Earlier than most, he foresaw commercial-political developments in Central Asia. A Yankee, he was no friend of the British or British colonialism.

His matter-of-fact description of British fiscal methods is filled with disgust at their tortures and inhumanity. He warns Russia against the British advance, emphasizing that Russia's vital interests must not be left in the hands of irresponsible adventurers whose behavior in no wise accords with their nation's good reputation.

He plans railways across the Russian steppes and the deserts of Central Asia. He proposes proper river traffic on the Amu Darya. Again and again he returns to his talk of the British. Their ruthless taxation and plunder intrigue him. But he also realizes the novelty of this commercial empire.

> . . . and the inevitable result of contact with the English, appearing first as mercantile adventurers, followed by armies and ending in permanent conquests, has impressed an unqualified conviction that the commercial enterprise of England is in fact the precursor of invasion and pretext of conquest.

Back in the United States, he becomes one of the men who urge the import of camels. He is a Yankee and a rationalist. He asserts that the deserts of the West cry out for camels. Right in the middle of the Civil War he applies for a government grant to explore Afghanistan, for a journey to collect the seeds and plants of vines and fruit trees. The Afghan fruits are superior, he says, and the climate in the western United States corresponds to that of Afghanistan. But no grants are obtainable in time of war.

His tragedy is deeper than that of adolescent dreams. His tragedy is that he was a heroic bourgeois, torn between his republican, puritan conscience, his rationalist pioneer spirit, and his greed for money; between his passion for intrigue and his craving for power. In the end none of these find satisfaction, and he dies as a quack doctor in the American Far West.

XVIII

The first time we saw Kabul, it was from the Khairkhana Pass.
The city lay spread out beneath us. All around that town, with its
greenery and vegetation, the mountains stood up red and sharp. Just
beyond Charikar, where we had come down out of the Hindu Kush
by the Ghorband Valley, the asphalt road came out to meet us and
led us through the wealthiest and most fertile agricultural district:
the fertile valleys of Kohistan and Koh-i-daman, where across fields
of ripening corn the white villages clamber up the mountainsides.
Now the road was leading up over the last pass, and beneath the
serpentine twists and turns of its asphalt lay Kabul.

There was a nip in the morning air as we drove in toward the
town. The houses stood yellow in their gardens, and in the clear air
the red mountains seemed very close. Slowly we drove through the
streets as the bazaars were opening.

Kabul is no monumental city. No city of memorials. Baber's
Grave, a couple of Buddhist cliff temples in its neighborhood, this
is all that is left after all the wars of all the millennia. These buildings have no style. Yet few cities resemble Kabul. We stayed long.
The city lies at a height of some six thousand feet above sea level
and the sky up here seems so high and free. In travel books I have
read how travelers after crossing the Hindu Kush from as far as the
Khairkhana Pass have seen a grey-brown treeless city, and afterward
driven into a dust-blown conglomeration of buildings stinking with
impurities. To read this always amazes me. For this city is as lovely
as Granada. Lovelier, for its air is clearer, its mountains closer, and
the contrast between them, so hard, so stern, so barren, and the city's
leafy gardens, its terraces of old houses clambering over the slopes,
its swarms of people, so strong, so sharp.

But now we were arriving in Kabul for the first time, and other
years and later journeys will only reinforce the impression we gain
of greenery and high-altitude air. We walk toward the bazaars, the
meeting place of all the peoples of Asia. Once, roofed over, these
bazaars were famed for their beauty. Then the British burned them

down and plundered their shops. Today the city's streets again pulse strongly with life.

But the street kennel through the bazaar quarters is a stinking open sewer, sluggishly flowing with a stream of filth. A boy scoops up the water in his hand, gargles, and spits it back into the kennel. A woman tourist in a flowery dress walks by. At the sight of the slowly flowing sewage her eyes widen in disgust; she purses her lips and hurries on her way, hunting for genuine carpets and silver-plated earrings.

"They are the dirtiest of all God's creatures. They do not wash after obeying calls of nature nor do they wash their hands after meals. They are as lousy as asses." This was not said of the Afghans, however. It was said of the Swedes, by the ambassador of the Caliphate, Ibn Fadlan, who in the tenth century made my ancestors' revolting acquaintance.

In the eyes of the tourist everything strange seems exotic. Exoticism turns into scorn for humanity. Other folks' culture, other folks' customs become distorted by our smugness. A normal European Christian can speak of the superstitions of the Mohammedans without for an instant reflecting on what a Moslem might have to say of a religion where divine service culminates in the believers eating up their god.

The street we are now walking down does not reach as far as the new buildings. It leads past no ministries or palaces. It is a perfectly ordinary street, in a town high up in the Central Asian mountain massif. In the wood merchant's turban the entire history of urbanization can be read—likewise his own. He has just recently moved into town. No longer is his turban six yards long, only four. For the cloth has been bought, and bought cloth costs money. His wooden-soled sandals bear witness to the cultural stream which has been sweeping Asia. He weighs the wood meticulously; for in a country with so few forests as Afghanistan wood fetches the same price as bread.

A pakhtou walks by. He is carrying a mother-of-pearl inlaid gun and wears crossed bandoleers on his chest. I enjoy being in a city where men have the right to carry weapons. In a world where right grows out of a gun it is pleasant to be in a country where everyone carries his own gun. It is a promise of popular power.

XIX

Early one morning we drive out of Kabul. We are on our way to India. The sun has just risen. The plain of Kabul still lies shrouded in darkness, but the mountains around us are all aglow. The air is fresh and chilly. There is a touch of autumn in the air. After we have left the city behind us, the morning light arrives. The shadows shorten, and in brilliant sunshine we drive straight for the red mountains. They open to receive us, and we follow the Kabul River into the gorge. We are en route for Sarobi, Jalalabad, and the Khyber. The water foams and froths beside us, splashes up across the road, and the rapids follow close upon each other. The way bends and twists, crosses bridges, and clambers up the mountain face. Bores into a tunnel through loose boulders. And ahead we see the mountains—beneath and all around us—as the road, veering sharply this way and that, plummets down the steeps. Rock faces and a glittering river. Sometimes we drive into a dark shade, and then out again into the brilliant light. The ground is hard and bare.

We pass a road-workers' camp. Then another. These camps turn into six-mile cities of tents. The Afghan army. It is building this new road down to the plain country. Communications with the outside world have become necessary. The new road is a good one, a broad gravel surface, soon to be asphalted. The contours of the landscape become softer, and we reach Sarobi. The new power station. Its stern concrete beauty melts into the contours of the landscape, and with giant strides the high-tension cables march away over the mountains toward Kabul.

The farming lands are enclosed by valleys. The lower one descends, the broader become the strips of plowed land. Then again long sterile wastes of stone and dry plains. Again the red cliffs approach, and the river flows more turbulently. But the mountains are not so high now. The river is crossed by an iron suspension bridge: the road up to the Kunar Valley and Nuristan. The bridge is guarded by a military patrol. The passengers have to get out of their bus on one side and cross it on foot to another bus which is waiting on the other. Then the Jalalabad plain. Far away the high snow-capped mountains. The air is heavier here. Dusty. Makes your throat smart. And hot. We meet the old road from Kabul and drive into Jalalabad.

It was on that old road that, on January 13, 1842, the British Army of Kabul reached safety in the British-occupied fort of Jalalabad. It was the year of the First Afghan War. The British had marched into Kabul, deposed Dost Mohammed, brought back Shah Shuja and placed him on the throne. Afghanistan had become an ally of Britain. On January 13, from the fort at Jalalabad, they caught sight of a solitary wounded ragged-uniformed man staggering out of the desert. He was the only survivor out of 16,500 troops and camp followers who had left Kabul a week before.

The first British-Afghan War was a failure. All historians agree on that. The British started the war, saying Dost Mohammed was pro-Russian and had to be removed. But in the end, so as not to perish in the chaos they themselves had caused, the British were obliged to beg him to resume his throne. Both as a strategist and a politician the Governor General at Calcutta was a failure. The general was senile. The ambassador was young, inexperienced, and too inclined to erotic intrigues, and no one gave ear to what wise advice he might have to offer. The staff was a wasp's nest of petty personal intrigue; the officers incapable; the morale of the troops doubtful; the confusion indescribable; and the home public kept thoroughly in the dark. Such are said to be the reasons for the British army's disaster—why the British met with their first, catastrophic defeat in a war against "natives." For the loss of the Kabul Army shattered the myth. An undefeated and undefeatable army had ceased to exist. Infantry and cavalry, gunners, staff officers, the general, the ambassador, the whores, the orderlies, and the profiteers, all were dead. And that was when the war was lost. The following year's pyromaniac expedition was no more than a gesture, albeit a bloody one.

But this does not explain the defeat. Merely establishes its great extent, the fact that the myth was shattered, and that even before it had finished being built the British Empire had met with its first serious reverse, its subsequent expansion being accompanied by ever greater and bloodier reverses.

None of this applies more to this war than to other wars. Ineffectual politicians, senile generals, intriguing staff officers, half-witted ambassadors, general confusion, and a public kept in the dark—all this has been part of the normal picture for all of us. Quite other factors lost the British their First Afghan War.

After this defeat the story of Afghan treachery was heard, for the first time. The specifically British version of the legend of the stab in the back. Afghans were not gentlemen. Afghans were treacherous. Afghans were uncivilized. The Afghans even refused to understand that they had lost. The British had come up against a free people. A barbarian people, who still retained their barbaric liberties. And the moment the British threatened the Afghans' vital interests, all their diplomacy, all their games of intrigue, all their legalism became meaningless.

The British signed a worthless treaty. A chieftain, a king, had no right to sign treaties. Without the approval of the popular assembly a treaty was not worth the paper it was written on. The British had intended to wage a normal war on a monarch and his subjects; and found themselves waging war against a people in arms.

But where in quite another historic situation the Romans had admired the free Germanic tribes, idealized them and held them up as a model for their own citizens, the Victorian British gentleman saw in the Afghan war of liberation a mere violation of the rules of the game. The British army was chased down through the mountains, was slaughtered in the passes, slipped in the wet clays, was plummeted from cliffs. All discipline vanished. In panic terror men hunted each other to death while the Afghans sat on their mountain crags and picked them off one by one.

As far as the British were concerned, this defeat helped to swell the hatred with which they saw the Afghans. Afghans being no gentlemen, no one need feel obliged any longer to abide by the rules of the game. Thereafter no action was too brutal or dastardly.

Power brutalizes, and turns men into soldiers. Kipling's gentlemen sang:

> For you all love the Screw-guns—the Screw-guns
>   they all love you!
> So when we take tea with a few guns, o' course
>   you will know what to do-hoo! hoo!
> Just send in your Chief an' surrender—it's worse
>   if you fights or you runs:

You may hide in the caves, they'll be only your
graves, but you can't get away from
the guns!

The Empire transformed the petty bourgeois Victorian gentleman into an "Übermensch." Not a superman, just a slave-driver.

For the Afghans this victorious war was a great step toward national unity. True, in the next half-century, the British managed bit
by bit to gnaw into Afghan territory; the frontiers were pushed further and further back. But they never succeeded in controlling this
people, and English literature and the memoirs of British officers
and administrators are filled with bitterness against this treacherous
people whose love they never succeed in winning and on whose word
they can never rely. At the same time they love those Afghans and
Pathans who, enrolled in the British army, fought for the British
Empire against their own people. These are the good Afghans: hon-
orable, honest, righteous, and altogether admirable—in British literature. But although the whole of Baluchistan was lost and the
British ruled from the Indus to the Khyber and although the British
Empire reached Spin Baldak and Quetta was lost, the British never
succeeded in conquering the country. Only in occupying it.

Afghanistan kept its independence, but at a high price. In order
to preserve that independence the Afghans were forced to close their
country to all foreigners. To prevent the British from running their
foreign policy on their behalf, their only recourse was to have no
foreign policy at all. Afghanistan became the closed country of Asia.
But as early as 1907 Afghanistan seemed once again to be strong
enough to adopt an open attitude toward the empires. In that year
the Emir, Habibullah, refused to ratify an agreement between Russia and Great Britain: the agreement which, for all futurity, was to
have regulated the two empires' mutual affairs. For this document
the British Government failed utterly to obtain Afghan ratification.
No one had consulted the Afghans. Therefore they said they would
sign nothing. The agreement, the British assured them, guaranteed
their independence. But the Afghan view was that, not having been
present, they could know nothing of the matter. The simple fact
was, they had become strong enough to refuse.

We drive away through the wide rolling grey-brown landscape.

The heat is intense. We are on our way down out of the mountains. Clay forts stand on the hillocks. Fortified farms. Massive towers of sun-dried clay dominate the buildings, but in this great open landscape even these forts seem tiny pinpoints. More and more the mountains disappear steadily behind the mist and haze; the soil flies in the wind; and we are on our way toward the Khyber Pass.

It was here the Third Afghan War was fought out. It was a queer war. An Afghan student had told me: "Twice the British declared war on us and lost. In the third war we attacked—and won!"

According to the history books, Afghanistan is supposed to have first demanded her complete independence. During the ensuing negotiations this is said to have been refused. They then attacked the British and were thoroughly defeated. Whereon the British, out of sheer magnanimity, it seems, granted all the Afghans' demands. It sounds too good to be true. It isn't.

On May 3, 1919, without any declaration of war, hostilities began with fighting at Torkham. The British forces of 340,000 veterans were faced by only 38,000 ill-equipped Afghan infantry, 4,000 artillery using antique cannons, and 8,000 cavalry. Just how it all began is shrouded in a certain darkness. The Empire of the British in India had always grown as a result of "incidents." The innocent British, if we are to believe the history books, were being eternally attacked, and in pure self-defense and possessed with a deep love of peace found themselves obliged to conquer half a continent.

In 1919 many leading British politicians and military men were hoping that Russia's Central Asian empire was on the point of total collapse. As for the British Empire, it had never appeared so strong. Russia, ravaged and torn by war, with British armies on Russian soil. Turkey crushed. The Caliphate stripped of all significance. A Middle East occupied by British and French military. The hour was surely at hand when all Asia would fall like a ripe apple. All over Asia the millennium of the *Pax Britannica* was about to dawn. Today, after the Second World War, after the disintegration of the British Empire and the great wave of national liberations, it seems almost beyond belief that people, only one generation ago, could have been thinking in such categories. But at that time, in the eyes of many British officers, the goal was within sight. At last the Central Asian market was to open up!

In this situation the victory of the Afghans acquired historical importance. Both in Afghanistan and Turkey the British had to yield to the new Asian nationalism. For, in spite of all, the Afghans *were* victorious. The chain of defeats and failures which had fettered the Moslem peoples for so long snapped at the very moment when the Empire seemed strongest.

The British offensive against Jalalabad had to be held up when Mohammed Nadir Khan (who later ascended the throne of Afghanistan) advanced on the central front. He attacked the British at their weakest point: their lack of real control over the peoples they had been ruling. The British had to flee from their fortresses. The Pathans rebelled. All India was in danger of bursting into flames. The British bombed with their airplanes; and opened peace negotiations.

We drive through the Khyber. A low, unimpressive pass, whose only significance is that it was here the British troops were stationed; here reports were written, and likewise ballads on British heroism.

Gun is ill. The change in atmospheric pressure as we had driven down from the high mountains, the sudden heat, the stifling humid air of the plains all made her feel ill. As we drove up to the Afghan customs station she was asleep up on the baggage. When the soldiers, young recruits in baggy uniforms and coarse boots, saw how poorly she was they became anxious. In less than a minute passport controls were over, there was no talk of inspecting our baggage. The officer said, "The woman mustn't travel if she's not well. She must rest."

With almost Spanish dignity and natural politeness, everything was done for us. They evacuated their own accommodation, saying, "You are our guests."

We were filthy, tired and sweaty. They gave us water and beds. They brought us tea and wondered if we wouldn't like something to eat. As we laid Gun down on a charpoy in the shade of the trees in the garden, the soldiers, not wishing to disturb us by their proximity, withdrew to a distance. A young soldier, he couldn't have been more than eighteen, brought a fan. As he gave it to me he said, "Khanum doesn't feel well. She must be cooled." Then he ran off, and sat down fifty yards away, among his comrades who sat there embracing their rifles, looking away toward the mountains.

"They don't want you to be embarrassed by being looked at,"

said the commander of the frontier post. He had come over to ask whether we were displeased in any way. Whether there was anything more he could do for us?

"But this is impossible," I said. "We can't take over your house, your beds, your food."

"You are our country's guests," he said. "Our house is yours. We must all help each other. And the woman is sick."

1959

INDIA

XX

DALA RAM'S JAIPUR, 1728

Of most cities in the world it can be said as the girl of her baby: "It just happened." Cities, like children, have their causes, chance is no more chancy than it can be treated statistically. But completely planned cities are about as rare as completely planned children. And India, of course, is no exception.

But Jaipur is different. Jaipur lies in Rajasthan. It is a region which hovers on the borders between absolute desert and lands which, if irrigated, could be made arable. Under the British the region was called Rajputana, and was the abode of several maharajahs. Here the feudal type of state was preserved right up to the country's independence in 1947. It is also the part of India whose memories are the most warlike and heroic. For a long while it resisted the Moguls. In it one meets with a certain scorn for other, less stern parts of the country.

Up to only yesterday Jaipur was the capital of the principality of the same name. Now it is the capital of the Indian federal state of Rajasthan. Its last maharajah, Man Singh II, ascended the throne in 1931, and had to quit it in 1949.

The city was founded in 1728 by the Maharajah Sawai Jai Singh II, from whom it also gets its name (Jai's city). This warrior prince and vassal of the Moguls was an Indian prince of the same type as the later Ludwig II of Bavaria. Jai Singh was a famous warrior; with the help of his astronomers under the leadership of the learned Vidyahar, he was himself an astronomer and author of the work *The Motions of the Heavenly Bodies.* He set up astronomical observatories at Jaipur, Delhi, Mathura, Benares, and Ujjain, equipped them with instruments of his own invention and had carried through a reform of the Indian calendar. After a glorious reign of forty-four years he died, and three of his wives and innumerable concubines threw themselves (or let themselves be thrown) onto his funeral pyre and as saints went one and all straight up to heaven. Such was the man who created the first city in India with an over-all city plan.

The old name for this region was Dhundar. Desert. Jai Singh's choice of the site was not merely for strategic reasons. It is true there was water there, building materials and potential drainage and communications. Also natural beauty. But Jai Singh's strongest motive was that the whole region was a desert. Here he would build his own city. A capital to be called after him, unique in the Orient. No one should contest his status.

Jaipur is known as the Pink City. This because the buildings along its main street are pink. This, however, has nothing to do with its city plan. It was a much later maharajah, Ram Singh II (1835–1888) who, influenced by Europe's painted houses, had each of the city's streets painted a different color. One green, the next yellow, etc. Only the pink remain. In doing this Maharajah Ram Singh II can also certainly be said to have taken his place in the history of city planning.

He can be seen as a spiritual uncle of some of our suburbs around Stockholm. But originally the city was white. White it was planned, and white it was built.

As to the planning of the city, it is true that Maharajah Jai Singh II sent for plans of European cities and ordered the work to be carried out. But the actual planner was Dala Ram, his chief architect, whom he borrowed from the Mogul court. He it was, together with the chief eunuch Panah Mian, likewise borrowed from the Mogul court, who had the honor of paying for it all.

Dala Ram planned the city as a rectangle, with its streets at right angles. Not a perfect rectangle, inasmuch as its northwestern corner is cut off by the Amber Hills, and one of the nine main blocks, or

110

nidhis, lies outside the rectangle, east of the city center. This devia-
tion from European rectangularity is not haphazard. Its irregularity
protects it from the absolute rectangle which, in the classical doctrine of Indian architecture, is regarded as evil and of ill omen. The
city is surrounded by a crenellated wall, seven ells (20 feet) high,
and embellished with seven beautiful gates.

The city's traffic plan has been thoroughly thought out; broad
main streets for through traffic, little local streets, without through
traffic, to meet the needs of its various blocks. The broad main
streets divide the city up into eight nidhis (plus one nidhi outside
the rectangle). The two central nidhis consist of the Maharajah's
palace and public buildings. The nidhis intended for the population are then divided up into quarters, blocks, or mohallas. Each
mohalla gets its name from the occupation assigned to it, all in
accordance with the traditions of the oriental bazaar and with
medieval European practice. The important thing about this division, however, is that for the first time we here meet with a conscious
attempt at giving the segregation and stratification of Indian society
a rectangular and "modern" framework.

It was Dala Ram's intention to enhance the squares created by
the intersection of the main streets with a uniform architecture; but
the Maharajah Jai Singh II died in September, 1743, and the city
which Dala Ram had planned and had had to pay for, but which his
prince had glorified with his own name, was never completed.

Later generations went on building planlessly, building in the
normal way. To the southeast the city outgrew its city walls, new
palaces were built, and a patch of British garden suburbia was
added; the street crossings were reconstructed into traffic circles—
efficient obstacles to motor traffic, but even more so to a traffic of ox
carts.

Within the center of the city many lovely houses were built.
The Hawa Mahal, the palace of the winds, is justly famous. The
population grew. It exploded all plans. Refugees arrived from Pakistan. The arcades became hidden behind marquees and rubbish. But
notwithstanding these two centuries of planlessness and population
overflow, Dala Ram's plan is still fully discernible at Jaipur. Its
stern astringency, it is true, was not able to cope with the population
increase. (What city plan ever has been? Or been planned for a

The mighty build their monuments. But they are not able to rob the people of art and decoration. Against the marble palaces of the rulers the people decorate their dung heaps.

population increase on a scale which has invariably followed?) Even so, the planless builders and the masses of humanity which came pouring in were not able to shatter his scheme.

Not only did Dala Ram build the most thoroughgoing of all Indian feudal cities; comparison even with the British-inspired districts to the southeast also shows how far ahead of his time he was. For good or for ill, he was the first and greatest modern city planner in India. That Jaipur bears a maharajah's name can never steal the real glory from Dala Ram.

XXI

THE CAPITAL OF IMPERIALISM—SIR EDWIN LUTYEN'S NEW DELHI

Half a century ago Britain was still a great power. Not only a great power, but *the* great power. Like the Spanish Empire a few centuries before, it knew no sunsets. The mere thought of the Empire being anywhere obfuscated by twilight was sheer heresy. The Empire was the kingdom, the power and the glory. All to the ever greater honor of the pound, parliament, and civilization.

In India—not in the potato fields of Mecklenburg—did the European petty bourgeoisie start to develop as rulers over others. Here, as never before or after, the ruling race attained to power and luxury. The British Empire was mighty, and its power brutal. So powerful and so brutal, that the home country could afford the luxuries of parliamentarianism, liberalism, and the rule of law. Something which Hitler, for lack of might—if not of brutality— could not afford his Berliners.

Its might seemed assured. Two generations ago rebellion had been crushed. One generation before, the crown imperial had passed to Queen Victoria. The scions of the petty electorate of Hanover (who had as yet not, for patriotic motives, adopted the name of Windsor) had been placed on the throne of the Moguls. Unrest and dissatisfaction in the country were regarded as having been canalized into safe channels (or at least reliably controlled) by minor reforms, instigated communal strife, and British education.

In 1911 the residence of the Viceroy and the capital of the Indian Empire were moved from Calcutta to Delhi. That was symbolic. The capital was moved out of the great commercial city on the Bay of Bengal to the old Mogul capital. India's historic center. The Empire had come to stay.

New Delhi, which was intended to be the proudest monument to British Imperial city planning, was not ready for its inauguration until February 15, 1931. But by then twilight had already begun to descend on the Empire.

To make democracy safe against Prussianism—or, more precisely, to secure the pound against the deutschemark, and its own possessions against others' claims to a share of the plunder—the Empire had fought and won a world war. But the victory of the pound had cost sterling its position. Now the pound was in retreat. No longer did the City lightly carry the White Man's Burden, the whole world, on its back. The City, too, was shaken by the great crisis; and in September that same year the pound loses all appearance of total supremacy. Great Britain is forced off the gold standard. A war and a generation later—and the British Empire is no more. Great Britain herself, sunk to the level of a nation of the third rank, begins to share the fate of the Spanish Empire, to experience the sunset of her power. At that moment New Delhi becomes the capital of the Republic of India.

Delhi is a distorted version of Dilli. That is how the name is pronounced, and how it should be spelled, inasmuch as the city gets its name from King Dilu of Kanauj, who ruled in the eighth century. Here lie the ruins of capital after capital. For Delhi is the new key to India. He who controls this city controls the immense plains of Northern India, and the roads into Central India. Here the Punjab plain meets the plains of the Ganges. And hither, century after century, conquerors have come to establish their empires.

Delhi lies on the west bank of the Jumna River. Or, more precisely, it lies to the west of the river. Delhi is not a unit. It consists of several units, of which at least two, Delhi and New Delhi, are also administratively separate (the capital of the Republic of India is called New Delhi, not Delhi) . Old Delhi is a typical Indian city. The population density is astounding. A street is a world. All wears a lively, fascinating aspect—albeit with an active TB rate of between 2 per cent and 6 per cent, depending on the density and general standard of any given quarter. Even so, Old Delhi with its monuments, its bazaars, its immense concentration of refugees and its unplanned network of streets, is a living city. A city which has grown organically, and which, even though it lacks the most elementary public hygiene, permits Indians to live like Indians. If the city could be cleaned up and rebuilt without changing its basic characteristics it would be one of the really charming and pleasant cities of the world. It is not its swarms of people, but its tuberculosis, its overcrowding, its poverty, its social structure which are evil. Any other way of seeing the matter is mere aestheticism; anti-human. An Indian city for Indian people in an Indian climate and an Indian culture will always remain Indian. Otherwise it is not a city; just a muddle of houses. However beautifully it may be planned on paper.

North of Old Delhi lie "the Civil Lines." Also the university, the old secretariat, and the better-class old hotels. Here the city wears quite another aspect. Even if built by Indian workers with Indian materials, it is not an Indian city. It is the old British cantonment in Delhi. Where the rulers lived, and from which they ruled until New Delhi was developed.

"The Civil Lines" belong to a type of town one meets everywhere in India where the British have had their abode. Already, as soon as we had passed the Khyber, we have met with it at Peshawar. It is the British garden suburb in an Indian climate. Hedges, winding roads where it is difficult to find your way, houses hidden away in gardens, plantations, empty streets, the isolated habitations of the upper class. But these towns are no mere British garden suburbs in an Indian climate, affording all the luxuries of the ruling class; they, in turn, have also influenced the British garden suburb. One can turn the question around, and say that Hampstead Garden Suburb is a shrunken and inept version of "the Civil Lines." The home country was poorer, afforded smaller possibilities. The relation between the cantonments in India and the garden suburbs in Britain is not uni-directional. There is a mutual influence. Britain outside Britain; but even the ruler's bungalow is squeezed into a sooty, poverty-stricken, and petty bourgeois suburb. And this brings our own Swedish early twentieth-century suburbs into a complex family relationship with "the Civil Lines," north of the squalor of Old Delhi. As soon as New Delhi was ready, "the Civil Lines" were evacuated by the British. Now the town is the abode of an Indian upper class.

New Delhi lies south of Old Delhi. The town was planned by Sir Edwin Lutyens and Sir Herbert Baker. It is a city of imperialist monumentality. Its architecture has touches of Mussolini. The very choice of Raisina Hill for the government buildings at the end of the endless show street of Kingsway (now rebaptized Rajpat), at whose other end the king's statue looks out from the Anglo-Indian triumphal arch, is reminiscent of Mussolini's study. The long empty space. At its end the ruler. Chilly. Splendiferous. New Delhi's site is said to have been selected with care. There is a lot of talk about the city's axis (east–west). Old forts are turned into metaphysics. In point of fact New Delhi consists of a number of show streets, broad, empty of people, bordered by trees. Where its streets cross, an infinity of traffic circles and de luxe bungalows hidden away in the shade of their gardens. Its distances are huge. It is virtually impossible to find your way about. But it is grandiose, monumental and—like the boulevards of Paris—easily defended against a mob.

This is not to say the city is not functional. Every city plan is functional. The statement is meaningless unless one says what function one has in mind. In this case, the ruling class's function as rulers.

To say that New Delhi is easy to defend against a mob is no jest. Quite obviously the city has been planned militarily. Between New Delhi's blocks, designed for a ruling class, and Old Delhi's swarming humanity, there lay—unexploited—an empty space. Communications between the two cities were limited to three routes. Nor do its grandiose street perspectives, in which, as if by magic, the individual vanishes, offer any cover to a mass of people. A couple of machine guns, and the Empire—should the Indian masses ever have

Chandigarh. The architecture of neo-colonialism.

tried to flood into the administrative capital—would have been saved. City planners propose, but history disposes. When the day came, even a million machine guns could not save the Empire. The Empire builders chose to flee rather than stand and fight a war they must inevitably lose. Paris was worth a Mass, and Britain's Indian investments worth a retreat.

One of the many things they left behind was India's capital.

There the British had carried one step further the tradition which began at Jaipur. They segregated the residential districts, the civil servants' districts, where the civil servant, every time he is promoted, changes his environment. A difference in salary scale means a different residential area, a different school, and a different number of square feet of floor space. Where, when you know a man's address, you know his salary.

XXII

LE CORBUSIER AND CHANDIGARH

"You foreigners!" said the Indian journalist. "The only thing you're interested in here in India is the Taj Mahal and Chandigarh. And the erotic temple sculptures, of course."

"Tigers, holy men, and corpse cremation interest them, too," said his friend.

"Foreigners!" said the journalist. "You come here, take a look around, and then go home and write about the soul of India."

"And our Chandigarhian future," said his friend.

"India," said the journalist, "d'you know what India is? Half a million dung heaps calling themselves villages. As Gandhi said. It's our villages you should write about."

"Our steelworks," said his friend. "Our great river regulation schemes. That's where you'll find our future. If we have one."

"Instead all you do is go to Chandigarh and write about the city's head and its belly and its feet. Soul and sun-breaks, cubism, and beauty. And call it functionalism in India."

It's true. I have read about Chandigarh in the daily and weekly press, in trade union journals and women's magazines, in building magazines and young people's broadsheets. It's true, what they say in India. Westerners are obsessed with Chandigarh.

Well, I suppose there is always a satisfaction (however unconscious) in finding the familiar in the strange. Chandigarh was also India's first great constructive propaganda item after the independence (extraverted propaganda, that is—not for consumption by the home public). And Chandigarh's fascination grows in geometrical ratio to the distance you are from it. It's also so very much easier, so much more natural to admire (or honestly assess) what is already admired. In European consciousness Le Corbusier and the Taj Mahal have their well-furnished niches. The Taj Mahal's is older; but Le Corbusier's has already begun to acquire its classic patina.

The first time we arrived in Chandigarh we drove around for

two hours, searching for the town. Then we heard we were already in the town. Had been for two hours. Chandigarh is said to stand at the foot of the slopes of the Himalayas. That sounds good. In clear weather one does in fact catch a glimpse of the hills, far away. The town stands on a plain. One of the largest plains in the world. The plainlands of North India. In summer it is one of the world's hottest spots. In winter, cold and windy. Sandstorms, monsoon rains. I doubt whether the scattered (very widely scattered) houses provide any protection either against heat, wind, sand, or rain. My personal experience suggests the opposite. In point of climate Chandigarh is one of the few places I personally should refuse to live in, and which I should seriously dissuade others from living in, either. Years and the green belt may perhaps lend a certain patina to its emptiness. But where, among Chandigarh's suburbs, can you find a city?

The fact is, Chandigarh is problematic, and its problems fascinate. Those problems do not lie in any narrow architectonic considerations, in how to protect oneself from the sun, or in its building materials; nor in Le Corbusier's surely rather speculative notions of city planning. Doubtless all these things have their interest and confront you in the town's very aspect. But the essential problem lies on quite another level. The question is not how it came about that Chandigarh was built in the style it was built in; but why it was built at all. The answer to the second question gives us our answer to the first, even to the question of how to protect oneself from the sun, and why it is built of the building materials it is built of.

An answer not merely historico-political, either; but politico-tactical.

India's partition was a tragedy. The everlasting imperial game of dividing to rule has yielded bloody dividends. It is hard to say just how consciously British policy aimed at the country's partition. But the acts of the British over two generations, the game they played vis-à-vis religious groups and caste groups made partition, if not inevitable (that is still being discussed in India), then hard to avoid. They played a hard game, and a clever one, a game which even when the Empire collapsed made it possible for them to retain their investments, the greater part of their economic power, and to turn independence into a legal formality.

122

These were not two countries, even so, which each went its own way. It was not like the dissolution of the Swedish-Norwegian Union in 1905. Now India was bisected by frontiers. Frontiers drawn straight through language units, cultural units, economic units, and historical units. The Punjab was no longer the Punjab. Lahore went to Pakistan, and the Eastern Punjab to India. In the feudal maharajah states, the maharajahs received princely pensions and princely privileges.

Of old, Lahore had been the region's central city. Its climate was bad, but its power and wealth were great. Now the Punjab is split in two. From which follows the simple—deceptively simple—answer, that since Lahore is out of the picture, the Indian Punjab must have a new capital. Whereupon they began to build one. Deceptively simple, inasmuch as cities already existed. Even capital cities.

There was Patiala. It had been the capital of the maharajah states of the Punjab. Now it was the seat of PEPSU's (Patiala and East Punjab States Union) administration. But Patiala—it was objected—was dangerous, as its maharajah still exerted power and influence. Patiala was a maharajah's city, built in the shadow of his palace. But other Indian cities, even though they were once the capitals of maharajahs, have remained capitals.

Others say Patiala was out of the question simply because it was so dirty. Chandigarh, however, has cost a great deal more than a sanitation department. The real reason why Patiala was not considered was that Amritsar—the city of the Sikhs—was excluded, and therefore no one dared give preference to Hindu Patiala. Rather, in that case, a new city altogether.

For Amritsar regarded itself as the obvious choice. It was the Sikhs' sacred city. There stands their golden temple. The city was founded by their fourth guru, Ram Das. Destroyed at the end of the eighteenth century by the Afghans, it was rebuilt at the beginning of the nineteenth by the great man of the Sikh empire, Ranjit Singh.

The Sikhs are a religious group. Also a militant one. Their religion is a compromise between Islam and Hinduism. What one might call a reformed Hinduism. The Sikhs are soldiers and policemen, administrators, taxi drivers, mechanics; but also peasants.

They constitute a community without castes. And the Sikhs never forget that it was under their leadership that the Punjab was made into an independent state, at war with both the Afghans and the British; and that if it foundered as an independent state this was less as a consequence of any Sikh military incompetence than as a result of clever British intrigues.

The Sikhs had desperately opposed the partition of India. When it came, it cut right through their community. They saw it as a threat to their existence. A divided Punjab was a divided Sikh community. When partition became inevitable, they took India's side—despite certain hopes that they would join Pakistan. So they felt they deserved a reward for having saved the Eastern Punjab for India. The Sikhs regarded Amritsar, therefore, as a self-evident choice as capital. For which very reason it became a political goal of the first order that Amritsar should *not* become capital of the Punjab. The Sikh had done his duty, and it was important to defuse him, before he could set up his own Sikhistan. Nor, on the other hand, must he be provoked to the limit by granting that honor to the Hindu city of Patiala. So, with both Amritsar and Patiala out of the running, the only thing that remained was to build an entirely new capital, as quickly as possible, to confirm Indian sway over the East Punjab, thus ensuring that no traditional bonds should cause the Punjab to gravitate toward Lahore, which now lay in enemy territory. And that is why Chandigarh was built. And why the Sikhs are now (1959) demanding an independent Sikhistan.

It was through this rather political-tactical than historico-political background, too, that Chandigarh came by many of its main traits (so fascinating to travelers). Hence its total absence of tradition and why a totally new city has been built plumb in the middle of one of the most traditional and historically important regions in the whole world, without a trace of any connections with its local culture, history, or traditions. Built, indeed, as if in terror of acknowledging any association with its surrounding reality. Chandigarh is a city without a memory. It has less character than the most humdrum Swedish railway town. Less historical than Salt Lake City. And when they wanted to find a name for Chandigarh all they could find, northeast of the city, was a village temple in honor of the goddess Chandi (the female demon who slaughters souls on the field of battle). All these background facts must be taken into account if one is to make a true assessment of the serious criticisms leveled in various quarters at the city's lack of traditions. No cubistic Potemkin scenery can conceal the fact that the city has been begotten as an offspring of foxy politics. A bend sinister goes right through Le Corbusier's city plan.

There is another reason, too, why the layout of Chandigarh is so sternly lacking in tradition. Its formal functionalism, which makes such an inhuman not to say un-Indian impression on a visitor—and for that very reason elicits so many words of praise from Europeans —is overdetermined. Psychological explanations of social events are always dangerous and uncertain. But not to recognize the horrified disgust with which the liberal political leaders of independent India and their whole generation saw the country burst into blood-stained lunacy would be seriously to underestimate them. With liberation came partition. The national future for which that generation had fought suddenly turned into a flood of millions and millions of refugees fleeing through the country. Through the streets of Calcutta, Utopia flowed in rivers of blood. The national struggle for liberation did not become a social environment; it became distorted into vendettas between neighbors, bloody revenge for imagined wrongs, and irrational religious feuds. They loved India. But there, suddenly before their eyes, stood India: hysterical, feverish, inhuman. The negation of their dream. A formal independence had taken the place of a social liberation. The aborted revolution assumed a horrible form.

For this reason one spot, at least, on the Indian map should be a refuge of logic, simplicity, strictness, and purity. Of one town, at least, should it be said: Here is the India of the future. A sane India. Or, as Nehru put it: "Chandigarh is the symbol of Indian freedom, no longer fettered by the traditions of the past."

This attitude, characteristic of the country's leaders of that time, gave Chandigarh's architects carte blanche to take complete leave of all Indian realities; drove them to create the unrealized (and never realizable) city plan which was to be Chandigarh's, an illusion in concrete.

Since then a great deal of water has flowed down India's river valleys. The years have gone by. India has been swept along the path

125

of her destiny. Her future did not lie in an administrative capital far out in the plains, but in her villages. There lie her problems and her great possibilities. Chandigarh is a future which is already passé. It was already passé in January, 1955, when the city began to function as a capital. The rationalist protest against irrationalism proved to be itself irrational. But by then the city and its city plan were fettered to an abstract scheme, already internationally famous. There was the place of pilgrimage. There the miracle must necessarily occur.

Chandigarh is not India's future. It is a mere aside, a diversion in India's development. The future will be found where real problems find real solutions. Chandigarh became a swarm of bureaucrats, remote from all reality. Since it had never been planned for an organic city life in an Indian environment, only a theoretical city life in a drawing-board environment, it did not even solve the refugee problem.

But history is seldom sparing in its ironies. Chandigarh, which was to have revealed a vision of the India of the future, but in reality was only a drawing-board product, was not even allowed to be "pure" drawing-board. It was obliged to compromise with all that is most retrogressive and dangerous in Indian society. It became an embodiment of what it was designed expressly to reject. Caste. Inequality. Scorn for humanity. Oppression.

It was Chandigarh's destiny to be planned in the tradition of Jaipur and New Delhi, one more step on the downward path which New Delhi represents compared with Jaipur. The Punjabi government—which in this case means the higher civil servants in the ICS, the Indian Civil Service, the British-schooled corps of bureaucrats—insisted inexorably on all its houses being built in categories. Here a colony for civil servants of salary grade X, with school and all. There a colony for civil servants in salary scale Y.

In Chandigarh this new caste system is stabilizing itself. Criticism of Chandigarh remains meaningless as long as such criticism dwells only on the details of its architecture. One must see that it is fundamentally anti-democratic. But also understand its history, and so not make the mistake of confounding Chandigarh with India. Neither the India of today, nor of tomorrow. Its sole connection with India is that it has adapted itself to, and compromised with, the higher bureaucracy's demand for salary castes in the administration and for discrimination between human beings. Chandigarh has adapted itself, not to the Indian present, but to the oldest and most dangerous of all prejudices. Least of all to that future which perhaps is even now being prepared.

XXIII

THE GREAT SLUM

Year by year the slums are growing. Beautiful cities are being gnawed away as by a cancer; and from a distance of six miles, approaching them across the plain, one can smell their sour smell of sewage. The slums are winning.

Slums are not, in the first instance, a city-planning problem. (What city-planning problem ever is?) The slums are a symptom of imperialism.

This is the root of the matter. Without it all talk of Asian cities, their clearance and their slums, remains nothing but a lot of empty talk. Or in reality—and whether due to ignorance or malice equally criminal—special pleading on behalf of the process which is turning them into slums.

A tourist reacts to Asian slums as to something strange and remote. Something "Asiatic." For him there is no immediate bridge between this "Asiatic" herd of rotting humanity and his well-ordered "Euro-American" suburbia. He who is rich enough to be a tourist—not a traveler—in India is rich enough never to see his own local slum. His only abiding memory of the slums is their stink and their beggars. After which he goes on to talk about soul and unchanging Asia. But the stench is no symptom of the Asiatic soul. It is always a by-product of that course of historical events which has raised the price of land, depressed wages, split up dwellings, and allowed rents to rise. In Asia as in Europe and in the United States. The profit system. Both symbolically and in reality it stinks. And if, furthermore—as in Asia—all the forests have been cut down to the last tree, all the irrigation canals and water supplies been allowed to fall into disrepair, and the old sewage system rendered unusable,

127

then one will arrive in record time at a point where any social group one may encounter is instantly recognizable by its smell.

Nor is beggary poverty. Beggary is an industry. Still, admittedly, at the manufacture stage; not yet, as with us, at the collection-in-aid-of-worthy-causes stage. (One of the USA's eight largest industries.) In Delhi, for example, a beggar's average monthly income is 200 rupees. Artisans get about half as much. Any parent who can place his child as a beggar can look forward to a safe future. He has every reason to give thanks to the gods (and the authorities and Mr. Peachum) for showing him such good will. The Asian slum is no special category of slum. If it differs from its European or American counterparts, it does so only in point of space. A slum's decorative aspect may vary somewhat from country to country, and from one culture to another. But it has never—all travel writers notwithstanding—been in any way the crux of the matter.

A ghetto in the United States, or a French bidonville, or an Indian basti all yield the same over-all impression. The shabby poverty. The vain attempts to humanize such an environment. The lack of cleanliness. The stench which surrounds the area like a wall. The tired, sick, and stupefied faces. These are not different simply because in one place the homes have been built out of wooden crates and corrugated iron, in another out of empty drums and bits of wood, and in a third of clay and twigs, and in the fourth place are a decaying old city block. Another important point. There is no such thing as Asiatic poverty. Only poverty in Asia.

But the slums are growing. To walk through Asia's cities is to walk down fine streets which are being eroded by slums. The slums are no mere shanty towns around the main part of the city. Slums have attacked the city itself. Only the upper classes' and the foreigners' bungalows with their gardens are sacrosanct. And even they only in appearance; for in its back yard where the servants have their quarters each sacrosanct bungalow is cultivating its own slum. In its gardens the overclass, too, is rearing slums.

Even the little villages are being eroded. The strict village plan is dissolving, yielding to the chaotic confusion of a planless slum. The classic ornamentation shrivels into rudimentary wall paintings, and only on dung heaps and the fuel stacks does the old décor survive. And only in certain villages. This is exploitation.

Its façade, gleaming like a Rolls Royce, is the profits which are the cause of the slums. And that is why slums are not a city-planning problem. Anyone could solve the city-planning problem of the slums: reduce the population density in the old quarters of the city, make them worthy of human beings and restore them to their normal function—simply by building new houses. Create new living space. Open up new opportunities for living. To solve the technical problems, drainage, water supply, communications, would be so simple. Even the most learned of apologists has not been able to find any better argument for the slums' survival than the Asiatic folk-soul (for which we have so many beautiful words).

Filth, both physical and spiritual, flourishes in poverty and ignorance. Spiritual filth, whether it takes the form of an ability to drink milk through one's rectum or a readiness to kill anyone who eats cow-meat, or pork, or meat of any sort, is not specially Asiatic. Nor is it peculiar to any one culture. Merely the hunger hallucinations of a starvation culture.

Slums mean being born sick, a life in sickness and hunger, an early death. Working for sub-subsistence wages. Being trained to say My Lord, Sahib, or Sir to anyone who looks well clothed or well fed. But slums are also the fine bungalows of the foreign experts and Indian high civil servants and merchants. Slums and bungalows fit each other like hand and glove. Only when the bungalows have been eliminated can the elimination of the slums be discussed. But by then it will have all become a simple question of city planning.

Black-tent nomads. Tribal Afghans.

AFGHANISTAN

XXIV

In the late winter, 1959, we drive back over the Khyber. The soldiers say, "Welcome back!"

The commander of the frontier post asks, "Well, wasn't I right? Down there you can't even live."

"But we're back."

They all laugh and wave us on. The plains open up ahead of us. We are past the Khyber. The nomads have begun their spring migration. We pass them trudging on beside the road. The camels sway along, calm and dignified. On the top of their load a basket filled with puppies. I remember the Indian officer who dismissed Afghanistan so scornfully: "Just a barbarian state! They should have had the British there. That would have taught them what is meant by law and order."

But I had no desire to think any more about all the poverty and misery, the luxuries and extravagance, down there on the plains, with their browbeaten population. The great Emir, Abd-er-Rahman, once scornfully described the Indian princes as the un-men with little bells around their ankles who betrayed their people to the British in order to enjoy a meaningless life of idleness and luxury.

We pass Jalalabad, drive up the Kabul River toward Sarobi.

Come to the power station. The cement supplies (to build the power station) via Pakistan were stopped, so that the cement had to be transported by boat to Klaipeda via the Baltic, and thereafter by rail all through the Soviet Union, down to the Amu Darya where it was ferried across the river, then transported by camel caravan to Kunduz, and so by truck across the Hindu Kush. Nevertheless, the power station went up. And now Afghanistan is building her own cement factories. At Sarobi they tell us the road up to Kabul through the gorge has been blocked by a clay landslide. Since it will not be reopened for several days to come, we have to take the road over the Lataband Pass.

Across the grey sky, black clouds sail heavily. A cold wind is blowing across the black clay soils and the brown gravel. Here comes the rain. It rattles on our roof, and the windshield is streaked with water. As we mount higher, the rain becomes mixed with snow. Behind the sweeping rain-squalls the landscape is brown and black, and suddenly heavy snow is falling. The road turns white, and the air grey. Under the melting snow the clay surface becomes slippery. Slowly we climb the winding, twisting road, and when the clouds clear again there, all about us, row on row, are the mountain chains. Naked crags. Then the clouds come sailing toward us, and once again we are driving in mist, haze, and snow. Snow-laden camels come toward us. Their shaggy coats are dripping, and their drivers greet us amiably. And now we are emerging onto the highest level of the pass. The clouds are opening and at a great height we are driving along a ledge on the face of the mountain. To our right, the receding valleys and the distant mountain crags rending in the mist. To our left the mountainside, down which the water trickles between stones, scoring furrows in the snow. The clouds close beneath us, and we drive into a cloud-grotto among the mountains. The motor roars, the wheels spin in the clay; but we get over, and soon we are gliding down the slippery soapy road with the engine in first gear and the wheels sometimes losing their grip on the clay; and beyond lie still more mountains, chain on chain.

In the evening we reach Kabul. Snow is falling gently on houses and streets. As we drive into town the mountains are invisible behind the low clouds. It is the snowy spring-winter. In the bazaar people are wrapped up warm in thick clothing, and a man is warming his hands over a tray of cinders. The Kabul River is rising and its waters are a foaming brown. The houses shiver, and rain alternates with snow. The clay sticks to one's shoes. One crosses the street clumsily and without agility. But now we are out of our car and the air, snow and clay notwithstanding, feels free and clean. We've come home to Kabul.

Here are no castes. Here is no scorn for humanity, no hatred of human beings. This is a poor and hard country, not without its difficulties, oppression, and other evils. But it managed to escape colonialism. They tell me how a dishonest tax-collector in the south was marched barefoot through the deserts under a guard of soldiers to stand trial at Kabul. What became of him after? No one knew. He had been extorting excessive taxes from the poor, and letting the rich get away with it. He arrived in Kabul, and disappeared. But the peasantry, the people in the villages, had seen what happens to a tax-collector who has no honor. In India he would have been taken care of by legalities. By trials, lasting for decades. By lawyers. A machinery for oppression inherited from the British. And what in all this legal machinery would have become of justice? The dishonest man would have got off, and sued his accusers for false allegations, for insulting a civil servant and every other device a society based on the rule of law can invent to protect dishonesty. Down there the lawyers, after a whole generation, are still wrangling over the embezzlement of the Burmese military funds. The legacy of feudalism and despotism is a lighter load than that of colonialism.

On our way up through Lataband we had spoken of the great Emir, Abd-er-Rahman. The man who made Afghanistan into a kingdom. Taking over a poor, distraught, and oppressed country which looked as if within a few years it must fall victim to the great empires, he left it a nation. His methods had been tough. In Jalalabad he had built a tower out of the skulls of captured bandits. At the highest point in Lataband he had shut up a couple of robbers in a steel cage, hung from a gallows. They hung there for twenty years as a punishment for themselves, and a warning to others. Justice ruled in the country. He held officials responsible for their actions. United the kingdom.

"The first thing I had to do," he wrote,

was to put a stop to all these innumerable robbers, thieves, false prophets and petty kings. I must admit it was no easy task; it took fifteen years of fighting before they finally submitted to my authority or left the country, either by going into exile or by their departure for a better world.

Abd-er-Rahman had seen what was happening in India. He had his warning. He enrolled foreigners to teach his people how to vaccinate themselves against smallpox, to teach them about dentistry, steam engines, and factory methods. But he did not surrender his people. It was the country of the Afghans which was to be developed, not the foreigners who were to grab a market. The experts were retained until they had taught their pupils all they needed to know. They were informed that if their pupils did not learn everything they, the experts, knew themselves, their pupils would be punished and they themselves forbidden to leave the country. Abd-er-Rahman points out that this announcement was an excellent way of making the experts get down to work. Having seen the swarms of experts who like grasshoppers are eating their way through the underdeveloped countries, one is inclined to agree with him.

But let us not lose our sense of perspective. Abd-er-Rahman was in no sense a democrat. Like our Gustavus Vasa * he was the master builder of his realm. He stood on the threshold between the Middle Ages and our own age, leading his country forward. But neither he nor his methods—no more than Gustavus Vasa's—could lead the country into the new age.

Like Gustavus Vasa, Abd-er-Rahman could have said to his people, "Attend to your houses, fields, meadows, wives, children, sheep and cattle, and presume not to dictate our goals; either in government or religion."

They carried out a piece of necessary work. They left behind them a state. But even under Abd-er-Rahman's iron hand (an iron people, as he put it, can only be ruled with an iron hand) the lowest of men was freer than an ordinary Indian under his present rule of law.

Now the heavy wet clay was clinging to our feet. The snowflakes were melting on our hands, the sky was dark and the wind howled among the low yellow houses. We had come back to Kabul.

* Gustavus Vasa (1523–1560) founder of the Swedish State.—TRANSLATOR

135

Decorated wooden coffin, Nuristani grave, Mundagal

XXV

At Mundagal, a little village in the Bashgul Valley, high up in Nuristan at the foot of the Hindu Kush mountains, the road came to an end. We had been driving north from Jalalabad through the Kunar Valley and on along the Bashgul River until we had reached the forest belt. And now the cliff was sticking straight out into the river ahead. The clear water squirted over the black rocks, and the eternally white mountain peaks stood up in sharp relief against the deep blue sky. The trees clambered away over the slopes and high up we could see the tree line and bare grey mountains merging into snowy mists.

To say the road ended at this cliff would, however, not be quite correct. It had just got as far as the cliff. Fifty men with sledge hammers and crowbars, pickaxes and spades, were clearing a way for it. A pneumatic drill was chattering against the rocks.

The workers gather around us and our car. They laugh and shout, patting the car's fenders and calling out to each other. We are the first private car to come up by the Bashgul road, and the first vehicle of any sort to pass over the latest, newly finished mile. Our arrival demonstrated that the road was passable to traffic, and that their work had been meaningful.

Actually, we'd taken a wrong turn. We hadn't been heading for Mundagal at all. We were on our way to Kamdesh, the capital of upper Nuristan, which lies a few miles further down the valley. No one had told us the road was being extended, so we had just driven on until it came to an end—as they had told us it would. The leader of the party approached. He was a young man with a round face, dressed in the same coarse boots, grey commissariat trousers, and khaki shirt as the others. He welcomed us and led us over to his tent.

"You are our guests," he said. "If you've got so far you must stay."

In the leafy shade of trees not unlike silver birches, the tents had been pitched in a cluster on the green meadows down by the river. The only feature distinguishing the foreman's tent from the others was the field telephone beside his bed. They offered us freshly caught

137

brook trout, grilled in the ashes of their fires. Afterward we drank tea. The workmen crowded into the tent to talk to us.

"Did you find it difficult, driving up here?" one man asked.

"Not too bad," said Gun.

"It's a bad road, a road for jeeps," said the foreman.

"Well, it was a road anyway," I said.

Up here, toward and across the peaks of the Hindu Kush, we realized what amount of hard work is needed to turn a donkey path into a jeep track. Now, in the twilight, the river was singing at the foot of the meadow and the sky was turning as green as the sea.

Beside the tents, an old Kafir grave. Carved wooden ornamentation. The air is fresh and cool, and the foreman is talking to us. He speaks slowly and simply, so we shall understand everything he is saying: "We're making a road here. The road is to go up the Bashgul Valley and over the passes to Badakhshan. When it's ready you'll be able to drive direct from Faizabad or Jurm to Jalalabad. That will save almost a whole week's journey. It will mean goods will come up here. Everything'll get cheaper. Now they are building a road through Wakhan, too. One day a car will be able to drive straight across Pamir. There'll be buses between Kashgar and Jalalabad."

He poured us out some more tea. Accepted a cigarette. Cupping it inside his hand so that his fingers formed a mouthpiece and his lips did not touch the cigarette, he went on: "This road isn't part of the major road scheme. Or of the government's five-year plan. We are a poor country. A small country. To build really big roads through the country we'll need foreign loans. After all we haven't the right machines. But for this road we can't get any foreign loans. You know what the Pakistanis say about it, don't you? In this frontier region we like to build our own roads. This one is being paid for by the province. The government isn't having to pay a single afghani for it. Now people will begin moving about. Life will be much easier. Already a bus goes to Kamdesh every other day. In a month or so there'll be one coming up here. The further we push the road, the further the bus can get. Now everyone's life'll be better. In one place, up to now, grain can be cheap and wool expensive, while in another wool is cheap and grain expensive. Now we'll be able to send the goods where they're needed, and everything'll become cheaper for everyone. The first thing we put up was the telephone

138

wire. See it? It links up the whole country. I can sit in my tent here, and whenever I want to I can pick up the receiver and talk to Jalalabad. As soon as the network's complete I'll be able to pick it up and talk to Kabul, Kandahar, Herat, or Faizabad. When the phone's laid out you can build a road. This isn't a road for a little car like yours. It's narrow and difficult and steep, has a lot of fords. We can't afford bridges where the road only floods in spring. Well, anyway, you can get along it. Afterward, in a few years, when we've bigger resources, we'll widen it. Come back in ten years and we'll have a broad asphalt road for you up here."

Fresh tea was brought in. Somewhere among the tents a couple of men were singing. A boy brought some trout. Outside, the compressor was heard no longer. The camp was beginning to settle down for the night. The foreman drew on the ground with a stick, and said, "Afghanistan is like this, you see. A country surrounded by other countries. We've no railways; and for a long while almost no roads, and we weren't too keen on building any, either. We didn't want the foreigners just to march straight into the country over the roads we had built. Now we're stronger. And we know we've got to build roads. In ten years or so there won't be a single village you can't reach by bus. Before, everything was remote from everything else. Now everything's getting closer."

We were standing on the slope, looking up through the falling darkness at the black cliff sticking into the river. The white foam was squirting over it. Fifty men were toiling here to break a road. A cool wind came off the snow-covered mountains. All around us the Hindu Kush rose up against the dark transparency of the evening sky.

XXVI

Nuristan is different. Forests and wooden houses. Paths lead up to villages of wooden houses, higher and higher, but without ever reaching the glittering white peaks. Timber houses clamber terrace on terrace above each other. There is not much arable land and the slopes of the valleys are too valuable to be used for houses or roads.

The villages climb up the mountainsides. In the meadows on the slopes of the foaming green rivers stand carved wooden coffins, and horses' heads, cut in wood, still watch over the dead. Here everything is different. Here people carve in wood. Here the men sit on carved chairs. Culture and language, customs, history, and until quite recently even religion, separate Nuristan from the rest of the country.

On a map Nuristan—the high mountain valleys south of the Hindu Kush watershed, east of Panjshir Valley and north of the Kabul River region—can be drawn into the eastern part of the country. But Nuristan is more than a geographical area. Nuristan is a culture on its own.

Nuristan—the Land of Light. The name, however, is of recent date. It got its new name only some seventy years ago, when its inhabitants were converted by fire, sword, and muzzle-loaders to Islam. Until then they had been called Kafirs, infidels, and their country was known as Kafiristan, the land of the infidels. It was Abd-er-Rahman who converted them; not so much for religious as for commercial and political reasons. Kafiristan, a region of high mountain valleys, acknowledged no real overlord. The Kingdom of Kabul had been little concerned with them. The Moguls had made a few minor armed incursions, nothing more. But now the British were forcing their way in from the east. A British agent settled in the Bashgul Valley in 1889. And it was he, George Robertson, who, by mapping the valley and entering into communication with the Kafirs on behalf of the British, precipitated the holy war. Abd-er-Rahman wanted no door left open to the British. He was also of the opinion that the Bashgul Valley could become an important trade route from the Indus region up to Badakhshan and Central Asia.

Today the old Kafir gods can only be seen in Kabul Museum. Hard, expressionistically carved faces. Nuristan still shows traces of an older, less differentiated culture than that of the rest of the country. Its society is more antique. The men hunt and wage war, and the women till the soil. Which has given the women greater power. Woman's position in society and in the village council created a morality different from Islam's. In his book—the only one to treat extensively of the Kafirs before their conversion—Robertson describes how the Big Dipper was known to them as Prusht, the bed;

and how they said the first star was a man, the second his wife, and the third her lover.

This more ancient form of society is still to be met with. It is visible at once in the landscape. The valleys are well irrigated, the patches of plowed land form terraces, and the women till the soil. Nowadays, since their conversion, the women of the villages are less independent, less forward in their contacts with strangers. But they are famed for their beauty; and beauty is a function of freedom. In any society where woman has been free she has another bearing, and her eyes speak another language.

Their culture shows other traits than those dominant in Afghanistan. Their society was still based on slaves taken prisoner in war. As in India, the artisans, the creators of commodities, were untouchable. The Kafirs have not lain outside the mainstreams of culture, merely in their outskirts.

Many tried to conquer their lands, and some attempted to convert them. But the valleys were too remote. Their conquerors were seldom persistent enough to waste time, troops, and gold on retaining such remote and poverty-stricken valleys. They were content to march through, burn a few villages, and carry off a few beasts. Carve their exploits, perhaps, in some rock inscription. Meanwhile the inhabitants looked down on them from their craggy peaks, and as soon as the conquerors had departed returned to their village, rebuilt it, and all went on as before. In poverty and isolation they were able to survive. No one bothered about them.

But it was not a peaceful society. Constantly at war with other villages and other valleys, attacking, plundering, pillaging, each village lived for itself. Each village was in a state of feud with every other village. Each tribe with other tribes. At times there would be temporary alliances, sometimes eternal peace would be declared, but more commonly war. All fought against all, and all fought the Moslems. No one was granted manhood unless he had waged war against the Moslem. So much pillage caused their region to shrink. The Moslems, down in the broader valleys, whose herds were always being carried off and their neighbors butchered, would march into the land of the Kafirs to wreak revenge. Slowly the Kafirs were driven back.

141

Through these valleys went one of the trade routes, between Badakhshan and the Indus Basin. Blue lapis lazuli was carried from village to village, down toward the plains of India, in exactly the same way as amber once wandered southward from tribe to tribe through Europe. But the British isolated and impoverished their India. Trade died away. The Moslems exerted pressure. Many Kafirs allowed themselves to be converted. By the time Robertson reached them their own culture had already begun to crumble away.

XXVII

"Tomorrow the Kuchis will again pack up to move;
The flowers in the wilderness will smell your skirt."

The desert is ochre yellow and the mountains pink. We are four hours' drive, over rough terrain, southeast of the road from Ghazni. Already, in early summer, the river beds and the ravines are dry, and the brief violent splendor of the spring colors is over. The sparse vegetation has begun to take on the protective coloring of the soil, preserving its humidity under a dry crust and turning its prickles outward. The sun is hot. We drive slowly, in first gear, rocking over the steppe, slithering down ravines, circumventing pot-holes. When the tussocks have been left behind and the ground becomes hard again, we shift up to second, and go bouncing away over the high plateau. Far away in the direction of the slopes, a herd of grazing sheep. The shepherd says his camp is behind the hills. Makes a sweeping gesture in the direction of the distant yellow slopes. As we drive on, the sheep follow us with their eyes.

We round the last hillock, drive down a ravine. A few patched black tents against the light hues of the soil. The big dogs rush around us, barking. Their jaws wide open, slobbering, they are protecting their herd. The men calm their dogs, capture them; tie sacks over their heads, muzzle them. Invite us into the shade. Under their sacks the dogs go on barking, tugging at their ropes, scenting strangers. The midday heat is intense. Men and beasts alike have sought the cool of their tent-cloths' shade. They spread out rugs for us to sit on, and the much-patched tent-cloth admits little sunbeams which play on the red and black costumes of the women. Silver earrings and bracelets sparkle. The tightly wound corkscrew braids gleam, a cool wind passes through the open tent, and we are among the nomads, the kuchis. Pashtun shepherds, on their way from their winter camps down in Pakistan up to Afghanistan's summer pastures.

They talk and laugh, offer us tea and food. Unleavened bread, salted sour milk, sugared goat's cheese. Two children are sent out to find the herd and fetch a lamb to roast in the embers. Their hospitality is self-confident and free.

The women are unembarrassed. Much less embarrassed than their settled sisters in the white clay villages. On their heads they wear their black chadars; but no veil hides their faces. Their features are of a sharp etched beauty.

Not only their glance and their way of carrying themselves, but also their clothing and art, are independent and beautiful. Costumes in red and black, with silver ornament. The family fortune transformed into a décor of sewn-in silver coins. The textiles have a geometrical—though never mechanically symmetrical—embroidery in red and gold. The firmness of the lines and the clarity of the colors are grounded in the same proud style as the lundaye, the folk song the women are singing:

> Come not to me with flowers, my belovéd,
> For I am more lovely than any rose.

These nomad women are freer than their sisters. For their life is harsher and makes greater demands on them. In their songs and their poetry are undertones of an individual sexual love that has been more strictly suppressed among the settled population. Here love can still—or already—form a relationship between human beings, not only a property relationship. They know, too, how to receive strangers as guests. Unlike the village woman, the nomad woman is not immediately suspected of infidelity the moment she speaks to a strange man.

Their culture has grown out of an obstinate daily struggle to master a beautiful, but inhumanly hard, nature. These kuchis belong to a folk who for centuries have had to fight to preserve their independence and their freedom against mighty kingdoms. Their pride is no mere personal pride, pride in their beauty or strength. It

144

is the pride of a people who have never given up the struggle to preserve their integrity. When the poet and hero Khushal, the khan of the Khattacks, was imprisoned by the Emperor Aurangzeb in 1664, he lamented his people's sufferings and his own misfortunes. But his song ended with the words:

> Yet in these misfortunes I am grateful to God for
>   two gifts.
> The first, that I am born an Afghan.
> The other that I am Khushal Khattack.

It is a people whose women have often had—and still have—reason to sing:

> My lover sacrificed himself for the homeland.
> I sew his shroud with hair from my locks.

We were guests in their black tents, guests of a people often maligned, often attacked.

> My kisses are for him who has broken the chains of serfdom,
> For him who is divorced from slavery.

All this is true. That is how it was. And that was how we experienced it. But every truth is capable of many interpretations. From the truth I have described to the romantic lie of the freedom of the nomad is but a short step. UNESCO took that step recently. In a press release they spoke of a freedom, a culture, an economy with old traditions, and of the necessity of preserving all this. Often have I not met with Europeans who say they dream of living the free life of the nomads. But their dream is only a dream. As well might they dream of the free wandering life of the train engineer. The nomad life was a specialized variant of the earliest division of labor, just as an engineer's is of our industrial one. The life of the nomad is no freedom to stray at will, to follow one's nose. In Afghan society the nomads fulfill special functions. By a myriad economic ties they are bound to the settled peoples.

The whole landscape is typified by their black tents. Wherever you go, you meet them. Their herds are visible afar off beyond the hills, and their great dogs watch over the encampment and the herd. The total population of Afghanistan is usually assessed at twelve million, of which the nomadic part is two million. Even if these are round figures, of dubious exactitude, the proportions would seem to be about right. Each sixth person in this country, at least, belongs to the kuchis; those who are forever on the move.

In Afghanistan the two great nomadic cultures, the Arabic-Persian and the Central Asiatic, meet. Not at any definite frontier. No borderline is anywhere staked out. Such a boundary would conflict with the economic and legal system of nomad life. Instead the nomads form pockets in each other's territory. One sees how the further north one goes the more the number of black tents dwindles, while the yurt becomes predominant. But the occupants of the yurt are tending more and more to settle, and the black felt tents are moving into the yurt's districts. Far inside Badakhshan we still met with black tents.

Often it is difficult to draw a hard and fast line between the settled peoples and the nomads. The mountain pasture culture, with its winter dwellings and its summer grazing grounds, is semi-nomadic. The desert regions and the dry steppes demand extensive grazing, and the borderline between a settled existence and a nomadic one often cleaves families. Not infrequently the nomads are attached to villages and the village council.

When spring has come and the time for nomad migrations is at hand, then the slopes around Kabul are black with nomad tents. The kuchis wander up toward their summer pastures. For the nomads, in principle, are shepherds. They drive their herds from the lowlands where they graze in winter to the high mountain meadows in summer. Slowly, they drift up from the plains around Jalalabad or down by the Indus in Pakistan. Their rate of march is slow. They take with them their kids, their newborn lambs and their young camels. Early in the morning one meets them out on the roads. The men are carrying the newborn lambs in their arms, and in baskets on the backs of the camels sit the small children, puppies, and kids. They drive their flocks of sheep. They are specialized members of a special community. Themselves, they only produce a small fraction of what they consume. They barter wool, meat, sheep's fat, and milk products for grain, metal, and tools. Yes, even their tents are made by others. They constitute one side of the great production triangle which is Afghanistan. Settled farmers, nomad herdsmen, and urban artisans.

That is to say, in principle. Some hold sway over enormous herds.

Others own only a few wretched beasts. Some rise to wealth, others fall into poverty and in the end own nothing at all. At that point the herdsman drifts into other spheres. The unpropertied nomad tends to become a migratory agricultural laborer. Free as the beetroot pickers in Skåne, Sweden. From the winter dwellings and the rice paddies they move upward, passing through the same villages year after year. They take part in the work, and move on. They have become a wandering proletariat of the soil, yet one that is organically involved in a community.

Other nomads drift into trade. The specialized culture which makes it necessary for them to barter, buy, and sell in order to obtain the necessities of life causes them to become peddlers and hawkers. They follow the routes, finding their way up into the remote valleys, selling the commodities of the cities to poor villagers. Yet these tadjars, travelers, do not constitute a firm and unified group. On the one hand, the poor peddler with his bundle on his back or in the saddlebags of his donkey. On the other, the wealthy herd-owner become merchant, money-lender, and landowner.

Klaus Ferdinand points out that during the last century the regions where the Afghan nomads follow their migrant existence have steadily grown. After the country had been united and pacified, the nomads were able to penetrate deeper and deeper into its interior. From having only really controlled the southern and eastern part of the country, their caravans now traverse it from end to end.

But the pacification of the country under Abd-er-Rahman did not merely give the Afghan nomads larger grazing grounds and oblige the Hazaras to give up many of their traditional summer grazing grounds to the Afghan nomads. The extension of the grazing grounds hastened the transformation of the herdsmen into traders. Peace and quiet in the country and protection of the settled population led to increased nomadization. Increased nomadization led the nomads up into the previously inaccessible Hazarajat, where the nomads arrived as civilization's advance guard. They brought with them the products of civilization and the crafts. And this interfered with the nomads themselves. They drifted over to trade, and the Hazaras became steadily more dependent on them as traders and money-lenders.

But the unification of the country, though its first effect had been

Victory Tower, Ghazni. In 1152 Ala-ud-din Husain of Ghor occupied Ghazni. He ordered the city burned down. He ordered the people massacred. While he watched the city burn, it is said he composed a poem: I am Ala-ud-din, the ruler of the world./I will conquer the whole world like Alexander./I had intended to make rivers of blood flow/But the children and old men beseech me to spare their lives.

This tower and one more tower and some tombs were all that was left of the capital of the Ghaznevid Empire.

148

to increase the nomads' power, soon swiftly reduced the range of their activities. Unity brought roads. As it gave impetus to more developed trading methods, the process which had enabled the nomads to become traders also limited their possibilities in this respect. The new roads shortened distances within the country. Now internal combustion engines and the great trading organizations are forcing the peddlers out of business. Only up in the high mountain valleys does their trade still flourish.

The rich and powerful among them, the money-lenders and the great merchants, are becoming part of the rich merchant class. The days of the nomad are at an end. It was their fate to be the advance guard, and this very fact has thrust them aside. It is becoming steadily harder and harder for them to count on being allowed to cross national and regional frontiers without let or hindrance, without customs and passports. Their freedom of movement is being restricted.

The black tents are to become the dwellings of a settled population, just as the yurts have. The new irrigation projects are to provide land which can be cultivated by kuchis who have been obliged to give up their nomadic life.

XXVIII

We had come from the grave of Mahmud the Great, and were passing the victory towers. There they stood, solitary on the plain. Silent witnesses amid the blue-flowering rice to great victories and everlasting glory. To protect them from wind and weather they had been given hats of corrugated iron. How to describe? Thus:

> 999–1150. The empire of the kings of Ghazni. Mahmud of Ghazni was declared Sultan by the Caliph and ruled over a great kingdom. His court was the meeting place of the great artists and poets of the age. After his death (1030) his kingdom began to decay.

That's one way of seeing our world. Then everything looks charming. Then even the victory towers can be appreciated at their true aesthetic value. But the history of Asia is not its rulers' history. Those rulers were the warlords of pillaging armies., All Mahmud's victories were the victories of pillaging robber hordes. He was the defender of the faith and of good morals. If his subjects died like flies, it was not only because they were addicted to heresy, but also because they supplied the taxes to maintain his army during its Indian campaigns.

Those campaigns may have meant wealth and eternal glory for Mahmud and his followers, but for all those who happened to come within sight of his army they spelled ruin. The court historian Utbi points out that whenever Mahmud needed money for a new campaign, the money was raised within two days. The populace were shorn like sheep, the farming districts laid waste, the irrigation systems allowed to decay. Subject or enemy, in either case a victim. In the environs of Nishapur, alone, a hundred thousand people starved to death. First they ate up their cats and dogs, then each other. To the greater glory of the ruler monuments were erected, poems were penned, and poets and artists were fetched to Ghazni, until Ghazni became famed as a center of culture.

The type of state which developed in Asia was a parasitic marauding army, based on an exploiting and corrupt bureaucracy. As for the people, in the eyes of Asiatic princes they were less than dung. When the inhabitants of Balkh resisted the Karakhanids, Mahmud wrote to them indignantly:

> What have our subjects to do with war? It is self-evident that your town should have been destroyed, and my property, which formerly yielded me such taxes, should have been burned. [Because they had resisted.—J.M.] . . . You should really pay me damages for this, but I have pardoned you. Just see to it it doesn't happen again. For if any ruler shows himself to be the stronger and demands taxes of you, then you must pay those taxes, in self-protection.

No, there is no glory in victory towers. Not even their artistic ornamentation can gloss over the fact that they are monuments to brutality, stupidity, and the oppression of a time-serving court. Just because it is archaeology, we must not romanticize all this thousand-year-old meaningless violence.

The sun is sinking. The shops and artisans' corners are still open. The men are sitting in their bazaar stalls, embroidering Ghazni sheepskin jackets. We walk on through the winding maze of streets

150

and Ghazni begins to go to its rest. Ghazni is not glory and castles and monuments and memories of prehistoric victories. It is what it has always been. A city of artisans, a trading city, a city of goods and embroideries and iron.

X I X

Only once does anyone spit after us. Little children are throwing refuse and stones after our car. They don't like us. We are *Feringi*. Franks. Foreigners. Perhaps British.

This happens in Kandahar one blazing hot summer day when the heat lies dense as a woolen blanket and the streets are roasting under a cruel blazing sun. The desert dust lies thick upon our clothes, clogs our skin, and sears our eyes. As we drove into Kandahar the men spat after us, and the children yelled insults.

All day we had been driving through an open landscape of wide, dry plains. The road had been a bad one. Broad but rutted. And all the bridges had collapsed. We had rested under some trees, been offered mulberries and tea. Now we were driving in through Kandahar toward the new city. It met us with its damper air and a feeling of well-being in our bodies. But as we passed they spat after us. In two wars British armies had marched this way, and Franks were still enemies. Assuredly our fathers have eaten sour grapes and the teeth of the children have been set on edge.

Sunday, August 28, in the year of 1842, the Reverend I. N. Allen, Assistant Chaplain of the Honourable East India Company's Bombay Establishment, who served with Her Majesty's 40th Regiment on foot, writes in his diary:

> About half-past eight a.m. we arrived at our encampment ground at Oba, and I hoped after breakfast for a little quiet, and divine service at five p.m. as on Sunday last; but very different was the fate that awaited us. Finding that the country had risen, and that we were not to have any forage by fair means, I sent a camel with a camel-man and horse-keeper, to join the foraging party, at about half-past twelve p.m. They had not been long gone, when there came a report that the enemy were in great force in our neighborhood, and I sent a man in all haste to recall them . . . As

151

I went, I learned that a report had been brought to Captain Delamain, 3rd Bombay Light cavalry . . . that their grass-cutters were being slaughtered by the enemy. . . . The cavalry, with Leslie's guns to reinforce them, again advanced over the hills to recover the bodies of their killed, while we turned with the infantry, Captain Blood's nine-pounders, and Captain Anderson's six-pounders, to the fort from which the attack on the grass-cutters was said to have been made. It was rather large, and with three towers within. As we approached, several unarmed people came out to meet us with supplicating gestures, and pleaded that the village had no share in the matter. The general listened to their tale and told them to remain quiet, and ordered Captain F. White, with the light company of H.M. 40th regiment, to proceed and examine the fort and ascertain whether there were any evidence of their having taken a part in the affair.

As they approached the gate, accompanied by Major Leech to act as an interpreter, the infatuated wretches, though they had professed to surrender, discharged a volley of matchlock balls at the company, one of which very nearly killed the major. The men upon this rushed in; the light company of H.M. 41st, another company of H.M. 40th, under Captain Neild, and some light companies from the native corps, were ordered to support Captain White; they had been enraged by the previous events of the morning, and one of those painful scenes ensued, which are more or less common to all warfare, and which, I fear, under such circumstances, it is almost impossible to prevent. The fort was found full of people and all armed and resisting. Every door was forced, every man that could be found was slaughtered, they were pursued from yard to yard, from tower to tower, and very few escaped. A crowd of wretched women and children were turned out, one or two wounded in the *melée*. I never saw more squalid and miserable objects. One door, which they refused to open upon summons, was blown in by a six-pounder, and every soul bayoneted . . . I drew gradually nearer and nearer, till at length, curiosity prevailing over prudence, I entered it . . . Destruction was going on in every form—dead bodies lying here and there—sepoys and followers were dragging out sheep, goats, oxen, and goods . . . European and native soldiers were breaking open doors where they supposed anything might be concealed—and every now and then, the discharge of a firelock proclaimed the discovery of a concealed victim, while the curling blue smoke, and crackling sound from the buildings indicated that the fire was destined to devour what the sword had spared.

The bugles sounded, and I retired from this painful spectacle.

152

It is difficult to ascertain the number that perished in the fort, but it is probable that no less than from eighty to one hundred were shot; and if any remained concealed in the buildings, they must have perished in the flames, for it was one mass of blazing ruin before we left it, and continued flaming all night . . . While the attack was thus made on the fort, the bodies of our slaughtered friends were recovered, sad, mangled remains, bearing mournful testimony, of the ferocity of these savages.

We now returned to camp, having been, including the morning's march, between nine and ten hours on horseback, the greater part of the time exposed to a grilling sun . . . Oh! what a day! Could my friends at home realize it, surely they would prize more highly their peaceful Sabbath blessings. It was now nearly midnight. I threw myself on my bed and obtained that oblivion of sorrow in sleep which a gracious God is pleased to grant, even in the midst of such scenes of excitement.

How true were not the words in which Reverend Allen described the situation in his sermons during that war:

And, lastly, if you have appreciated the great redemption wrought for you by Jesus Christ from the grasp of the great enemy of mankind make it a proof of your gratitude to spread the glad tidings of it among all nations of the earth. We have all seen the merciless and savage cruelty, the unblushing treachery, the vices not to be named, which prevail among the votaries of false religion, in which the pure and peaceable doctrines of the gospel are unknown. Let the personal experience of these horrors be an additional motive for aiding by your prayers, and your contributions, every effort to diffuse among them the light of life. (Kabul, October 9th, 1842)

Who can look upon the small space occupied by our native islands on the face of the globe, and then turn his gaze to the vast extent of our foreign possessions, upon which it is literally true that the sun never sets, and not confess that the Lord our God must have gone before us signally and specially. And what nation is there that hath statutes and judgements so righteous, based as they are upon the pure principles of the gospel, securing peace at home to the whole realm, and to every man the quiet possession of his own. (Kabul, September 18th, 1842) .

Now the children are stoning us. Because all this has been committed in villages like the one where we were given tea in the shadow of the high trees.

153

What difference is there between the British officer and gentleman and the German SS? The one was successful and the other not. That is all. The German SS did to Europeans what the British officer and gentleman (and the French, and the North American, and the Italian, and the Dutch—it is not a question of nationality) did and does against people after people outside Europe.

If Hitler had won, and got his Reich to last a hundred years, there would have been assemblies of "Aryan leaders" talking as learnedly as the parliamentarians of London or the senators of Washington. But the crimes would have been the same.

X X X

Kabul, the mountain city, is Afghanistan's capital. There Baber, the Mogul emperor, lies buried. It also became Afghan at an early date. Ibn Battuta calls it an Afghan city. But Kandahar, the Kandahar of the plains, the steppes, and the southern deserts, is the heart of Afghanistan. Kandahar is the capital of the Afghan tribes. With Peshawar the city shares the honor of being the center of Afghan culture. But now Peshawar lies in foreign territory.

In Kandahar lies buried Ahmad Shah Durrani, the first Afghan monarch and the founder of the Afghan State. On one's way from Kandahar in the direction of Girishk one passes through Maiwand: the battlefield where British troops were defeated in the open field during the Second Afghan War.

Thus Kandahar symbolizes a great period in Afghanistan's modern history.

The Afghan tribes had always been turbulent subjects. Indeed, they had seldom been subjects. The cities were in the power of the great states, but the Afghans in their mountains remained free, and the roads could only be traveled under armed protection. Sometimes the tribes came down from the mountains and established their own dynasty of rulers in some foreign country.

Over the centuries the land of the Afghans came to lie at the point of intersection between the Persian and Indian empires. The Afghans could play off one great power against the other, until even

154

the cities—in a long series of intrigues and counter-intrigues, re-
bellions, revolutions, and a diplomacy sometimes directed against
Persia, sometimes at India—fell progressively under Afghan influence. More and more the Afghan tribes' plunder raids began to take
on the aspect of national uprisings. Their poets began to sing of the
Afghan name and what it required of a man. By playing off one great
power against another, the Afghans began to gain control of their
own country. But not until the middle of the eighteenth century,
out of tribal revolts, did they succeed in becoming a nation.

The Turkmen Shah of Persia, Nadir Shah, went from greatness
to glory to madness, falling at last to the hand of an assassin. The
great Persian families, terrified, had turned on him before he could
exterminate them. His empire fell, and his Afghan lifeguards, surrounded by Persian armies, fought their way out and began to march
home.

It was in the course of this march the legionaries were transformed into the core of a national army. In 1747 their young commander, Ahmad Khan, chieftain of the Saddozai family of the Abdali
tribe, was crowned Shah Durr-i-Durran: the Pearl of Pearls, or the
Pearl of the Ages. He was only twenty-nine.

A warrior and a commander, he had already taken part in many
slaughters, and pillaged cities and villages. Now he became the first
Afghan monarch, the first who had no desire to utilize Afghan military skill to set himself and his men up as rulers in a foreign land,
but to establish an independent Afghanistan. His greatness lies in his
realization that the state could only be based on tribal democracy
and the popular assembly. His power was derived from his intimate
contacts with the tribes. He was never a Badshah, never a Great
King; he was the chieftain of all the Afghans.

True, he was a commander and a warrior. From Bactria to Delhi
he allowed his followers to plunder and pillage. But it was no part
of his goal to become a new Baber. From his letters and from con-
temporary memoirs it transpires that what he was aiming to establish was an Afghan state which should also control Balkh and the
Punjab. And that is why he is so important. His state was different
from the Moguls', or Nadir Shah's. It was no mere ruling military
machine and tax-collecting apparatus. And what began to grow up
was the first modern nation-state in this part of the world.

155

He did not attain his goal. But his attempt to conquer the Punjab hastened the putrescence of the Mogul Empire. When he crushed the Mahrattas' military machine he smashed to pieces the last power capable of resisting the British, and therefore paved a way for the British. His attempt to retain the Punjab led to a steady increase in Sikh power. In the long run his policies resulted in the Afghans losing their lands between the Indus and the Khyber. But it was through him the country had first achieved unity. And his northern conquests were to be permanent. Kandahar was his capital, and that is where he lies buried.

This was the first step in Afghanistan's modern history: the establishment of an Afghan nation-state. It occurred at a moment when most European countries still had not achieved their national unity and independence. Germany and Italy were split up into petty principalities or were provinces of the great powers. The Balkans lay under the sway of the Turks. Poles, Czechs, Slovaks, Hungarians had no country of their own. Norway was a Danish province. Ireland a British. Afghanistan is not "a new state."

The second step in Afghanistan's development was taken during

the defensive wars against British attempts at colonization. In that struggle the lands of the tribes became a kingdom. At Maiwand, on July 14, 1880, the British lost more than a battle. Until then it had been said that Afghans and other uncivilized peoples could only win a guerrilla war but not a regular war, since they were not gentlemen and did not follow the rules of warfare. But on July 14, 1880, a British army was defeated in the open field.

The victor at Maiwand, the pretender to the throne, Yakub Khan, won the battle but lost both the war and the throne. Abd-er-Rahman had seized power in the country. But history is not decided by the fates of individuals or the good or bad luck of pretenders to thrones. The main fact remained: here, for the first time, a trained British army, well prepared, properly forewarned, splendidly equipped, and fighting with the sun at its back on a field as open as a barrack square, had been thoroughly trounced by an Afghan army. For the British the choice had been either flight or annihilation. The myth of their unconquerable military machine was shattered. Even the best-drilled British soldiers could be defeated by a people in arms.

It was only long after the Afghan victory that the full significance

of the Battle of Maiwand became obvious. It rendered impossible all further British advances, and it had kept Herat and Kandahar in Afghanistan.

XXXI

The new road to Girishk is broad and gravel-surfaced. Its pebbles rattle against our fenders. We are driving fast, but all around us the wide steppe stands motionless. At sea and in plain country the horizon is close, the range of vision limited. Even now, in the early morning, the air is hot and dry. Grey-hot. A car appears at the limit of vision. We get closer, and it grows into a big American station wagon, standing across the road. Two people stand beside it, waving. An American engineer and his wife, on their way from their project to Kandahar. They've a puncture.

"I suppose, we'll have to take the wheel off," she says.

They have a jack. But no pump, no tools or tire-mending kit. So I take the wheel off for them. The nuts are stiff. I lever the tire off, take out the inner, locate the hole, patch it, check the inner again, re-insert it in the tire, get the American to stand on the tire as I lever it on again, screw the wheel on tight. Then they help me remove the jack.

"It must be just wonderful, being handy like that," his wife says.

"My driver was ill this morning," the engineer says, by way of excuse.

The wind burns, the sweat sears my skin, my hands are black. Already the sun-haze, the dust-haze, are lying over the plain whose colors are dry and lifeless.

"We're living at the project," she says. "It's nice. Almost like home. Refrigerator, plumbing, water you can drink, the lot. In fact if we don't look out of the window we'd think we were back home."

"Sure," I say. "Home away from home. That must be nice for you."

Then we drive off, each in our own direction. We drive through Southern Afghanistan. Through Technical Aidland, through Morrison & Knudsenland.

158

This is a poor part of the country. Deserts, steppes, burned slopes. Drought, dust, and heat, all the way down to the distant—the infinitely distant—sea. Ever since the Mongols wrecked the irrigation canals the country has got drier and drier, ever poorer and more wretched. In the deserts as the dunes roll onwards, great castle ruins stick up through the sand, remains of ancient cities and villages, fragments of their walls and stone-paved yards. Once this was an agricultural district, and fertile. Now drought and heat. But when the snows melt in the mountains the river waters come roaring down, rush through the deserts down to the shallow brackish lakes near the Iranian frontier.

For a long time now irrigation schemes have been planned here. To restore the country's fertility, reconquer the land stolen by the desert. Japanese and Germans were working on these irrigation schemes before the Second World War. Morrison & Knudsen after the war. All this country was to be transformed. Seistan and the deserts of death were to become a paradise on earth, the granary of Asia. During the last ten years, on an average, twenty per cent of Afghanistan's state budget has gone to this project. The rivers were to be regulated, the soil irrigated, roads built, electric power was to have made industry possible, and the country modernized. The nomads were to be settled on the land irrigated by the Helmand.

Such is the great dream. The desert is to blossom. Other irrigation systems, in other parts of the country, are less expensive, and yield almost as much; but being cheaper they remain unknown. For this project is costing money. The poor man always has to pay heavily. Only the rich get long-term credit. Afghanistan is poor, and the project is swallowing more and more currency. And what is currency? Sheep's intestines, dried fruits, karakul!

It's a high price Afghanistan is having to pay. If help is to be worth the helper's while, the recipient has to pay double. Nor has the project come up to expectations. The soil wasn't as rich as the irrigation engineers had promised. The whole thing became Afghanistan's biggest political issue.

Day and night the water flowed through the canals. The basis of the old sort of existence had been removed. The rich peasants became richer, and the poor peasants were turned into an agricultural proletariat. The forces which had led the nomads up to new grazing

159

grounds in the mountains turned shepherds into traders and wandering landowners, gave them soil to settle on, ground them all together and then divided them up again. And some became wealthy landowners, and some became lowly hired laborers. And all the while the water goes on flowing through the new channels. The power lines sing their song, and over the steppes the sun blazes down.

Girishk meets us with its greenery. A great castle, and an Italian engineer. He sits in his jeep in nothing but a pair of bathing trunks and big sunglasses. A stocky man, bald, hairy, sweating. He stops our car.

"Welcome to Girishk," he says.

He's glad to see us; wants to talk; asks if we'd like some iced water; takes us up to his house. Between concrete walls water is trickling in the canal. All this water is easy on the eyes. The gleam of water always cools them.

"A bit lonesome here," he says.

He shows us the regulation dam across the Boghra Canal. The water is rushing through in a silver stream. In this dry landscape the strictly functional concrete constructions are imbued with a living beauty. Here he sits, all by himself in his concrete house, beside the regulation dam, making sure everything is working properly. Great drops of sweat stand out on his forehead; run down his arms; pour over his hairy chest.

"If only it weren't so hot," he says. "It's not too bad in winter. But all the rest of the time it's just as hot, day and night."

He pours us out some iced water and the radio squalls in the big naked room. There is a lot of static. Kandahar is calling someone. All around us the concrete walls are grey-white from the salts they precipitate. The radio rumbles.

"It's not for me," says our Italian. "But I have to keep it on all the time. Though there's rarely anything for me."

We ask how long he has been working here.

"Three years," he says, "I've been sitting here all on my own, the whole time. Nothing idealistic about it, though. It's for the money. All the time I'm saving money. And so are M & K saving money, too, because it's cheaper for them to employ an Italian than an American. We don't cost so much. But now my wife writes from Venice we've enough at last to buy a restaurant. Here I've been in

160

this desert, sweating and saving up. And there she's been with the kids, saving up. And now we're going to get our restaurant. Oh well, such is life."

From a white cardboard box he takes out a bundle of thumbed letters and frayed snapshots. His wife is beautiful, with dark heavy features. All three children are the spit and image of their father.

"Her name's Maritza," he says. "We've been married twelve years. But we never had anything over to save. Always poor. Italy's a lovely country, but not one you get rich in. So I took this job. And now I'm off. Three years I've been sitting here. The Americans are allowed to bring their wives and children; but Italians and Filipinos have to stick it out on their own. It's just as well. She's stayed behind in Venice, and now we can be free. Always been my dream, it's been, to have my own business. The kids write to me every week. They're good kids. Next time you're in Europe you must look us up in Venice."

The room's baldness is terrifying. Two chairs with worn covers, a table, a radio. On the table three glasses and the white cardboard box full of letters and photos. Outside, the water flashes against the concrete, and everything beyond is desert. The Italian offers us lunch.

"Really I'm supposed to live on canned foods from M & K's commissariat. It's in my contract. Well, I buy chickens, even so. The company hasn't found out yet. There must be some limit to their power, after all. Three years of my life they've bought. But what food I eat is my own business. Anyway, the inspector's hardly ever here. As for the Filipinos who come by now and again, I can trust them. They're trying to save, too, and don't like canned food either. The Yanks are harder on the Filipinos than they are on us Europeans. At least we aren't Asiatics."

Beside the functional beauty of the regulation dam an Italian engineer sits in a naked room with a bunch of thumbed letters and a howling radio receiver. Longing for his wife and kids and a little restaurant all of his own in Venice. Whenever he thinks of the company he spells it with a big C.

The Afghans have accused the project's contractors of being wasteful. They've complained. They say the company has given them incorrect information. The company has made too much out

161

of it. Afghanistan has had to pawn her exports for years to come, and the project isn't paying off.

A poor country is having to pay the price for help. Having the shirt taken off its back. Being cheated. Profits are being reaped.

XXXII

The heat is grey over the steppe. Cliffs stick up like jagged scorched islands out of the rolling dry desert. Over its dusty surface the dust-devils form pillared halls, and where the heat deceives the eye with mirages the ground bathes in water. Man is an insect, crawling over the roasting hot surface.

Beyond the solitary island of cliffs the road changes direction, turning down into a narrow valley where the underground irrigation channel, the kanat, bursts forth into vegetation. The houses with their protective walls and vaulted cupola roofs cling tightly together. At the mouth of the kanat, a few women are standing under shady trees. Then again the horizon, weighed down by hot greyish brown air, over which flow mirages of water, magnifying little prickly bushes into great forests of greenery.

Yet this poor village in a scorched landscape is architecture. An architecture of sun-dried clay. Pisé, adobe, handmade brick dried in the sun, together with the beaten brick, likewise sun-dried, gave us our first architecture. It is then man first began to create something new. Then for the first time he shatters the hard immobility of wood and stone.

Here, in the dry countries, man erected his first civilized buildings. And it is here, too, that good architectural form has survived. These clay villages can be an architectonic experience. The villagers, poverty-stricken, wretched, and downtrodden though they are, still create an architecture rich in future possibilities. Here the great Persian building tradition lives on.

But clay architecture creates no strict monumental forms, to last for millennia. Its castles collapse. Its massive monuments, eroded away by rain and wind, melt back into the earth, into the landscape. If clay architecture survives, it is in its functional, human tradition.

162

Its material is clay. Wet clay, reinforced with straw and pressed into wooden forms. The humidity being so low and the sun's heat so intense, the brick sets hard. It is the local building material. With water, clay becomes its own factory. To fashion one's own bricks from one's own soil presents no difficulties. As a building material it is foolproof. You can't go wrong, building with sun-dried brick. On the other hand it does not lend itself to speculative or risky projects. Houses of sun-dried clay are easy to maintain. And properly maintained, plastered with straw-reinforced clay, whitewashed, these houses will live as long as any of our new suburban dwellings.

The thick walls exclude winter cold and summer heat. The house can breathe. Is insulated against sound. Living is pleasant in a house of sun-dried brick.

The form arises out of the materials. Vaulted roofs, cupolas, free surfaces, soft lines. One works in forms and surfaces. A closed building, open nevertheless to humanity, and alive. Within it one shuts oneself off from the tormenting hot desert winds, from nature's ferocity. Opens oneself inward, to a community of human feeling.

But only in appearance is this form free. If it is free and good and human it is because it so closely follows its function, and because its materials permit no extravagances. Its form is obliged to yield to strictest necessity. And this makes its freedom of form a real freedom, no mere weak evasive formlessness, enclosing men within narrower limits than those dictated by necessity. Unlike the fanciful drawing-board artifacts of Chandigarh or Stockholm suburbs, this is a human way of building.

Everything has been thought out, developed in the course of millennia, to create for man a human environment. The tall cupolas create air cushions under the thick clay walls, and in the rooms the air, even in the hottest desert summer, is fresh and cool. The entrance faces south, so that the winter sun can light the rooms and warm them; as for the summer sun, it is too high in the sky to get in and overheat them. Water, splashed over raffia mats outside the door, evaporates and cools the interior. Indoors, too, the house's humidity is maintained by sprinkling water everywhere. Its yard is a patio. Even the blistering heat of July days cannot penetrate to the sardabs, the cold rooms beneath ground level.

The American and European experts build inhuman compounds,

full of machinery for cooling and humidifying the air. They sniff and snivel and suffer from the heat, meanwhile, using up enough energy to run a small factory. For they have no culture. They have divorced form from function. They aren't rationalists. Were they rational, they would study the clay villages, and begin to build rationally. But they can't. For they are obsessed with their idea of their own superiority. If they lose that obsession, then they lose the ideological defense of their neo-colonialism and imperialism. Air conditioning is ideological and political—not functional.

But the villagers do not live as long as the Europeans and the Americans. The village is poor, wretched, oppressed. We see the poverty, the bad health—and nothing else.

Yet new ground has been broken. Water has been fetched, and the desert is being forced to yield a harvest. People say how nothing of all this ever changes. How it will go on repeating itself forever. And is therefore standing still. Kanats are dug, get choked with slime, are cleared, collapse, and are reconstructed. One bad year follows another, year after year, seldom interrupted even by one good harvest. Only by hard obstinate toil is enough bread wrested from the soil to last until the next, and scarcely so much. Under this hot sky one year follows another and nothing is ever new, and no thought ever reaches further than the mirages of green forest on the horizon—forests which are no forest. No one comes here from the cities. Only the tax-collector, the forager, and the landowner demanding their due. The village is eternal; and the villagers and landowners are forever the same, no matter how often individuals come and go. Each is born into a life staked out from the beginning. The peasant, plundered and dispossessed, forms the third side of the triangle.

Yet even this immobility is illusory. In the long struggle for this soil, burned brown under the hot pallid skies of millennia, kanat-diggers and peasants have been butchered, flogged to death, hanged, burned, and quartered. No soil in the world is deeper drenched in blood than the soil of ancient cultures, this ancient farming land.

Time and again the peasants have revolted. In late Sassanid times their struggle, which lasted for three centuries, shattered the aristocratic regime and the slave economy. But even today the demands of the old fifth-century Mazdahkites still haven't been met. What they demanded was a real land reform, a community of wealth, liberation of the harem women, and the introduction of monogamy. A political and social revolutionary movement in religious guise. Everywhere they had their sympathizers. The best-educated and most knowledgeable men of the age said with Burzoe, Croesus's court physician:

"Our age is rotten through and through."

The peasants marched away to bloody battles. The nobles' castles were razed to the ground, the land was divided up, women were released from the harems, the property of the wealthy was distributed—and a cry went up to heaven at the outrage suffered by culture, and at the anarchy prevailing in the land. Destroying the nobles, the people augmented the royal power; and when they threatened that power they had to be smashed in the name of culture and order. So the monarchs, the generals, the bureaucrats, and all other pillars of society joined forces with the various priesthoods in a holy war against the uncultured heretics. They were hunted through the streets of the cities, flayed alive, chopped in pieces, their books were burned, their children massacred, their property seized. And then the king, who had used them to crush the nobility, restored order in the land.

But for a long time to come the Mazdahkite organizations persevered. Although their leaders were dead or in exile they could still gather their forces for attacks on the established order; an order, however, of another sort than that which had preceded the great conflicts. And stronger. No longer were they faced only by a lot of quarreling landlords. Now they had to deal with despotism. Again, fifty years after their defeat, at Bukhara far away in the northeast, the poor rose in revolt. Aristocrats and the great merchants were expelled; but the revolt was crushed and its leaders chopped in pieces. As late as the early eighth century armed conflicts took place. Khurzad, brother of the Shah of Khoresm, seized power. The aristocracy were punished. Their property, their herds and their wives were seized and distributed among the people. But the king called in the Arabs, who crushed the revolutionaries and restored order. The new order. Of all the many leeches who had bled them before, only one remained; but he insatiable: the tax-collector. He who, to pay for the despots' armies and their ever more glorious exploits, laid waste the villages.

XXXIII

From North Africa to the Turfan depression in Sinkiang, through the whole of the old world's drought belt, the deserts seem pitted by smallpox. It is as if huge moles had been burrowing away under the scorched lands, at regular intervals flinging up mounds of earth beside their tunnels. Deep pits, miles from any vegetation or human abode.

But a closer look reveals that these deep holes are not scattered haphazard over the desert. They fall into a pattern. Range themselves in rows. At regular distances from the hills or mountains they go marching out toward the yellow clay villages and the green fields. These are the karezes or kanats, the underground irrigation channels. The whole of this part of the world is athirst for water. It isn't soil which is in short supply. It is water. These kanats are one of early engineering science's most magnificent achievements.

My grandfather was something of a water diviner. One summer, twenty years or so ago, he tried to teach me to use a hazel twig. Wanted me to feel how the veins of water tug at it. The kanats would have delighted him.

Nothing is more sacred than water. Water is life. Without water, in these parts, there is only desert. Out here on the steppes and in the deserts the subsoil water lies deep. Evaporation from open canals is tremendous. A little rill of water cannot be carried many miles across these parched lands without evaporating, being absorbed, and vanishing. Yet everywhere there is water. Deep beneath the soil is all the water it needs for bearing crops.

The climate is dry, rain a rarity, and snow only lies on the highest mountains. Water from rivers and streams runs down from the mountains and the nearer it comes to the plains the more the rivers and streams dry up, are absorbed by the loose soil and disappear. Before ever they get as far as the desert regions, the streams have vanished. Toward the hills and mountains the plains shelve gently upward. Deep below their surface, water is flowing over clay strata and impenetrable layers of rock. And this is the water which must be brought to the fields and villages.

If one follows a kanat from its mouth in the village to its source, one finds one is following a ditch which gets gradually deeper and deeper until it becomes a tunnel. From one well to the next the kanat can be traced up toward the mountains. And the nearer one comes to the mountains, the deeper it lies. The last well is at the water-bearing strata.

In theory all this is simple enough. Merely a matter of digging a tunnel with sufficient incline for water to flow along it, but just that much less precipitous than the slope of the plain for the tunnel to reach the light of day exactly at the village needing its water. In practice this is difficult and specialized work. The kanats stretch for miles. The main well, where each kanat collects its water, must be as deep as a mine shaft. In Iran five-hundred-year-old kanats exist, with main wells more than three hundred feet deep. The soil is loose and sandy. Everything must be calculated to the nearest inch.

Show me the Swedish engineer who, without any instruments, was given the job of digging a tunnel two feet in diameter through thirty-one miles of sandy soil, at a gradient of one-in-a-hundred! Yet the feat is achieved. We were with the kanat-diggers, and saw them at work. First, they had established the summer level of the subsoil water at the foot of the hills, twelve and a half miles further on. By running out galleries in various directions they had created a water reservoir. Now they were burrowing their way from well to well. One man lay inside the tunnel. Filling leather sacks with soil, he was passing them out to an assistant who stood at the bottom of the well. At its mouth two men were taking up the full sacks and lowering the empties with a winch. At regular intervals segments of the burned-clay vaulting were wound down. The soil was loose. There was a constant risk of the whole kanat caving in. The man inside the tunnel was digging and facing, digging and facing. Sixty-five thousand feet, more than twelve miles at a precisely calculated gradient.

Every spring the kanats are cleaned out. Sooner or later a section

167

collapses. Then a new stretch has to be dug. In the end the whole thing caves in. Then a complete new kanat has to be dug. Villages and fields follow the kanats.

In the shade of the poplars a carpet has been spread for us. Beside, the kanat flows along. Its cold clear waters pour out of the tunnel mouth, forming a shady dam; thence on into irrigation canals through the village and so out into the fields. The men treat us to tea and melons. Beyond this little oasis of greenery and human habitations the blazing desert, bald and bare, stretches away to hills which sway and flicker in the heat. Suddenly they rise, swell, bob about like balloons. Lose touch with the ground. One can clearly see them floating high above its surface. Beneath them there is blue sky. A heat mirage. As we drink our tea our hosts sit beside us, dipping their hands in the water, playing with it, allowing it to trickle between their fingers. This is one of mankind's great victories. The triumph of thought and work over nature.

No one knows for certain where the kanat was invented. Supposedly it is a construction originating in the high Persian plateau. Large-scale construction of kanats was regarded as one of the great achievements of the Achaemenids. Kanat irrigation is expensive. Calls for much labor and highly experienced specialists. A great investment both of labor and materials. A short kanat, no doubt, can be built by a village's own efforts. For a larger one professionals are needed. The kanat-diggers we met were craftsmen, proud of their art. Masters, descended from old families of kanat-diggers, whose knowledge and trade secrets have been passed down for generations.

The "western" experts seldom have much use for the knowledge of the old kanat-diggers. They have bulldozers, motors, instruments. They say they can build huge dams, plan for entire countries. Why should they bother about men brought up in a thousand-year-old tradition, who know how to burrow their way through narrow tunnels beneath deserts to bring fresh clear water to the villages?

But such scorn for tradition is both unscientific and irrational. Irrational, inasmuch as its roots lie in the whole complex of superior attitudes which a "western" expert drags about with him. Half-educated, with only the vaguest notions of other lands and other

168

cultures and no real feeling even for his own or its background, ignorant of most things and cruelly indifferent, he equates horse-power with reason. Outbursts of rage against anything he doesn't know, anything disturbing to his own vicious circles, are rationalized into scorn for "Asiatic backwardness." Of which kanats, like clay houses, form part.

It is also deeply unscientific. The theory of subsoil waters is far from complete. To ignore the knowledge of subsoil water conditions on the high Persian plateau which generations of kanat-builders have labored to bring to light is waste of knowledge. Not to utilize the kanat-diggers, these water-craftsmen, in the new irrigation projects, not to teach them the new techniques and so put them and their local knowledge of the country and its potential in a position to exploit such techniques, is political; helps the foreign dominance.

Some "western" technicians, it is true, do not suffer from this superiority complex. Individuals who see clearly and rationally. But their opportunities of influencing the powers which are providing the machines and capital are few. A company like Morrison & Knudsen has only a job to do. Discussion of the kanat-diggers' techniques, their knowledge, their usefulness to the country, simply doesn't concern them. Morrison & Knudsen are not Afghanistan. To them, the kanat-diggers are just "natives."

In these countries climate and geographical conditions have determined social development. No peasant of the desert could set off for the horizon, start building his own private kanat, and manage on his own. Cooperation has always been crucial. Slaves could construct kanats for a landowner. The village council for the village. A governor, the state, a monarch could build them. But no individual.

Kanats supported the state. The struggle for the kanats was the struggle for power. The kanats decided the limits of that struggle. Landowner, village council, despot. But a landowning peasant was an impossibility. A contradiction in terms.

The immense new irrigation schemes are changing all this. A new technique, placing clear water at everyone's disposal, has unleashed a scramble for land. And as land is now available the peasants will lose their rights. The new water will increase productivity and make poverty deeper. The Asian village crumbles

169

Paddy fields near Shahidan

with the arrival of the irrigation water; out of the bitterness grow new struggles, sharper and more violent than those of the Mazdahkites.

Cool and clear, the kanat water trickles through our fingers. We play with the water. Our hosts proffer us more tea. This time we take no sugar with it; that would be impolite. All the men of the village are sitting around us. At the house-corners the women stand peeping out at the strangers. The children, too, throw us surreptitious glances out of the corners of their eyes, but are sharply reprimanded by their fathers. Curiosity, forwardness are bad taste. And all the while the cold water is pouring out of the mouth of the kanat.

XXXIV

The grey hot steppes lay behind us. On the road across the rolling deserted steppelands from Tashkurgan to Kunduz—where the tracks diverge and disappear into the distance and the road widens out for a half-mile on either hand—the wind had blown grey rolling balls of entangled vegetation toward us. These were thistles. Their branches bend in such a way that, dried up and torn loose from the soil, their remains hook on to each other and they come snowballing toward us across the wide hillsides, pursued by the hot wind. Enormous balls, six feet in diameter, they go rustling past, away over the wide-open spaces.

We had passed through Kunduz and the rice fields; now we were driving northeast up toward the mountains. Jagged mountain peaks pierced the horizon. As we climbed the slopes this jagged, thorny horizon opened out. There, broad and calm, flowed the Khanabad River. On its other side green farming districts, and down by the river, sandy meadows sloping upward to grazing grounds. A man on an inflated goatskin was floating across. On his head he carried his clothes in a bundle. We saw how the current caught him and spun him round; but he kicked out strongly with his legs and swam on, reaching the black muddy shore beneath those smiling green farmlands.

Valley follows valley. The river flows more swiftly. We drive through our first town since Band-i-Turkistan. Now the river bed at the fords is slippery clay; there is a great depth of water, and the grey vortices all around our hood are heavy with soil. But we get through. And then it is Marco Polo writing: "Pleasant country all the way, densely populated and rich in fruits, grain, and grapes."

But all around us stand the mountains. The first snow-covered peaks stick up through the haze of the plains. The valley grows ever narrower and the water beneath us clearer. We come to the end of the road. Have come too far. Turning, we make our way up out of the Khanabad River valley in the direction of Badakhshan. The route clambers up a dried ravine—the road itself has been washed away, several spring floods ago. Our wheels spin round in pebbles and gravel, but after a few miles we reach the watershed; and now the high brown plateau stretches away on every hand. Grey villages, built of stone and clay.

The road passes the salt mines. Salt caravans come toward us. Heavy-laden donkeys. Down in the cities men are sitting hammering this mountain salt into a grey powder. We descend between brown hills. The road drops away steeply, cuts through a mixture of stone and sand. Herds of sheep. Beneath us, another green valley. In the evening twilight we drive into Kishm, where the air is thick and heavy with the scent of flowers. Mosquitoes are singing and water trickles in streams and irrigation canals.

At long last, next morning, we reach the Kokcha River and follow it up into Badakhshan. The landscape hardens, becomes sterner and more barren. The mountainsides grow balder. Now, in late summer, melting glaciers are turning the gold-bearing Kokcha ever greyer. It boils and eddies beneath us. The road clings to the cliff edges and the river flows swiftly. Having cut its way down through the mountains it roars on down toward the Amu Darya and the plains. From the east comes a stream of clear green water, stabbing the Kokcha's grey-blue waters with emerald green. Blue rivulets run across its green surface, and its edges eddy whitely. Strung between knobbly poles, the telegraph line runs on ahead of us. The villages along the river turn a stony grey. Again the landscape hardens, but where it opens out into vegetation it is rich and moist. Behind the stone walls apple trees are growing.

172

"This kingdom," writes the Chinese monk and geographer Hsüan-tsang, in the seventh century,

> belonged of old to Tu-ho-lo; it is about 2,000 li in circumference, and the capital which stands at the foot of a cliff, measures some six or seven li in circumference.
>
> It is intersected by mountains and valleys, extensive regions of sand and stone; its soil is suited to wheat and beans; it produces grapevines, Khamil peaches and plums, etc. The climate is very cold.

Now, on the other side of the river, we can see Faizabad. Under the bridge the water foams and as we drive into the town the rock beneath us trembles slightly. This is earthquake country. And still the Hindu Kush is crumpling into ever deeper folds to rise to ever greater heights. A few years ago Faizabad was laid waste. The earthquake dammed up the river waters, and when the barrier burst, the town was shattered by the flood wave. We had got used to tremors at Kabul. Whenever the shocks began and we felt the Hindu Kush straightening itself out, my typewriter used to go squealing away across the table. But the seismic center lies up here in Badakhshan.

Badakhshan is not a rich part of the country. Its gold and precious stones go, as always, to the great cities. Its soil is stony. Its people are rugged as the country itself, and its women famed for their beauty. Its folk art has lively colors. In the mountains the shepherds go about with naked, wrapped legs.

Today Badakhshan is an out-of-the-way district in an out-of-the-way country. But not so long ago the great trade caravans eastward-bound along the Silk Route used to traverse it. The old route up the Kokcha toward upper Amu Darya, Punjab, and Pamir goes this way. Of Badakhshan's precious stones Marco Polo says how fascinated he was by the idea of mountains consisting of nothing but precious jewels; but being a practical merchant, adds: "Here are also mountains which contain veins of silver, copper and lead in great quantities."

Badakhshan is one of the country's poorest provinces. But potentially it is rich. Here is water power. Here are minerals. When people talk about Badakhshan today, they speak of lapis lazuli or the high mountain air. Badakhshan is said to be one of the healthiest regions in the world. This reputation, which it owes to Marco Polo, is exaggerated. Poverty means bad health. Poverty-stricken villages are seldom health resorts. A future Badakhshan will be known for its iron mines, its lead, its silver, its zinc, its real wealth. Then it will really be one of the healthiest regions in the world. Its air is high and clean, and when poverty has been smashed its villages will recover their health.

We continue up the Kokcha, pass Barak. And now the river divides. We follow its northern branch, the Wardouf, up toward the watershed. The landscape becomes harder, but also more Scandinavian. Strange it is to meet one's homeland's flora, not by journeying to the Arctic Circle, but after climbing up toward the high mountains, deep in Central Asia! The mountains are as bald as very high mountains, and in the ditches grows the baby-slipper flower (*Lotus corniculatus*). And ahead the telegraph wires lead on and on toward the northeast. The white cow parsley (wild chervil) is waving in the breeze, and the fields are a mass of blue campanula. The very air in one's lungs seems Swedish, damp and chill.

This is a new road. The river throws itself from one reach to another, roaring against its banks. The road is in constant danger of being undermined and collapsing. This makes for difficult driving. Precipitous slopes cross its ridges where the river has eaten away its embankment. At one point the entire embankment has been washed away. The cliff ledge sticks straight out into the foaming waters. We are obliged to descend into the river bed. Though attempts have been made to protect the water passages with wattles, the foam splashes our windshield. To get up to the road again is a troublesome business and the long climb up into the mountains slow and arduous. The river gets narrower and narrower, the mountains rise to ever greater heights, the air becomes clearer, and the peaks, grandiose above the narrow valleys, are covered with white snowfields. We drive through rock gorges where great sand dunes have strayed across the road. Wind erosion.

High up on the black mountainsides the villages cling to the rock ledges and beneath them is a chessboard of verdant terraces.

Mountain Tazhiks near Zebak

174

After a wearisome drive we reach Zebak at dusk. High mountain country now, and marshes. It is cold, damp, and gusty. Here the snow has only just melted, the swamps are still muddy, and the mud bottomless. The very road is boggy. Water seeps up between green tufts and a grey woolly mist is falling over the valley. Contours are erased. Only the coldly sparkling sky is black and starry overhead.

During the night I muse on Badakhshan. It is a remote land. Not often visited nowadays. But in the twilight the landscape was so like ours in Northern Sweden; and I wonder whether Charles XII's soldiers, after their failure to conquer the world, and when they entered the service of Peter the Great and civilization, really visited this land or only mapped it by hearsay. The one real achievement of our Swedish Age of Greatness was its contribution to the exploration of Central Asia and Siberia. None of our campaigns were half as glorious as our commonsensical defeat at Poltava, which placed our officers at the service of humanity.

Now the evening mist has blown away. In the chill air the robat at Zebak, the caravanserai beneath the mountains, faces out over swamps and the dark valley.

XXXV

On the clay-plastered stone wall of the robat the paraffin lamp throws a warm yellow glow. Beyond its yellow cone of light, darkness lurks in corners. Over the roof a cold wet mountain wind is blowing. One listens to the sound of the wind and feels the damp draft hissing down from the roof. But the lamplight is mild and human.

The low ledges are covered with kelims, brightly colored mats woven in simple patterns. They are much worn. The central corridor's grey shiny surface of trampled clay has been polished by many feet. I take off my anorak. My knapsack is propped against the timber beam. We've unrolled our sleeping bags, eaten the food of the rich. Roghan. Rice with mutton fat. They've served us our tea. And now all the men go out, so that Gun can slip into her sleeping bag.

Outside are the cold and the wastes. But in here one feels safe. A community of human feeling. Here we all sleep side by side, rolled up like chrysalises on the low ledges, and the thick walls protect us against wind, cold, and other nuisances.

Along every route and road stand the robats and caravanserais, ready to receive visitors at the end of their day's journey. This is a group-travel culture. And up here at Zebak, where the road from Faizabad meets the road from Chitral and continues toward Ish Kashim and Wakhan, the robat is strong and well kept. Just before reaching Zebak we had passed the crossroads where the signpost pointed to Chitral. According to my British map, it should be a "road," while we ourselves have been traveling along a "track." But it was no more than a narrow plank bridge, thrown across the rapids. In the distance beyond, the high white mountains of Chitral.

When I awake in the morning I find myself gazing up at the roof of the robat. And now, in the morning light, where last night nothing but darkness was visible, I see the roof. A lantern roof. Beams ingeniously forming a timber dome. A wooden cupola with smoke-holes. The last time I saw such a roof was in Bamian. In Buddha's cave temple. But cave temples were only stone facsimiles of wooden temples. Between the spurious lantern roof in Bamian and the genuine functional dome at Zebak there is a direct link. This is no mere stone hut on the outermost outskirts of the inhabited world. We are still on the great culture routes.

The lantern roof was developed on the high Persian plateau and with the artisans and the merchants wandered across Asia. This lantern roof at Zebak inspires in me a feeling of happiness. I cannot take my eyes off it. Like a well-designed link it fits into the great chain of culture. Nor was it an ordinary plank bridge which carried the Chitral route across the Wardouf. It was a console (cantilever) bridge. A construction of Chinese invention, brought across these mountains to India and Europe.

Up here in the mountains the great streams of culture have had their point of confluence. Nothing abstract about either the streams or their meeting. It took the form of everyday artisans' daily work. Abstract speculation, religious meditations, notions of the gods, all lose their interest. Earth-bound, they lack elevation; they never transcend the narrow limits of that which already exists. But to

177

learn a technique and with it overcome nature, exploiting nature's powers in the service of humanity—that's important.

This road, which has climbed over ridges, clung to mountainsides, which has been built out over the low swamps and thrown across rapids, is old. Ingeniously made of wood and stone, the bridges we have been driving over have had to be rebuilt almost every year. This victorious human struggle to keep the route open, in spite of the masses of water from melting snows and the thunderous landslides, has been going on for millennia. Which is why the console bridges over the upper Wardouf and the domed lantern roof at Zebak are such great monuments.

They rise high above the wooden roofs of mountain huts and the plank bridges of mountain streams. No temples, no art can match them. Temples and arts are mere reflections of reality. The lantern roof at Zebak is no abstraction, no piece of cultural history; it is human life, human activity. Today, as two thousand years ago.

The morning is sunny but cold. Ragged clouds are flying over the peaks. Beyond the swamp the valleys are still dark in the mountains' shadow. Mountain Tadzhiks with conical back-baskets go by. Carrying butter down to the cities.

We drive on through the cool morning, following the river upward. At the foot of the cliffs lie conical heaps of tumbled boulders. Above our heads, water and the cold are bursting the mountains asunder. The heavens grow deeper and the air acquires a fresh healthy sharpness.

We are still in inhabited valleys. The villages are getting poorer, but their greenery at the same time is becoming more vivid and fruitful among the grey mountains. The children turn to look as we go by, and behind us the shepherds' dogs bark their suspicion. Cloudbanks surround us and the high mountains themselves begin to acquire the bare severity of high peaks. At our side, cliffs cracked by frost. More vivid green valleys. Tents huddled beneath high fields of black sand. Once again we have to drive down into the river. This time we have to wade three miles at a time. Occasionally we drive through deep channels, the water rising against our doors. We get up onto a gravel bank, and I go ahead on foot to stake out the shallows.

178

The water is freezing cold and the current drags at my legs. It's hard to get a foothold on the rolling stones of the river bottom. A shepherd is leading his sheep across the river. Bleating pathetically they step down into the water, are caught by the stream and struggle for their lives, their eyes black with terror. Reaching the other shore the flock stands huddled and shivering. The lambs refuse the water. The ewes call their lambs. The shepherd throws them in. Little grey bundles of terror, they go spinning round in the eddies. But the youngest he carries over. One lamb slips from his grasp, falls into the stream, and is swept away. White foam covers it. Just at that moment I am standing out in the river, water up to my waist so I know how strong the current is. The stones rustle around my feet. All around us now the mountains are jagged crests projecting from gravel ridges. This time the water rises above the hood, splashing the windshield. The wheels are lifted off the bottom, the car rocks violently in the waves and Gun takes an anxious grip on the steering wheel as it spins round in the rapids, and the water comes seeping in through the windows as the car is pulled across. Jagged bald mountains, yaks, and a clump of poplars. We're on our way up in the passes over to Wakhan.

But now we are through, and the road leads onward and upward. The river has shriveled to a stream. A saint's grave. Then soft meadows, leading upward. Tadzhiks on horseback greet us amicably. Now only the last pass remains. The Sarda. A gentle pass through high mountains where, the higher one gets, the more the mountains seem to sink into plains.

Now the stream is no more. The ground is marshy. On the mountain ridges which sink away to the west snow is lying. We go over the pass, and at once the scene changes. It is as if we had not moved at all, but one stage scene had replaced another. The ground is still swampy, but the white mountains appear ranged in a semicircle in front of us. Pamir and the Hindu Kush. Straight across the valley lies the Soviet Union; to the east, Pakistan; and now the Ab-i-Pandj twists serpentine through the valley below. A great basin of green meadows, where the upper Amu Darya, coming from Wakhan and Pamir, turns northward.

The clouds are flying over the mountains and we drive down into an amphitheater. A long green slope redolent with spring flowers, its long sweeping lines are broken by high black mountains, white-topped: Ish Kashim. The key to Pamir.

Here the road goes up to Pamir. The new motor road, which one day will continue right through Wakhan to Sinkiang in China. The wind is bitingly cold, but the fields are green and they tell us we have brought the spring with us. The snow has just melted in Ish Kashim. Higher up it is still falling. It is July 16. Our odometer shows we have driven 37,480 kilometers—23, 226 miles—since leaving Sweden.

XXXVI

The old saying used to be: "If you want to die, go to Kunduz!"

The whole of Kataghan province was formerly Afghanistan's place of exile. At Kunduz, Khanabad, and Baghlan malaria raged. In the swampy valleys between the Hindu Kush and the Amu Darya anopheles mosquitoes buzzed. There the plasmodia broke the wills of refractory officials, and troublesome mullahs departed for a better world. The rich green vegetation around the rivers was nothing but a mask over the face of disease, lethargy, and want.

The new road over the Hindu Kush had been opened. It had direct and convulsive effects on the state of people's health and their economy. The province, now linked with Kabul, became both possible and profitable to cultivate and develop. Now Kataghan is Afghanistan's industrial region. Kunduz, Khanabad, Talikhan, Baghlan, and Pul-i-Khumri; everywhere industrial towns are coming into being. The route from the steppes turned into a properly dug road through the hills. The countryside on either side of the frontier was just as dry and just as hard, but as we approached Kunduz we found we were driving on a properly made and planned road. Across the steppes from Kunduz reason was forcing its way in. Building is reason. The road was lined with trees, and we crossed the river on a ferry. The ferry was old, an antique model, drawn across the river by a winch. But the people were new.

The Kunduz we saw was a developing town. The people were open, malaria almost exterminated. The white, the weary, and the old, both walls and ideas, were on the way out. A cotton industry had been started. This new reality was giving the town another face and quite different inhabitants. In the hotel hangs a huge city plan. We look at it a long while, admiring the beautifully planned industries and parks. Two gas stations were marked on it. We drove to Gas Station II. Drove straight out into the steppe. As yet nothing had been built. We returned to the town and to Gas Station I. But this very fact—that plans had been drawn up, that there was confidence, that the future was shown even before it could be realized—that was good, that was lovely.

Kataghan has begun to base its industries on cotton. Cotton and rice are cultivated. Between the rice plants fish were swimming. Anopheles-eaters! The big new industry, the one which began to be constructed before the War and which today absorbs the cotton, from harvest to finished product, is at Kunduz. The cotton is exported. There it stands in long rows, pressed like great toy bricks. But the cottonseed is crushed into oil, refined for cooking oil, forms the basis of the new soap manufacture. The ugly green soap we wash with makes a poor lather. The technicians apologize: "This is only a first experiment. We haven't started production yet."

But it *is* soap, and it cleans. It smells good, and is Afghanistan's first industrial soap. It is symbolic of a long development, a symbol of the new order, of industrialization which systematizes, rationalizes life. Nor is it an exceptional product, but the final phase of an extensive production process. Cotton growing by new methods. Cotton harvest. Cleansing. Preparation of the cottonseed oil. Soap manufacture. A process involving thousands of people. That's the great thing. That the soap makes poor lather is beside the point. This bit of soap is a hope of a new and richer life.

The roads have opened up the country. Now the industries can begin to be built. The difficulties are still enormous. Industrial workers and technicians are still few. But these new industrial towns are hopeful places. Their atmosphere is one of work, intensity, and health. Already the industrial worker is living a freer and richer life than he knew as a peasant or nomad. But it isn't only his personal life which has changed. The whole of society is changing with him. The new power stations, the new irrigation canals, the new industries, all are transforming any part of the country which lies in their path. As yet the industrial workers can only be numbered in thousands or tens of thousands. But these new industries have already led to a shortage of labor in the country.

On the old Silk Route over the Hindu Kush the villages are building schools. And even at a distance from the industrial towns children are being brought in to be taught, being given the tools to master reality. We stopped where one of these schools was being built. As yet only the foundation walls had been put up. But the teachers already existed, and the children had learned to read.

The road through Kataghan is the highroad through Afghanistan's future. Pul-i-Khumri's modern workers' blocks are a new form of Afghan town. In the center of Pul-i-Khumri boys in blue overalls stand outside the teahouses. As yet Afghanistan has no trade unions. But nomads and agricultural workers are being transformed into industrial workers. They have gained a new view of the world, and are making new demands on it. They are already asking, "Who takes the profits of our work?"

XXXVII

The sky is grey and driving rain-squalls obscure the mountains. Pouring, foggy weather, reminiscent of home and the North Swedish forests. The roof drips, and we've had to move our charpoys so that the drips shan't fall on our sleeping bags. Put empty cans to catch them instead. Above my writing desk the roof is still watertight, but Gun has had to move her easel into my room. We're waiting for the men who are coming to pour roofing clay over the roof, to stop it leaking. The grass in the garden is a deep green, and when we walk out to the car in the garage shed to go and fetch our mail our shoes sink in the mud. The water splashes about the tires and the wipers sweep across the windshield.

People, hunched to avoid dripping roofs, walk far out in the street. The gutters are full of brown water. Where the street is still not asphalted it has turned into a bottomless bog. Such liquid clay is too much even for jeeps.

New showers come driving in over the city from off the mountains. The rain lashes down. Leaving the car we crouch double and make a dash for the doorway to fetch our mail. Two letters and a parcel from Sandberg's bookshop in Stockholm. The Kabul River is rising. Sitting in the car we watch the flood pouring down from the mountains and notice how the river is climbing up the bridges. Streets in the bazaar quarters are so muddy as to be impassable. People clutch their shawls wound around their faces, and in the grey rainy streets women's plastic raincoats shine in bright patches of color. Gun buys mutton and potatoes in the fruit bazaar by the park. A cold biting wind drags at our legs as we come home again. But the rain has stopped. We cross the garden to our low white house. Soaked by the rain the wall plaster around the doorway is flaking off in great chunks. Straw and clay are exposed, the straw heavy and grey from the wet. In the rooms there is a smell of damp mildew. Now the roof tramplers have arrived. They are laying new clay on the roof, stamping it down hard after the rain to stop the leaks. Now it should hold again for another six months.

We put our mutton on to simmer, I don my dry sweater, and we get down to work. The trees are still dripping, but over the mountains to the south the sky is clearing. I have my books in the packing case which serves as an extra place to put things on. It is covered in plastic to stop water getting into the books if the rain should get in.

In the evening a flute is playing in the next house. We hear it every evening. A man is singing. As evening darkens into night the flute ceases. We read, or listen to the radio. Next morning I drive back to the library of the French Archaeological Delegation in Afghanistan. It is Kabul's nicest library. The British have more books, but won't loan them to anyone who isn't British. The Press Department's library is good, so are those of the Ministry of Education and the Ministry for Tribal Affairs. But the French Archaeological Delegation's is the nicest.

I read about Afghanistan. Fetch new books at the post office. And the more I read, the more astonished I become. Gradually, I realize I shouldn't be astonished. If most of what has been written about this country only awakens disgust, that was to be expected. Really, we don't take the same view of reality, these writers and I. I read Brigadier General Sir Percy Sykes, K.C.I.E., C.B., C.M.G.X: *A History of Afghanistan:*

> Nothing could check the gallantry of the troops who stormed through village and vineyard with such a rush that the defenders of Istalif were seized with panic and the hillside beyond was covered with men and white veiled women fleeing from the town. McGaskill, with true British gallantry, allowed no pursuit, but two guns and much booty fell to the victors.

When I read that, I think of the Istalif I know. A little mountain village on the road to Charikar. A place we make excursions to on Sundays to drink tea and walk in the bazaar where they sell blue china and beaten silver. Then I see we have a basically different way of seeing people and their lives. The General and I.

These gallant British officers are long dead. But their deeds are not. Take another text:

> Frank had been instructed that a signal act of retribution should fall on guilty Warsaw. He realized that if the fortress were destroyed there would be even less chance than at present existed for the restoration of law and order in the "Generalgouvernement." He therefore decided to blow up the Ghetto in which the mutilated corpse of Müller had been exhibited. But anxious to keep retribution within reasonable bounds, he sent a strong detachment of SS troops to protect the inhabitants from plunder and outrage. However upon the sound of the explosions being heard "the cry went up," to quote Bühler, "that Warsaw was being given up to plunder. Both camps rushed into the city, and the consequence has been the almost total destruction of the town."
>
> These excesses are to be deplored, but when we consider that the soldiers and BDM-girls had been eye-witnesses to the massacres perpetrated alike on SS and non-combatants by the Jews, the fact that the guilty city lay at their mercy and the rumor that it was to be plundered, feelings of vengeance, which cannot be severely blamed, would naturally be aroused.

If Hitler had not been defeated, so would the German historians write today. If you change "Frank" to "Pollock," "Warsaw" to "Kabul," fortress to "Bala Hissar," "Generalgouvernement" to "Afghanistan," "Ghetto" to "main bazaar," "Müller" to "Macnaghten" and so on, you will get to the text as it was written by the imperial historians of Great Britain.

184

You can transform the text once more. Many times more. You can place the destruction in Algeria or in Vietnam. The pattern remains. It is the same pattern. These gallant officers are not yet long dead.

City gate of Khiva

186

1960

SOVIET CENTRAL ASIA

XXXVIII

In the summers the winds blow from the hot dry Kara Kum. From its black sands they blow westward, toward Krasnovodsk and the Caspian Sea. They blow southward, across Khurasan and Herat toward Seistan. They blow eastward, along the Amu Darya, away over Mazar-i-Sharif and up toward the high mountains. The black sand is on the move, and the air is heavy with dust.

Two summers we breathed the desert of the Turkmens. It met us as the Wind of a Hundred and Twenty Days, at Herat, in July, 1958. It followed us across the steppes beneath the Amu Darya the year after. Then the sky was grey with loose driving soil. The Kara Kum was in one's pores, layer on layer in the car's air filter, turned one's hair stiff and grey. But even when we had reached Badakhshan, in 1959, and the high mountain range suddenly opened out its wide valleys to the westward where the smell of the desert stung our nostrils, we'd still never been in the native land of that wind.

Twice we saw the border of Soviet Central Asia. The first time was in the spring of 1958, beyond the Gorgan, just east of the Caspian Sea. We'd driven out across the steppes toward Alexander's Wall, succeeded in slipping through police chains and the barriers at the frontier posts. The steppe, Turkmen Tara, hung in mirages before our eyes, the low creeping white saksaul bushes rose up like great trees and ahead the water mirrored itself, as if offering to quench

187

our thirst, only to run away, nothing but illusions born of the heat.

More than a year later we crossed the high mountains, drove up river valleys, left them behind, and went over the pass; there the Ab-i-Pandj glittered beneath us and ahead of us rose the mountain chains, wave on wave, away across Gorno-Badakhshan. The waters from the melting snows ran across the track, yet summer was at its height.

For nearly three years we were on our travels, here in Asia, before ever we crossed the frontier to the Soviet Republics of Central Asia. Not that three years had passed before getting into Central Asia itself. Central Asia is a vague concept, but the land north of the Hindu Kush, where all the rivers run inward, obviously forms part of it. The deserts, the mountains, the peoples and their culture, all these we had experienced long before entering the Soviet. Which is important. The same peoples live north of the Amu Darya as south of it. They sing the same songs, speak the same languages, have identical traditions. Equally important: Central Asia is not a unity. There are great differences. At least as great as between the European peoples. On both sides of the frontier they speak the same languages, but this is not to say the same language is spoken along its length.

We'd been traveling in Poor Asia, living in Poor Asia. Seen much that was hopeful. Felt an affinity with its strictness, with Afghanistan's stern and manly tradition. But we had also seen, and been embittered by, the oppression and want in Iran and India; that poverty beyond belief which gives the few and well born such incredible wealth that life tastes like ashes in your mouth. When you live in the poorest parts of Asia you have moments when all you want to do is pray for the Day of Wrath; you become religious as the poor in Europe were religious in the sixteenth century, dreaming of the day of God's wrath, when the sheep should be separated from the goats and the whole world should be cleansed with fire.

It was with that basic attitude we reached the Soviet republics of Central Asia. And here—over old Russian Turkistan, Western Turkistan—a fire had already passed. In 1916 the Mohammedan population had revolted against Russian rule. Before the revolt could be crushed, Russia was herself ablaze with revolution. Of the 1916 rebels, some joined the Reds; some the Whites. The long hard struggle, decided militarily in 1920, continued in the shape of sporadic fighting up to 1931. A civil war, often cruel, sometimes wild and confused, in which yesterday's friends would be today's enemies and tomorrow's allies. A struggle which, when it was over, had also thoroughly changed life and society.

The words, the dreams, the words of command; the Red World Revolution; the dream of a Pan-Turan empire; the Holy War against the infidel; fleeing white armies; British armies of occupation; the fall of the Emir, and the khanate which became a people's republic. All this long ago. Yet no longer ago than that, this time of transvaluation of all values, this time of change in all that had been fixed and eternal had become the decisive experience of all older people we spoke with. In their conversation this revolution, even more revolutionary for Central Asia than for Russia, was ever-present. No human being, no generation can ever "begin all over from the beginning." One inherits a given situation. Here the *données* were the revolution—and the transvaluations.

XXXIX

"Russian Central Asia" isn't Russian at all. It is Turkmen, Uzbek, Tadzhik. Anyway connected with the Iranian and Turkish traditions and cultural regions—not the Russian or Slav. What ties the region to Russia, today, is the central state power. There is a common alphabet—but that is a practical matter. The attempt to retain a common alphabet throughout the Union facilitates schooling. India's language difficulty is more a difficulty with its many alphabets than with its many languages. In Russia, it would certainly have been more rational if a transition from the Cyrillic to the Latin alphabet had been effected immediately after the revolution, when the huge majority had no alphabet at all. But that is another matter.

Politics, too, are common to Soviet Central Asia and Russia. But Central Asia is not on the way to becoming more and more Russian. Only now are its own cultures, its own nations, being built up. That this is occurring within the framework of a world-wide technological civilization, an international Communist ideology, and the Soviet

189

State's over-all economic and social planning, does not close the gap between the various Asian federal republics, but steadily widens it. Differences in the good sense, and individuality of their peoples and cultures. Turkmens, Uzbeks and Tadzhiks are all developing into nations.

To come flying in to Soviet Asia from Poor Asia is therefore to arrive in a rational world. That anyone arriving direct from Scandinavia can see Turkmenistan as mere poverty, dust, clay houses, bureaucracy, sun-stricken days, and hot dry nights, is due to lack of perspective; he has no valid points of comparison. Coming from Asia one experiences the Soviet Republics as reason and prosperity. The nomads have become a nation. The women have become human beings, citizens, grown-ups. Illiteracy is gone. Disease overcome. The standard of living high. The individual, no longer shut out by caste, inhibited by extreme poverty, not nipped in the bud by long-antiquated taboos, enjoys freedom. The future's promise; the great canals, the massive industries, an ever-rising productivity, the huge universities.

That we cannot see all this in Scandinavia is a pity. More for us, however, than for them. A steady stream of delegations, students, politicians, is always arriving from other parts of Asia than the Asian Soviet Republics. Everywhere—in India, in Afghanistan, in Pakistan, in Iran—people spoke to me of the Soviet. And they weren't referring to Russia. Russia lay far away, was merely a great European power. What they meant was the Soviet Republics of Central Asia. Where the neighboring countries' plans had misfired, their plans had succeeded. Their living standard is rising where the others' is falling. That's why the Soviet Republics are always becoming more important in Asia.

In the night, after we have been sitting long together, eaten our fill and drunk still more, and become friends, the chicken farmer of the collective asks me, "Say, how are our brothers the other side of the frontier getting on?"

I tell him about the Turkmens in Iran. The chicken farmer says, "That's really strange, what you say about how the Turkmens have

Street, Khiva

it in Iran. It sounds like something we could have read in our newspapers. But if you say so too, well, then it must be true.''

Soon two generations will have passed away since the revolution, and the frontiers have long been closed. But the wind off the Kara Kum is still felt far beyond the frontiers. Nor is it only the wind and the loose soil which are coming from it, or its black sand. From the Soviet a revolutionary wind has been blowing down over Asia. The example of Asia's Soviet Republics weighs more heavily for every year that passes.

The power of example is also to a great extent independent of the Soviet Union's foreign policy or the propaganda of Moscow Radio. For apart from what is done or not done in Moscow, the Soviet example speaks with a loud voice.

An example which ties in with traditions and dreams of peasant revolutions of many millennia.

X L

"Take it easy, comrades,'' said the air hostess. "Women, children, and Swedes first.''

The plane was full of Uzbek collective farmers, Turkmen women who had been into town to see relatives, agronomists, and secretaries on party errands; people with chickens in baskets and great bundles. The two-engined plane was one of those air buses which go between the cities of Central Asia. The fare, too, was what you might pay on a bus.

We were on our way to Khiva. Or, to be more exact, Urgench. From there we were to go by road to Khiva. This town nowadays is small and insignificant. Hasn't even an airfield. Furthermore, it lies in Uzbekistan. The majority of its population have long been Uzbeks. But no one can say he has seen Turkmenistan who hasn't seen Khiva. Here, in the days of the khanate, 170,000 nomad and semi-nomad Turkmens used to live. And the desert Turkmens have always fought against and bargained with the power which controlled the oases along the lower reaches of the Amu Darya. The khanate of Khiva was the heir of a Chorasmian kingdom. If anyone in mid-nineteenth-century Europe had wanted to name an example of a really backward and "Asiatically" cruel city, probably he would have said, "Khiva."

The Khan of Khiva was the archetype of an Asiatic despot. Vámbéry, who arrived in Khiva dressed as a dervish a hundred years ago, writes:

> All the evening I had before my eyes the image of the Khan with his deep-sunk eyes, his chin and his thin beard, his white lips and quivering voice. "How fortunate for mankind," I often thought, "that dark superstition sets a limit to the power and bloodthirstiness of such tyrants."

The limit set, according to Vámbéry, to his bloodthirstiness was however a most liberal one:

> As several of them were led away to the gallows or the block, I saw close beside me how eight old men, at a sign from the executioner, laid themselves down on their backs on the ground. Their hands and feet being tied, the executioner put all their eyes out, one after the other, then kneeling on the chest of each wiped his blood-dripping knife on the beard of the old he had just blinded.

In 1872 Khiva became a vassal state of the Tsar. It was the governor of Turkistan, Adjutant General von Kaufman, who after a swift campaign bombarded and took the city. The Russians then took from the khanate all land east of the Amu Darya and full freedom to trade. In addition, the khanate was to pay two million rubles in damages to Russia. These war damages so totally laid waste Khiva's economy that in this way and with no further formalities the country became a vassal state. The Russians—according to their own statement—had gone to war to free Khiva's slaves. But more important than the slaves was the right to trade. And most important of all was the cotton of the Khoresm Oasis. As early as in 1902 cotton production had reached 10,450 tons. Its fertility was the khanate's undoing.

But the Khan was allowed to retain his domestic power. The only restriction was that, while he was allowed to execute, blind, and tax his own citizens, he was not allowed to hang Russians, carry on an independent foreign policy, or disturb Russian merchants and officers in their way of business.

Thus relations between the Khan and the Russian authorities was on the whole marked by understanding and mutual respect.

Not until February, 1920, did the revolution reach the khanate across the deserts. The Khan is overthrown. Civil war. The People's Republic of Khiva is declared. In 1924 the People's Republic becomes a Socialist Soviet Republic. Thereafter is absorbed into the Soviet Union as a part of Uzbekistan.

But with the revolution Khiva had also lost all importance. When the Khan had disappeared and his henchmen—tax-collectors, courtiers, and executioners—had all fled, when the beys and the merchants had lost their land, their water rights and their power, then Khiva became a remote and grey little town. A small, vegetating provincial town, the trading center of an agricultural district on the outskirts of the Kara Kum. The new industries and the new investments were made in cities where Tsarist Russian investment had already commenced. The new Urgench became the industrial city, the center of communications, the growing city. Khiva, it is true, got schools, a movie theater, a museum, a bookshop, and jubilees of the revolution. But the town had lost out.

The Khan had not encouraged tourists to visit his Khiva. Of all the cities of Central Asia, it held most closely to the true faith. He was not going to have it infected. Any tourists he discovered he had slain. Nor did the Tsarist authorities regard it as suitable for any foreigner to be in touch with the population of the khanate (their security organ was—with a certain justification—always busy looking for British agents who might have slipped in from India). The Soviet authorities shared this attitude, and in general could see no reason to show off this totally non-representative city of old mosques and walls. Freighting delegations across the desert was also an expensive business. Khiva remained a closed city. As far as I know (but I may be mistaken) in 1960 we became the first foreigners for many decades to go there.

We arrive in Khiva, and the experience is tremendous. This is the classical city of Central Asia. Certainly it is dusty, sun-scorched; certainly it is characterized by the white windowless walls which enclose its houses. But for that very reason, just because minarets, cupolas, closed-in houses, and echoing cool bazaars set their stamp on the town, it is a town of peculiar beauty. It is the only city of its kind still extant. A city never Europeanized.

In Afghanistan and Iran—not to mention the Soviet Union—the newly trained city planners have been busy. The bazaars have been exploded into avenues. "Hygiene and reason" is the city planners' motto. And it is true. Hygiene has triumphed. Anyway, hygiene of a kind. But it is also good to see that this city has been allowed to remain as a monument to the recent past.

The city is being restored. Now that Uzbekistan has grown more wealthy, this city, preserved because forgotten, has been declared a national monument.

Khiva is a lovely city. Its architecture is sternly beautiful. Even the Khan's summer palace—rebuilt just before the First World War and now a museum with revolutionary flags, a boarding school, and a library—even this building is a strict and beautiful work of architecture. In its yard stands a statue of Lenin, raised at his death. It is only fourteen years younger than the summer palace itself.

What is not to be seen in India, in Iran, nor in any other emirate or khanate in Central Asia, is to be seen here. A national, highly characteristic architecture from the end of the nineteenth century and the beginning of the twentieth. A great and thrilling architecture. Strict in form, clear in ornamentation, unified in conception. The whole city plan to be seen at Khiva is a nineteenth-century creation. The beautiful tile-work is the work of the same master who is now supervising the city's restoration and teaching the young artists.

Such architecture was beyond the power of the Emir of Bukhara, of the Shah of Iran, of the Afghan kings, of the Indian princes—all were equally powerless to order anything but facsimile buildings. How did it come about, then, that this cruel, sparse-bearded, white-lipped Khan could?

How had this rotting society, alone, the capacity to create a strict, honest, developed art and architecture?

If the question cannot be answered it is because I am putting it in the wrong way. The khanate was cruel. It was medieval. Its wealth and power rested on the toil of an exploited peasantry. But that was not the whole truth. Another bit of the truth was that the

195

peasants' houses were white. The country—according to travelers' impressions—was prosperous. And that the khanate of Khiva, like the emirate of Bokhara and the khanate of Kokand at the end of the eighteenth century, was developing a statehood; was part of the development which was leading to the forming of nations in Central Asia. They were Uzbek states, where the feudal power was limited in favor of the Khan or the Emir. One must see these khanates in their time and age. So it was mendacious of me to write "a rotting society." To point to the despotic, white-lipped, and sparse-bearded Khan and in him see the whole picture, is wrong. Anyone who does so has stuck fast in a nineteenth-century image of empire. The image which represented all Asiatic states as decayed and rotting. The one which provided the great argument for every expansion: British, Russian, or German: "The white man's burden."

Bukhara, too, had an architecture in the early nineteenth century. Char Minar, for instance, is closely related to the architecture at Khiva. But thereafter, Bukhara's building style became falsified, a monstrosity of European imitation-oriental. The summer palace at Bukhara is a horrible building. There must be some explanation, then, why the summer palace at Khiva, built at the same time, is so beautiful.

Khiva remained hidden away behind its deserts. In spite of all, Russian imperial influence was weaker there than at Bukhara. For thanks precisely to its backwardness, its isolation, Khiva was safe and therefore able to develop its own traditions even when the Russians were controlling all territory surrounding their vassal state. There lies the explanation. The same cultural havoc did not strike Khiva as struck the cities and states where Europeans—Russians or British—ruled. And the religiously colored conservatism characteristic of Khiva in Tsarist times also played a role. Introverted onto its own traditions (the religious likewise) and hostile, scornful, indifferent to the foreigners, these, the most conservative of all traditions, helped preserve the nation against European levelings. If Afghanistan—even more closed-in, even more conservative if possible, and a good deal more successful in preserving its independence than Khiva—did not succeed in creating any architecture during the nineteenth century, this is because Khiva was conquered while Afghanistan was victorious. Khiva's defeat cost the state two million rubles and the concession of all its trade and cotton. Afghanistan's many victories cost that country so many lives and such havoc that neither capital nor workers remained for building work.

In 1960 Khiva was being restored. Hundreds of young Uzbek students were working on its various restoration projects. The old Khivan masters were teaching their young colleagues. But today's students are tomorrow's architects and politicians. Uzbek architecture and future culture can and might be marked by continuity with the Khivan ideal of form.

Khiva could then become a catalyst for the Uzbek national tradition, crystallizing in prosperity. The city whose continuity was never interrupted by Europeans.

The colonial lords built their mansions in India; now those
lords are gone and their mansions are being pulled down. This
one in Madras was demolished in 1962. It was no longer modern.

But the new lords and their governors and their presidents and their officials of high rank and low . . .

199

*. . . what difference have they made
for the people?*

The regulations are all there. Some of them purely stupid,
as this one in Ajmer; others, more vicious.

*For the ruling class the step from colonization to Coca-Colonization
has been one from much wealth to more wealth.*

For the people the poverty remains.

SOVIET CENTRAL ASIA

XLI

The superphosphate factory at Chardzhou is modern. It is intended to meet the entire needs of Turkmenistan. Since 1959, 22,000,000 new rubles from the Union Budget have been invested in this factory. At present at Chardzhou an oil refinery, synthetic-rubber works, etc. Six hundred million new rubles are to be invested. Between 1961 and 1965 investments for the republic as a whole were estimated at 1,670,000,000 new rubles. Of this, 15–20 per cent came from the Union budget. During the period 1966 to 1970, 2,100,000,000 new rubles are to be invested. Of this, 30 per cent will come from the Union budget.

Turkmenistan has oil and gas. The Soviet Union is extremely short of fuel. Oil output must be doubled. Gas lines are to be carried up into the European parts of the Union. Its petrochemical industry is to be expanded. Electrification completed. Agriculture—progressively more specialized—is to deliver more cotton, more fruit, more grain. From the Union's side great efforts are being made. The Kara Kum Canal, desalinization, irrigation. Turkmenistan is no "underdeveloped country." It is a modern industrial republic, closely involved in the Soviet Union's industrial structure.

It is also a republic which is developing more swiftly than the Union average. The prospect for the Union as a whole is an annual growth of 9 per cent for industry and 5 per cent for agri-

culture. In RSFSR the rate of development—according to plan—will level off at the Union average. In the Ukraine, growth will be slower: 8.6 per cent for industry and 4.4 per cent for agriculture. In Turkmenistan things are to move more quickly: 13.6 per cent for industry and 6.3 per cent for agriculture.

This picture—with Turkmenistan's relatively swifter development—was the same in earlier plans. Ever since the end of the twenties there has been a steady flow of capital from the European parts of the Union to the Central Asian republics.

But the same day we arrived by train at Chardzhou, the Mexican correspondent, stationed in Moscow, also turned up in the town. We were met by five persons; he by eleven. (An index of status value.) We were placed in one hotel. He in another. We were not even to know of each other's existence. In each other's eyes we were to be state secrets. Yet we inspected the same factories, the same kolkhozes, the same day nurseries and the same workers' dwellings. All this was all right. Later, in the local paper, I read his paean. And it made me dubious. Of course, I didn't know what he had really said and how much the reporter had printed as his words. For even if it was true that all this had been built on a socialist foundation, to a socialist this did not necessarily mean it would be a model, for example, for the people of Mexico. (Unless, of course, Mexico became a minority republic attached to a powerful USA.) For such progress was ambiguous.

When we got to the superphosphate factory, the workers stood to one side. There we went, looking at them, Gun, myself, the personnel chief, the assistant manager, the departmental chiefs, a whole patrol of observers. Gun wanted to photograph the Turkmen workers. But the personnel chief didn't wish her to. He was ashamed of them. When he entered their social rooms, conversation fell silent. Only after he had gone and Gun went back by herself did the workers behave like human beings, joking and laughing. Well, that wasn't so odd. The blond-haired personnel chief had been one of Beria's men. When his boss fell into disgrace and the whole organization was dissolved, new work had to be found for him. Since he was used to dealing with people, it was the most natural thing in the world to appoint him personnel manager.

206

I tried to get an interview with someone in Chardzhou who could make some authoritative statements on economic planning. After two days the chairman of the Soviet sent word that the only person I should be allowed to speak to on that subject would be himself, and that he—on condition he received my questions in writing twenty-four hours in advance—could give me exactly thirty minutes. I declined. Sent word that I really hadn't the heart to cause extra bother to someone who was laboring under such pressure of work. My questions were later answered by the head of the Turkmenistan planning commission instead.

On the new Moscow kolkhoz, north of the Kara Kum Canal, Director Nurgeldi Chungusov could at first give me no clear information as to the number of workers, the number of families or the number of children. I was told he had only recently been appointed. But this sovkhoz is one of the gigantic agrarian projects in which millions and millions of rubles have been invested. After a while an Armenian from Ashkhabad took over the conversation. He knew. He was from the central administration.

The Kara Kum Canal is an immense project. It leads off the waters of the Amu Darya out into the desert, irrigates the Murghab Valley and the Tedzhen Oasis and the Ashkhabad region. Already it has cost about 235 million new rubles out of the Union budget. The stretch currently being excavated beyond Ashkhabad, in the direction of Krasnovodsk, is estimated to cost another 100 million rubles out of the Union budget. Already 25 million cubic yards of soil have been moved. A hundred and sixty-five cubic meters of water are being taken out of the Amu Darya at Kerki. Every second. When the canal is finished they are counting on a thousand cubic meters a second. That is no small part of the waters of the Amu Darya.

Back in 1960, I had asked the leaders of the canal work what consequences this would have for the Aral Sea and for Central Asia as a whole. For I had already seen what happened in Iran when the level of the Caspian Sea had fallen—irrigation systems on the Volga had ruined peasants in Iran. The reply then had been that the rivers of Siberia were to have their courses changed. Now new men were in charge of building the canal. Their answer was that all that about the Siberian rivers was just now no longer on the agenda. There was no real reason to worry, they said, about the Aral Sea.

But a few weeks later, up by the Khoresm Oasis, further down the river, the collective farmers were complaining about how hard it was to get enough of the Amu Darya's waters for irrigation. The water level was too low. The inflow canals were now at too high a level. I wondered what was being done about it, what was being discussed, whether anyone was even connecting this with the outflow at Kerki and whether the influence of the Kara Kum Canal on irrigation in Khoresm was even mentioned? They said, "That's not our business. We're just local collective farmers. That's for Moscow to trouble its head about."

Another way of expressing the point is to say that there was no opportunity for the farmers to hold an objective discussion with the authorities as to which solutions would, in the long run, be most rational. Nor did the big plan seem realistic in its effects. That is to say, neither popular self-government and democratic planning, nor grandiose "continental planning." Nor are the "liberals" in the Soviet asking to know the reason why. For a solution would also threaten their positions.

The collective farmers' enthusiasm for government's agricultural policy seemed cool. The new reforms from the spring of 1965 were dutifully stressed. But after talking things over a while, a Baluchi collective farmer in the Yolotan district, in the Murghab Valley, said, "I remember when Khrushchev introduced his agricultural reforms after Stalin's death. Then our average income fell by 12 per cent per annum, simply because the planners didn't grasp the difference between long-staple and short-staple cotton when they fixed their norms."

Everyone nodded agreement. Their suspicion of the reforms up there seemed both genuine and "peasant-like"—and thereto justified. The Party secretary, a sensible fellow, said, "In the thirties and forties this used to be the richest agricultural district in the whole Union. So they say."

The extreme demand for cotton production, ever since the Tsarist conquest and more particularly since the thirties, had brought about a monoculture in the oases. To get better harvests there had been intenser irrigation. Which had raised the level of the subsoil water. When the subsoil water rises in a dry hot climate, you get a salt desert. For capillary attraction sucks up the water to the surface. The water carries with it a solution of salts. Evaporates. And salt is left on the surface of the soil. About 1960, this salinization had begun to take on catastrophic proportions at Khoresm. Already, in recent years, after five years of plenteous water supply from the new canal, the Murghab Valley had begun to salt up. Which was why they were now being forced to implement a crash program, in which millions and millions of rubles were having to be invested in drainage and desalinization. Which, of course, still further increased water consumption, and to an extreme extent. In the classical Central Asiatic irrigation agriculture, one avoids salinization, but gets lesser harvests. I asked whether they had really studied the profitability of irrigation, whether their calculations had taken all factors—including drainage costs and double water consumption—into account. And I never got a really clear answer. This is not specific to Turkmenistan. The costly American and Soviet irrigation projects in Afghanistan have gone the same way; caused the soil to salt up, and for the farmers have meant economic catastrophe.

The new sovkhozes were said to be the outriders of Communism. This because their "European" agricultural cities brought together people of all nationalities. Russians, Ukrainians, Soviet Germans, Uzbeks, Turkmens, Baluchis and so forth, were all working together there. There they were to merge together into one Soviet people. The Moscow kolkhoz—it gradually became clear—had 4,500 inhabitants in one town-like village. The dwellings—Soviet standards—were good and roomy. But they didn't suit the climate. They had also been expensive to construct. Expensive; requiring too much materials; smart; and impractical. The self-service store would have suited Northern Europe. Its great glass façades, its low roof level, its faulty planning and its poor ventilation made it insufferably hot, even in April. Nothing was being planned on the spot by those who were to live and work there. Everything was being done centrally. Even people were being moved there by central directive.

Of the 4,500, 750 were engaged in productive work. The rest were "family members." But there were no light industries. No handicrafts. Nor were there going to be, for here nothing was to be carried on but industrialized agriculture over very great areas. I wondered what would happen in the future. One day, after all, Soviet agriculture must begin to be productive. Then they would be forced to provide this "agricultural town" with a more variegated economy. But no one seemed to have reckoned with the possibility of a rising output, or realized that these agricultural towns, without handicrafts or light industries or any possibility of a flexible labor market policy, might have been invented to create problems. As it was, they mostly gave the impression of being a form of organized underemployment.

The new agricultural policy—which is costing such enormous sums—is every bit as terrifying a piece of faulty planning as the earlier policies. All along the expensive new canal vast sums are being expended on constructing new and catastrophic agricultural crises for the Soviet Union.

The problem is not—as many people in the Soviet still console themselves by thinking—that there are individuals sitting in various offices, sabotaging the development of the Soviet Union. Nor is the trouble—as many in the West would like to believe—that no society can function without private capitalism. But that this type of planning, since it is not based on the people's own decisions, infallibly leads to failures and faults. Decisions, that is, which rest on practical experience. It is technocratic planning, by experts at various levels in various bureaus. And these bureaus combat and intrigue against each other. The technocrats, I'm sure, do their best, as they understand it. But they understand so little in relation to the people themselves. In the Soviet as in other countries.

The people, Turkmens or Russians, are not against the legal situation over property. They don't want any Alfred Nobel as the owner of their oil. They don't want capitalism. They are not against the country's development. But since they have no institutional possibilities for taking charge of their own socialism, they become victims of regularly recurring crises. The basic fault of the Union of Soviet Republics is that the Soviets—the councils—have not the powers they in theory possess, and the Party is not a party but an apparatus.

The circumstances under which swift industrialization was

carried out in Stalin's time led to the creation of a privileged caste, controlling the entire administrative apparatus, and this caste is today nullifying all possibility of efficient planning, quite apart from whether it is "old Stalinists" or "liberals" who are running economic policy. For just as during his later years Stalin's policies came steadily more into opposition with the system and the group of privileged Stalinists he himself had helped to create, so does this group now conflict with the economic structure they themselves have built up. From being builders of a system they have become its brakes. The crises in industry and agriculture, the bad planning, and the unsuccessful investments are not just "faults and mistakes" to be corrected by abrupt and violent reversals of policy. They are expressions of the deep contradiction which exists between, on the one hand, the Soviet Union's highly developed economic structure and socialist ownership of means of production, and, on the other, the privileged caste's monopoly of power. Since by controlling the party apparatus the privileged also control the only political organization permitted in the country, and in which changes and struggles merely reflect shifts in power *within* that caste—this blocks the channels through which needful transformation could take place.

In the long run the question will find its solution. No political and social structure can, in the long run, resist the requirements of its economic structure. And the newly educated generations are also demanding their rights. The many are demanding the rights they are already supposed to possess. If taken seriously the official ideology too—even though for the most part it has become no more than an empty phrase—also speaks out against the power of the technocrats. (Sometimes I wonder whether all the forced feeding with Lenin and Marx doesn't have the secret purpose of immunizing Soviet citizens against Lenin's words. For in today's Soviet society, if one reads them as they were written they are sheer dynamite.)

But during this process of transformation much can happen. And much depends on the extent of the unawareness with which those in power seek to preserve their own positions.

XLII

When taking her photos at Chardzhou, Gun was stopped on the street by an Uzbek. The man said, "Don't only photograph what is good. Show what's bad too."

But the problem of Turkmenistan is no simple question of good and bad. The good is obvious. Any visitor can see it. Everyone admits, today, that the Soviet epoch has given Turkmenistan social and economic development, greater equality, more civic rights, a longer life expectancy for its citizens, better schools, and a demand for a brighter future.

212

When the revolution was victorious in Turkmenistan forty years ago, its victory was not solely due to the strength of the Red Army. It also had the great mass of the people behind it. By no means the whole people. But a great many. And in the struggle between White Russians and their British allies, on the one hand, and the revolutionaries on the other, there were many who remained neutral, who tried to stay out.

Afterward, the armed struggle continued, right up into the thirties. But the Bolshevik policies won support. Particularly when, supported by the Khan of Bukhara, by the mullahs and the British, the armed counterrevolutionary forces—the "basmachis"—forced their way in across the frontier, many Turkmens who had been dubious about the Bolsheviks joined forces against the raiders. All the basmachis could offer in the way of a future was the past. Counterrevolution was a return to former misery. The policy of the British failed. For they had no insight into the inevitability of the revolution.

Even individuals so hesitant in their attitude to the Soviet power as the Baluchi chieftain Kerim Khan, in the Murghab Valley, fought against the basmachis. Then—during collectivization—Kerim and his tribe packed their bags and departed over the Afghan border.

"It was class war. The rich fled and the poor stayed," said the Party secretary.

"Yes," said the old man who had been Kerim Khan's bard, "and we poor wretches, who had neither horse nor mule to clear out on, had to stay behind."

In the whole of Turkmenistan I don't believe there is anyone who wants to have the khans back. Nor anyone who wants his country to be like Afghanistan or Iran.

The conflict now growing up is the conflict of the abortive and sidetracked revolution. Strong social forces would like to see the revolution carried further—or perhaps, rather, see its phrases turned into social reality. The conflict is not—as in Soviet propaganda it sometimes seems to be—a conflict between socialists and "bourgeois nationalists." I don't even think it is a conflict which has yet attained any clear organizational form, though it is already finding its reactive ideological expressions and in the future can find its organizational. Nor is it a conflict which necessarily imperils the

213

Union. Rather it is a conflict between those groups which for their own technological and privilege-preserving reasons pursue a policy which is making the Union into a formal shell around a centralized "Russian" state, and those who want to see the Union realized. But if official policy continues to follow the same course as at present, then its result will be centrifugal and separatist movements.

One should also bear in mind that the Stalin period wears quite another aspect if one looks at it from Turkmenistan from what it does if one looks at it from Moscow. (From the Baltic States or the Ukraine is even one step further from Moscow.)

Notwithstanding all errors and all reverses the period up to the mid-fifties was a period of progress. Even those who now are labeled "Turkmen nationalists" supported Stalinist policy. They did so for self-evident reasons. The policy was developing Turkmenistan economically and socially. It was at that time the great projects now being realized in Turkmenistan were planned.

It is all far from being as simple as it seemed to the Russian journalist who, after jesting about Stalin but without getting any applause from his audience, turned to us and said, "Here in Turkmenistan it isn't popular to make jokes about Stalin. Well, these orientals anyway need someone to look up to. They've always been used to despots."

For Turkmenistan the Stalin period meant economic and social development. It also gave a life to Turkmen culture. At that time this culture acquired a secular and national form. But in Stalin's lifetime the economic level in Turkmenistan was still rather low. Here therefore the destructive tendencies—which had already made themselves felt in these economically more highly developed republics—only found serious expression after Stalin's death, when the economic and social development began to raise the country to a "European" level.

I can exemplify this by the question of the relative status of the sexes, and feminine equality. Since the Turkmens were a nomad people, the Turkmen woman's position in traditional society was not so miserable as it was in India or in the city cultures of Central Asia. I am not even convinced it was as bad as in the Russian villages. But the Turkmen woman, too, was oppressed. Even she could only be regarded as half a human being.

214

The October Revolution in Russia, nearly half a century ago, meant the greatest victory to date for the demand for equal rights for women. Again and again Lenin returned to the question of the equality of the sexes.

> Of all the squalid laws which perpetuated established woman's lack of equality, divorce difficulties with their shameful procedure, non-recognition of extra-marital children and so forth—all these laws which still largely stand in the civilized countries—we have in the most literal sense swept the field clear of them. We have every right to be proud of our progress in this field.

(He also pointed out—naturally—that this was only one aspect, the formal aspect, of woman's equality.)

Twenty years after Lenin's death the stones had all been replaced. Not, this time, to protect a bourgeoisie, but a privileged group of bureaucrats and top *apparatschiki*. The new family legislation from the forties had two express goals: to "preserve" the family and increase population growth. In the latter respect it was realistic. Just then—in 1944—the Soviet Union was undergoing a blood-letting of one-tenth of her population. Twenty million people, mainly in their most productive and reproductive ages. But the way in which it was carried out, by making divorce difficult, costly, and by hedging it with a "shameful procedure" which meant that no man need longer pay for children born outside wedlock—the state would pay the mother for these—became in reality a fulfillment of an old bourgeois demand: that both the married man and the whoring man should be legally safeguarded.

But while, in the Soviet Union, laws were moving crabwise, the women of Turkmenistan were following a long, a very long path. The 1920's were their heroic age. Girls who went to school were then still liable to be stabbed or murdered. The women teachers were Turkmenistan's heroines. But thanks to their hard work woman's situation improved. She was on the way to becoming a human being. Thanks to schools and equal wages and chances of getting jobs, women, in the thirties and forties, and in the process of industrialization and urbanization, began to become men's equals. Women began to be victorious in the struggle for the right to love (free choice of husband, as against the arranged marriage), the right to education, the right to work, the right to be treated as human beings.

215

But the women one meets in leading positions in this country are still the women of that pioneer generation. And they are still fighting. Social equality is still remote. At the superphosphate factory in Chardzhou the average income was said to be 150 rubles a month. The lowest, 60 rubles: the charwomen's wage, and they were *all* women. (The dirtiest, heaviest and worst-paid work—as in all countries—reserved for women.) Of the workers only 30 per cent were women. Of the management, 5–10 per cent. In the highest management level of the factory there was no woman.

In the hospital at Takhta in the Khoresm Oasis I had a discussion with the head doctor, Tatar Jasmuradov. He was a local man. A fine type of doctor, with soft gentle hands. He pointed out that the birth rate here was one of the highest in the entire Union. The average at first childbirth was nineteen.

Thereafter the women have one child a year. Those who have weak hearts or suffer from TB are advised by the doctors to use contraceptives. But they don't want to. They want children. And so they, too, go on childbearing.

Child mortality had dropped, but was still among the highest in the Union. The life expectancy of the women was shorter than that of the men (i.e., the opposite to what is normal elsewhere in the industrial countries). They die younger than the men. That is, they begin bearing children in their nineteenth year and are worn out.

There are several reasons for this. In the first place the old traditional family situation. A woman's job was to bear children—sons. In the second place—possibly—the will of a small people to increase and multiply in order to safeguard its own national existence. Again and again the Turkmens, with a certain pride, came back to "we Turkmens have more children than the Russians."

But that the situation should still be the same forty years after Lenin's death has political and social roots in *today's* Soviet society. The state of affairs at Takhta can still be described in Lenin's words about "woman's de facto suppression." The situation of these women —a worn-out reproduction apparatus—is wholly unworthy of a society which has declared itself socialist.

But—apart from the worthiness or otherwise of the situation— its social causes, as I have said, lie in today's Soviet society. Traditions do not live outside society. Woman's liberation in Turkmenistan has been slowed down. In Turkmenistan the reactionary family policy which has reigned in the Soviet Union during the last two decades as an expression of the interests of a privileged group (not forgetting those of their heirs) has kept artificial life in certain of the bad old traditions from the feudal epoch. In a situation where to break with this family policy would conflict with material interests of the dominant group, neither the party nor society is capable of formulating a progressive policy for the women of Takhta. For such a policy to have any value, namely, it must, for the sake of the women's health, concern itself with contraceptive techniques and measures to limit the number of children. Anyone who did not mince his words but stood against the prevailing situation—leaning on Lenin's words—would be a threat to the positions of the privileged and their legalized structures and therefore—oddly enough— be stamped an "anti-Leninist" and an "enemy of the people."

Even so, this Soviet family policy did not have any very serious consequences until economic developments in Turkmenistan gave women an objective chance of achieving equality. Then—and only then—did the bars become barriers. Even in the early fifties, the economic situation was such that this policy had still not become an effective socially harmful barrier. At that time it was a future obstacle.

Now when it is one—as it is, most tangibly, all over the Union —voices are being raised in favor of various modifications in family law. But no one dares utter the simple truth: that reactionary policies are condemning the working women of Takhta to a premature death.

But Turkmenistan's generation of pioneer women, working in various leading positions, are trying to produce another generation of educated women. Female Turkmen students are given priority. They get higher grants than male students. A lenient view is taken of their exam results. For the new technological society needs women's work at a high level. There is a clear and open clash between the policy of these women—which also expresses society's real needs and is in line with Lenin's policy—and the existing state of affairs between the sexes in the Soviet.

Women are out in the labor market. But just as there is a big majority of women among textile workers, so is there a great major-

*The boots of J. V. Stalin. Back yard of the School for
the Blind, Khiva, Uzbek Soviet Socialist Republic.*

ity of women doctors. In both cases it is a question of low-paid work,
the one in "production" the other as "intellectuals." Women have
the lower-paid jobs and rarely reach executive positions. Then the
formal equality of wages does not play so great a role. For real equality of wages implies equal access to the highly salaried posts.

The attitude to women is also expressed in education and schooling. The newspapers one sees stuck up on walls mock girls who "have made the acquaintance of the bottle" and who are "immoral." They scorn them by name, because they are *women*. A man is mocked when he's a drunk; but a woman when she has merely tasted the stuff. "Women don't do that."

In schools the pupils spend their English hours reading Emily Post's *Etiquette*. Not as queer stories from the capitalistic past, a sort of anthropology; but to learn English and know how to behave. In the pioneer organization, too, the etiquette of the bourgeoisie is taught. Boys must give up their seats to girls. Girls shall help Mom with the housework. In children's and young people's hobbies there is a strict division between the sexes. Girls occupy themselves with "feminine hobbies": children, sewing, and cooking. Boys have "manly" hobbies. At Chardzhou Gun asked if no boy ever took a cooking or sewing course. This was taken as a joke. When I told them how we do things in Sweden the joke seemed to have turned sour—had become a joke in bad taste.

The tragic thing for Turkmenistan is that the country now has the economic conditions for achieving the original goals in the sex equality question. But now the bureaucracy has put the brake on. This is doubly tragic, because the causes of such backwardness are not to be found in Turkmenistan itself, where the great wave of enthusiasm from the first stage of social reconstruction has not yet had time to ebb away, but are due to social developments and their consequences in the metropolitan parts of the Union. In Turkmenistan the attitudes of the privileged have united with residual prerevolutionary attitudes.

XLIII

When officials in our countries rejoice at the Soviet cultural thaw it is usually because the only alternative they can see is between "cultural thaw" and "cultural freeze." Unerringly, the interested critics follow Soviet developments, cheered by each sign of a "thaw," disturbed at every sign of a "freeze." With Kafka again being discussed in the Soviet Union—with Babel again permissible reading and with Soviet cultural exchanges again passing through the official channels, then all these things are taken as a sign that Stalinism is being overcome. However, it is perfectly possible to envisage a type of Stalinism that reads Kafka.

I can go a step further—if a "mature" and "sensible" Stalinism reads Kafka, it is for the same reasons as a "mature" bourgeoisie reads him. All this assuming one regards Stalinism as a social phenomenon maintained by an existing social group in the Soviet.

The thaw, the "de-Stalinization" of Soviet culture, is ambiguous. This one notices particularly in Turkmenistan. One night, just after two o'clock, there came a knock at our door. It was an older Turkmen. I had met him earlier in some official context. He had been one of the Red leaders during the basmachi war, during the five-year plans and reconstruction. (Now he has been laid off.) Under his arm he had a bottle of champagne.

"It'd be nice to have a chat," he said. We sat silent. Drank each other's healths. After a while he said, "You've traveled a good deal in Asia, haven't you? Seen the different countries? So have I. I've seen Turkmenistan before. Don't you find the people of Asia, in India for example, oppressed? Exploited? Downtrodden? Well, here we had a revolution. And it was hard going. Lots of mistakes were made. But don't let's talk about that now. What you must understand is that, if we took all those struggles in our stride, it was because life was so hard on people. Yes, I've done my bit of traveling, too. Then they let you make official speeches about peace."

Again he fell silent. Then said, "Skål, Gun Khanum. Guncha!"

We laughed, drank, fell silent. After a while he went on, "I've been in Moscow. Nowadays I don't understand the things they say there about Asia. They talk as if there weren't any poverty. As if everything were going fine. A lot of mistakes were made under Stalin, of course, I realize that. From my own experience. But Moscow has forgotten the world's poverty. I don't like the things I read in our papers any more. They aren't true. They don't tell us how horrible the world is. And perhaps that's why the young people there don't understand any longer why we Turkmens joined the revolution. I just wanted to tell you this. You've seen a lot of Asia. You've been about. You should understand our situation."

The ideological revaluations are not—as we are told in Scandinavia—an adjustment to reality, but themselves constitute the real breach with reality. The choice—as the old Turkmen revolutionary saw—is not between Stalin's methods (camps, police terror), and a thaw implying a diplomatic and mendacious denial of the real state of affairs: that Asia is starving and that Asia is faced with peasant wars, revolts, hunger risings, and revolution. But today—in an atmosphere of thaw—it is the small bourgeoisie in Asia the Soviet Union is relying on and supporting.

One reason why the Stalinists—as a "mature and sensible" privileged group—feel solidarity with the middle class of the poorer Asiatic countries today, is that this middle class is the only "Europeanized" group in those countries, and therefore shares the Stalinists' view of, and prejudices against, the Asiatic cultures. And for Turkmen cultural life this pro-European attitude of the Stalinists is having interesting consequences. Let us look at the carpets. It has been during these very years that they have been exposed to the "thaw's" effects.

Of the three great oriental carpet traditions—the Chinese, the Central Asiatic, and the Persian—the Turkmens' art was perhaps the strictest and purest of the geometrical and Central Asiatic group. The carpet was the beauty of the yurt. For the people of the yurts —the round tents—they were equally articles of art and for use. The art of the carpets—in the best sense of the word—is a popular art; a collective creation of beauty within the nation's decorative tradition.

The bureaucrats could see nothing in non-European art traditions but ethnography. Their view of art is strikingly reminiscent of that of the British Victorian bourgeois. (Stalinism's social role had been equally "heroic," equally "progressive"; and during the current "thaw" is also following in the footsteps of the Victorians' twentieth-century conversion. All of which, socially, is precisely what one would expect.) A typical expression of this way of seeing things is to be found in the final volume of the first edition of the *Great Soviet Encyclopedia* (Volume: *Soviet Union, 1947*):

> In most of the eastern republics of the USSR no realistic painting, drawing or sculpture existed until after the Great Socialist October Revolution, since feudal backwardness and the long religious oppression had *paralyzed art's development for*

centuries . . . In the Soviet east Russian artists who have been working in the republics of Central Asia have played a great role both in the development of art forms and in educating new cadres . . . [My italics]

Thus to define "art" in such a way that Central Asia's art "for centuries" is simply conjured out of existence, is—I cannot help repeating—profoundly subjective. Just as unobjective, whether one applies "bourgeois" or Marxist criteria to the history of art. Analogously, the art of the carpet-weaver was reduced to "handicraft," thus exempting the carpets from the charge of being part of an art which had "stood still."

This denigration of the carpet-weaver's art had no serious consequences, however, until the beginning of the sixties. There are several reasons for this, not least among them the impossibility of getting the Turkmens themselves to see their national art as "non-art." At Ashkhabad the Turkmens set up their own carpet center, a unique arts and crafts school. We had visited it in 1960. Over the years an attempt was also made, naturally enough, to reach a compromise between the Turkmen tradition in art and the Stalinist view of art. The carpets were given "realistic motifs." (Described in the same encyclopedia thus: "In the carpets, more and more portraits of V. I. Lenin, J. V. Stalin and V. M. Molotov are being woven, surrounded by fine and elaborate ornamentation.")

Five years ago it was pointed out that the carpet institute's work was of the greatest importance to Turkmen culture. Since women were now coming out into the labor market, they no longer had time to weave carpets. Half the nation could not occupy itself with carpet-making. The carpet institute was to create a national art out of popular crafts. This year, when we visited the carpet institute, it had been turned into a state factory. Carpets had become an industry. An export industry.

This development is overdetermined. The Soviet needs currency. And the more the harvests fail, and the greater the failures in agricultural policy, the greater must be the strain on Soviet currency reserves. Yet the Soviet must also meet its population's demand for consumer goods. So it becomes a matter of political necessity that Turkmenistan's carpet output shall be exported.

At the same time the carpets have been definitively classified as

222

"non-art." For the women who knot the carpets this means the end of all specially commissioned carpets. From artists and craftswomen they are turned into employees. They do not even know any longer whom they are working for—or where their carpets are being exported. (They are being alienated.) The thaw which looks so pretty when seen from the Swedish horizon—where the liberals fancy they can descry the youth of Moscow reading Kafka—does not look so nice in Turkmenistan, where it takes the form of a great attack on the national culture. Proudly, they told us it was now possible to train Ukrainian women, Russian women, and others to knot carpets in factories.

"Which proves it isn't something only Turkmens can do."

What they did not say was that no one is saying Turkmens are born with "carpet-knotting genes"; merely that their carpets are an expression of Turkmen culture. That this is occurring in an economic situation where carpet-weaving in people's homes is coming to an end is a serious example of cultural chauvinism.

The connection between the artist and his public has been broken. This time our hosts were even unwilling to admit the existence of any "Turkmen markets." Five years ago they had proudly, gladly, taken us to see those markets, the meeting place of all the people from the villages—the old men in their black fur caps with long white beards, the women in their Turkmen-red costumes, talking, drinking tea, eating shashlik, selling and buying popular art—homecrafts—ornaments, carpets, and embroideries.

"We Turkmens love to be many."

This time the markets had already been classified as "backward." Backward because belonging to an out-of-date trading method. And there is not much to say about that. Or there wouldn't be, if this had been the Turkmens' own view of the matter. But it wasn't. And as long as the markets fill many social needs for the overwhelming majority of the Turkmen population, I cannot see them as "backward" or out-of-date. The markets, it was said, also had to be combatted because they interfered with the trade of the new socialist department stores. But inasmuch as these stores only offered such decorative articles as expressed a lax petty bourgeois—and, to the Turkmen tradition, wholly foreign—decorative degeneration, I could not see that this attempt to turn the people's taste toward such "kitsch" was indicative of anything but cultural chauvinism. Finally they told us the markets had been closed. We didn't believe it. And of course they hadn't. After a certain amount of trouble, and having got rid of our guides, we found them.

In Ashkhabad the market had been exiled to the suburbs. It was hard to find. That our hosts had sworn blind it didn't even exist amused us. Either our hosts had no contact whatever with reality, or else they were telling lies. And if they were lying, the question at once arose: Why? and the answer to that question was even more painful.

The market was a big one, and just as lively as ever. But there were no carpets. That's to say, no Turkmen carpets. The old carpets had all been bought up, repaired and exported, and the new ones never came onto the home market. Those old carpets which were exposed for sale were either of the felt type (beautiful, they too, but valueless for export) or factory-made carpets from Germany which "speculators" had bought up in Moscow and freighted down to Turkmenistan to sell at a big profit. It struck us that the policy being applied, so far from abrogating the profit motive, was on the contrary creating a whole new batch of profiteers. Since the policy clashed with the people's demands, profiteers were forced into existence. None too brilliant a specimen of socialist policy. It also struck us that the Turkmen people's one chance of keeping its art alive for the future now lay in the despised felt carpets.

Many touching stories were told about how happy the Turkmens were to be able to sit on chairs instead of carpets. My own preference —ever since I was little—for sitting cross-legged, was regarded by every Russian I met as an insult. To sit cross-legged with Turkmens was—I noticed—a political act. To keep within the pattern, one should get oneself a chair.

In their homes the Turkmens obviously preferred their own traditional way of sitting. Among much else it has shaped the style of their social intercourse, their meal rituals, their ways of being sociable. The story of the carpets and ways of sitting could be protracted. But the crucial point is that in the prevailing situation, and in every cultural conflict in Central Asia, the Russian bureaucrats are convinced they represent "progress." This can often express itself in the most distasteful manner. On the train to Repizek we were sitting in a crowded third-class section. An old Uzbek farmer was sitting cross-legged on the hard seat. After half an hour a fifty-year-old somewhat drunken Russian came along. Pointing at the Uzbek, he remarked that it was uncultivated to sit like that. The Uzbek didn't hear him. The Russian spoke louder. Appealed to all the other travelers. In the end he tried to lift the Uzbek off the seat, to pull his feet down on to the floor. But the Uzbek sat there as if glued to the seat. Didn't bat an eyelid. Didn't move an inch. But no one in the whole car tried to prevent the Russian from committing this act which—as I know for certain, and everyone else in the car should have understood—could only be described as a gross insult.

Another example of the cultural conflict is the shape of toilets. Since excretion, in our culture, is loaded with powerful affect, I must point out that the Russian behavior I am describing is not "Russian." It is typically European. It isn't the "Russians" who are dirty. It's the European chauvinists who have such a strong delusion of their own superiority that they would sooner die than adapt. As follows:

Asiatic latrine construction—also found in Mediterranean countries—really only consists of a hole in the ground. One sits squatted over it. This construction can take various forms. With tiles and foot-plates, flushing water and every imaginable sort of hygienic refinement. Our own North European toilet construction, on the other hand, is a further development of the bar in the wall. We do not squat, we hang with folded knees on to a bar over a ditch, or sit on a chair with a hole in its seat. This construction, too, can be provided with refinements. You can see them in your own bathroom. However, this construction has three disadvantages: it brings one's skin into contact with the seat, which, particularly in hot climates, means risk of infection; it creates inaccessible corners behind the seat, hard to clean, which, in most European toilets, means a bad smell; and it is sensitive to weight, can get cracked, and lead to leakage. In Central Asia the Russians, of course, are introducing this construction. It is also more expensive, and therefore has status value.

The Swedes, too, are trying to spread the toilet seat all over the globe. Sometimes our representatives are truly heroic. A Swedish diplomat's wife once told me that during a stay of many years in the Orient she had patiently stood on the oriental toilets, and therefore had to urinate in her shoes. When I wondered why she hadn't squatted (she wore no stockings), she said, "Well, I'm not a native, am I?"

Culture, that is to say, consists in pissing in one's shoes.

The Russians are behaving like this Swedish diplomat's wife. At Tashauz there are only oriental toilets in the hotel. We arrived one afternoon after an excursion among the villages. There the toilets were clean and neat, as they are all over Moslem Asia. But in the hotel at Tashauz we got a shock. No one appeared to have used the toilet. Everyone had done their business on the floor. It was a little troublesome to use the toilet. So next morning we tried to get out as soon as the toilets had been flushed clean. Then, in the morning, we saw what happened. It was a cultural conflict. The Europeans and the higher bureaucrats felt such disgust at having to squat ("like natives"), that they preferred to stand in the doorway and just stick their backsides into the toilet room. In that way they could shit standing, like human beings. But the villages were clean, the peasants were rational.

There's nothing typically Russian about this. I've seen it in every country where ruling Europeans meet a foreign custom. And sure enough, Tashauz was stricken with the cholera epidemic which swept over Turkmenistan in the summer of 1965. The ruling Europeans' inability to adapt to other cultures constitutes a health risk.

That the thaw also mostly takes the form of an extension of Russian cultural dominance to become a dominant "European" influence, suited to a modernized and European-conscious privileged group, was also evident in the new architecture to be seen in Turkmenistan. During the Stalin period the official buildings were given architectural forms designated "national Turkmen." Not always so successful—even if the purity and sternness of the Turkmen traditions did not permit such excesses as the Russian. There were no pastry cake buildings, anyway. And the buildings were not wholly without sense. Whether it was due to shortage of building materials, or to wisdom, I couldn't say, but the walls were thick, and suited to the climate. Nor was there any campaign against "Asiatic walls."

But today they are putting up "modern" buildings, Italianate. When we were looking at the new palatial bank in the center of Ashkabad, one of my Turkmen friends said, "It'd be a fine house for growing melons in. The architects have done that in Moscow. They don't know our climate."

The great glass walls of this palatial bank were among the most perverse things in the way of architecture I had seen in all Asia. And there is plenty to see. This type of modernism, which is only modern in its outward form, but not functional—this "modernistic décor" —sets its stamp on all the new building going on today in Turkmenistan.

"Backwardness" in building—of course—is also being combatted. If used in the right way, sun-dried brick is a cheap, handy, and functional building material in the Turkmen climate. With sun-dried brick one cannot (the material forbids it) build anything but thick insulated walls. If the modern houses become intolerably hot in summer, it is because they are no longer—officially—being built of sun-dried brick.

When we drove out to the great sheep sovkhoz of Baharden, we saw abandoned villages. The houses had been built of sun-dried brick. They had lovely cupola roofs with Persian ventilation drums. They were correct for the climate. I discussed this with the shepherds on the sheep sovkhoz. They had been given new modern dwellings and had been moved away from their cupola houses. (Most shepherds never had, and still do not, have houses. They lived in yurts. An attempt was made to get them to live in plastic yurts, instead of felt yurts.) They said they preferred houses of sun-dried brick with proper cupolas. This irritated our hosts. The shepherds were "backward." Didn't appreciate the bureaucrat idea of progress. But I agreed with those shepherds. The shepherds were rational. Sensible. I've lived in both sorts of house, in the same sort of climate. Providing they had the same amount of space, the cupola houses were superior. In building, too, the real question in Turkmenistan is who shall make the decisions. The people—which would be rational— or the privileged technocrats—who are irrational.

At Tashauz people had been given permission to build their own houses of sun-dried brick. The result was a beautiful and well planned suburb. But the Turkmens had built walls around their houses. The street was planted with trees and the white walls flanked the pavements on either side. Here—as in the greater part of Asia —one sleeps out of doors on summer nights. The walls protect against dust and peering eyes. The yards are dwelling rooms. But now progress was to reach Tashauz. The mayor wanted all the walls pulled down and replaced with Russian fencing. I wondered whether this wasn't rather stupid.

"No," they replied. "Nobody sleeps out of doors here at nights. It's old-fashioned. Besides, we're living in a more open age. Walls mustn't separate people any more."

Which, in reality, was just empty words. Words and culture-chauvinism. "What's good in Texas is good anywhere."

Examples could be multiplied. In Chardzhou they put on a "demonstration of popular art." The ensemble was from Tadzhiki-stan. A noisy—and bad—jazz band and a vulgar belly dancer danc-ing something called an "Egyptian folk dance." But in some of their numbers the artistes really tried to show off their paces—a mountain chalet dance with drums. But to get these numbers to go over the artistes had to make a mockery of their art.

I've nothing against strip-tease. In Calvinist Geneva I've seen a nude dance with a nun's veil, and in socialist Chardzhou I've seen a nude dance with a Mohammedan face veil. It is piquant, but it goes against the grain—in either case it tells too much about the realities of the situation. But I don't give much for a cultural policy which suppresses real folk-dancing and replaces it with low-class night-club numbers. Not that I'm running down the artistes. We made their acquaintance. They worked like dogs when out on the road, and their job was to give the public what it wanted. The public, in this case, being the decision-makers, the bureaucrats.

The thaw may very well turn out—in my opinion it already has —to be nothing but a new variety of bourgeois double-culture. A real "thaw" which recognized the cultures of other peoples, which gave its citizens a chance to absorb culture from various quarters and which recognized that socialism is based on reason and not on preju-dices or privileges, still does not exist in the Soviet Union.

What is left of Stalinist formulae is merely the dregs. The new ideological campaign against religion makes a painful impression. It corresponds—in its own way and with similar social motivation —to a Swedish "radicalism" which sees the religious question as its own main content. But the present Soviet campaign is more vul-gar. Since the critique of religion doesn't constitute one of the ele-

ments in a rational and critical discussion at all levels, its main results are merely socially destructive.

In 1960 we had visited the Sultan Sandzhar's mausoleum at Old
Merv. At that time it was still being restored. When we came back
in 1965 the mausoleum had been abandoned by its restorers and re-
searchers. Its guards had all been removed. Inside the mausoleum
two Turkmens were praying at a new tomb. The sign declaring the
building a national monument had been damaged by having stones
thrown at it. It had been used as a target. While the Turkmens
prayed, blond Russian children were playing about on the abandoned scaffolding. They were breaking out pieces of the—world-
famous—brick ornament and throwing them at each other. Gun
asked one of the Russian boys, who was about fifteen, whether there
was no guard.

"There was an old man here for a while, but he didn't have even
a bread knife to defend himself with."

All the children laughed at the smart answer—and went on
breaking out bricks. I asked a Russian if people were allowed to
carry on like this in the Kremlin. Astounded, he said, "But surely
there's a difference!"

Sultan Sandzhar's mausoleum is older than the Kremlin walls,
and has had considerably more influence on the history of world culture. I spoke to every authority I could in Turkmenistan, telling
them they ought to detach some of their guards to protect the
mausoleum. I don't know whether anything has been done about it.
That at the moment they can't afford to restore it I perfectly understand; but to permit vandalization—that's another matter.

Sometimes it's said to be typically intellectual to bother more
about monuments than about people. In this case it is not so. I know
what my Turkmen friends have told me, "All Turkmens want to see
Sultan Sandzhar's mausoleum once in their lives. They come there
from as far afield as the Caspian Sea. He was the greatest of us all."

And while the blond children went on throwing stones, the old
Turkmens were praying. In such a situation even a fake anti-
religious maneuver can have dangerous consequences.

This is the bureaucrats' policy. But it is not itself Stalinist. The
cautious old Georgian could be harsh—but he wasn't stupid. And
this policy in questions of culture and nationality and economics

will have as dangerous consequences for the Soviet Union's inner cohesion as it has already had for the Soviet Union's position in Asia.

Nor is it any great consolation to know that all this is happening just because the bureaucrats are such prisoners of their own privileged status that they are unable to implement socialist policy. Scant consolation indeed. For where, in the teeth of their opposition, do the Turkmen and Soviet peoples have institutions capable of implementing such a policy?

Necessity forces its own way. When the institutions are corrupt the institutions have to be smashed. When the people in Turkmenistan, in all the Soviet republics, take their socialism seriously then the *apparat* crumbles.

But when things have gone so far that the bureaucrats are seriously threatened, then ink will be found thicker than water. What help the bureaucrats will get they will get from their colleagues in the West.

1965

AFGHANISTAN

XLIV

Outside Herat the Soviet Union has put up a hotel. It looks impressive, even luxurious. At Lashkargah the USA has built a magnificent hospital (with marble floors) where—says the idealistic young doctor—doctors are to be educated for private practice.

"We must help them to get into private practice. They're so badly paid. The Afghans have been holding things up so long. But now they're beginning to see the light."

Outside the palatial hospital, the polyclinic patients with their diseases and sores are sitting in the sun. There is no waiting room.

At Kandahar Gun and I are invited to a meal in the American restaurant. But my Afghan friend is turned away.

"Americans and Europeans only."

So I refuse to eat with the Americans, and we go to the bazaar. I ask my Afghan friend, "Why do you put up with this? Have you no pride left? Are you going to let them discriminate against you in your own country?"

He laughs, "They've got money—they've got dollars. Lots of dollars." He rubs his thumb against his forefinger.

At Kabul the experts' quarters have grown bigger. The experts' villas better. Their servants more numerous and better drilled. The expert structure has been reinforced, and its service industries have stabilized themselves.

Where the old bazaar used to stand, the Spinzar Hotel now stands. At the top, in its restaurant, I drink Czech beer from Pilsen with the American ambassador. His view is that things aren't too bad: "As a matter of fact our Soviet foes agree with us as to which economic policy Afghanistan must adopt. Younger men have arrived from their side now, people you can talk to."

Afghanistan is being invested in. Its transport network is being developed. There is an altogether new prosperity. For the few. True, the American aid program in the Helmand Valley is just as salted up as it ever was, and has become an even more costly error—for Afghanistan; but the Soviets have learned from the Americans' experience and introduced a clause into their contracts for irrigation projects freeing them from all future responsibility.

The country is also to introduce criminal legislation. An expert from West Germany is just figuring it out. A trusty civil servant, with many decades' experience of criminal elements and how to combat them.

Afghanistan is also to get itself a constitution. Such things are important. The Herat district has been informed that eighty-five new lawyers are on their way from Kabul. Unfortunately no nurses were to be had. They would have been preferable. But the lawyers are necessary, for the statistics of trials in the Herat district have been making depressing reading. They have been showing a tendency to fall. From 1,200 cases a year to 120. With these eighty-five new lawyers it will be possible to get the curve moving upward again.

But the people—they're as poor as ever.

The slums which have been banished from the center of Kabul have fled up toward the hills. They're bigger than they used to be. True, their inhabitants have further to go to water—but water isn't good for the health anyway. The great thing that has happened in Afghanistan isn't the new roads and the new constructions; but that its egalitarian trait has been erased. The rich have got richer, and the poor poorer. And the rich are rich in a new way, and the poor are poor in a new way. In the wake of aid programs a monetary economy has hit the country, and hit it hard.

The international aid program has good traits—for a certain class of society. The new middle class of entrepreneurs and bourgeoisie. Whether this help comes from the Soviet or USA or UN, its social effect in Afghanistan has been to strengthen this new class. Irrespective of where the help is coming from, or what shape it takes, its effects are the same. This new class is growing stronger and becoming richer and remodeling Afghan society to its own needs.

Now, one might say that in spite of everything, all this is good. That the way to progress must go through dirt and want and misery for the masses. In which case the aid is good, just as the British, according to this way of looking at things, were good for India. They were shattering the old order. Creating a transport system and industries, they were also creating such insufferable conditions that the people, in self-defense, would be forced to democratize their society. The sad thing about this captivating line of thought is that nothing indicates it is making haste to come true. The people remain sunk in their poverty.

What is arising in Afghanistan is not what the pretty speeches in the UN and at development congresses pretend—human solidarity. It is neo-colonialism. Developmental aid becomes a revolution—but a revolution influenced and steered from without. But when people in Sweden spoke of aid their idea, surely, was not that every country should be thrust into a new British 1830's?

It isn't easy to write this. For it means I have to cancel out much of what I've believed in. But if what I believe doesn't accord with what I see, then I must cancel it out, and change my views accordingly.

This is what I myself experienced—with a shock—when I got back to Afghanistan. And if that had been all, then I should have seen the whole thing as hopeless. But the young Afghan intellectuals were saying the same. And various Afghans in the administration were also pointing it out. In their work in Afghanistan, the Soviet Union, the USA, and the UN were all—they'd said—leaning on the same class; a class which the aid-givers were supporting in order to line their own pockets. And poverty had now become worse, because a few were now in a position to live in luxury.

This Afghan point of view was clearly formulated. Partly, it was expressed in national terms. People were reminding themselves of Abd-er-Rahman's warnings against the foreigners and of his observation that the Afghans themselves must keep control. In their choice between economic investment with outside control or a smaller economic investment with native control, the latter alternative, he

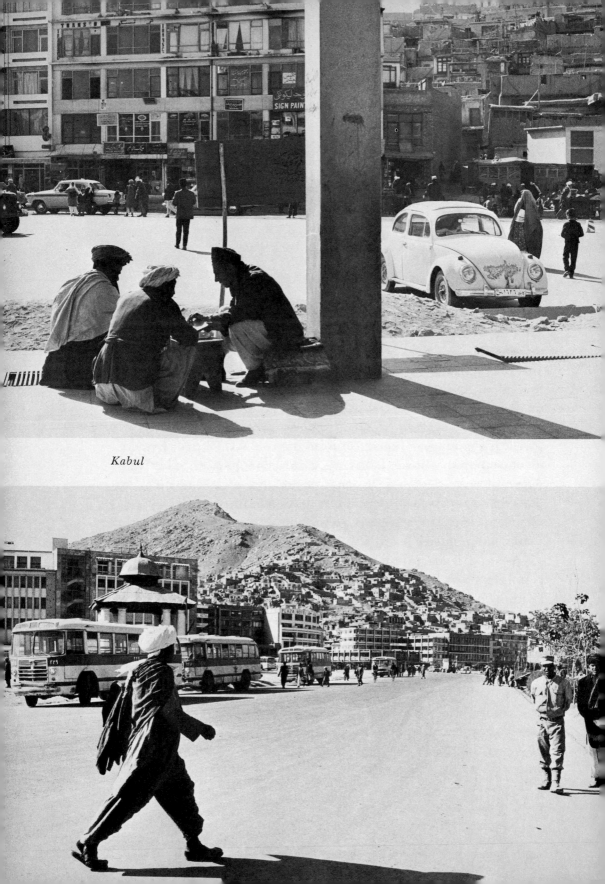

Kabul

had said, would in the long run yield the swiftest development. Where they differed from their old rule was in seeing the class issue in Afghanistan as crucial.

Yet—as an American said, "Everything's going ahead now. You can't imagine what a difference there is. Before, the Afghans hardly dared speak to me. Now we drink together. Liquor is becoming free in Afghanistan."

XLV

To become indignant over white westerners getting rich on aid to poor countries is often called cheap radicalism. Expressed in this way, it is. To get a given job done it can be perfectly rational for any given country to pay—or allow someone else to pay—a given foreigner a hundred times the annual income of one of its own inhabitants.

Nor is the Afghan problem merely the problem of that little privileged group, the experts. It is more general than that. Development run from abroad is having social consequences. These consequences are largely independent of the will of the individual experts or their personal qualities. By and large the result is the same today, whether those experts are idealistic saints or black-market sharks and profiteers.

As my friends within the administration pointed out, foreign planning aid is undermining the country's own ability to plan for itself. The various foreign aid organizations, the US, the Soviet, the West German, and the UN, present different plans and give priority to different projects. (When I talked to them, however, they alleged they were now trying to coordinate their plans.)

This causes the Afghan administration's planning department to split into different factions, enjoying different foreign aid and intriguing against each other.

At the same time, the country was exposed to strong foreign political pressure to get it to accept the plan—so important to the aid-giver's status—which the various Great Powers' representatives had presented.

"If we say to the Soviet Union," said one highly placed civil servant, "that their new project is too expensive for us and suggest its postponement, then the Soviet government asks, 'Are you anti-Soviet?' If we're dubious about some US project, similar pressure is at once exerted by the US embassy. A small poor country, today, is in no position to select those projects which are economically the most profitable. All the time we have to respect the Great Powers' demands. Our only way out in the end will be to say no to all of them. Get the foreigners out."

The foreign aid program's destructive effects on the administration of the receiving country should be comprehensible even to us Swedes—whether conservative or socialist.

At Herat, the Governor was busy arranging a reception for the American Peace Corps. Houses were evacuated and put in order. He was skeptical.

"But they mean so well," he said. "It's all so idealistic and well-intentioned."

When we got to Kabul, the Peace Corps were quartered in the Kabul Hotel. They'd been given all the rooms with baths.

Other countries, too, wanted to send peace corps. The Czech ambassador had informed the Afghan government of the great idealism of the Czech government. They would gladly do their bit to build up Afghanistan. They wanted to send Czech youth to Afghanistan. When the Afghans had pointed out that it was not people they stood in need of, he was both astonished and hurt.

"Afghans," they said, "are best suited to Afghanistan."

To me they said, "We could say that to the Czechs because our trade with them isn't so important they can bring pressure to bear on us. We can't say it to the USA or West Germany!"

But the effect of foreign capital is not only politically and administratively corrupting. It also leads to direct bribery. One of the companies which is doing most building in Kabul is Hochtief. Hochtief is strongly supported by the West German embassy. The ambassador's job, of course, is to promote his own country's economy. For several years Hochtief has been building villas for the Afghan ministers. Their method was direct bribery of high civil servants of the state.

236

At top administrative level the growth of bribery keeps pace with the interest taken in the country by foreign capital. And this high-level corruption distorts all planning and makes it difficult to develop the economy. (Hochtief is by no means the only example.)

At present a direct trial of strength is going on within the Afghan administration. On the one side are those officials who are foreign-influenced, corrupt. And, on the other, the young and still idealistic administrators who have just completed their studies. The young administrators who want to establish an independent economy—at the price of limiting foreign aid—come from influential families. Their ideology can be called "conservative" or "nationalist"; yet they are giving expression to the needs of the whole Afghan people (the entrepreneurs and the corrupt excepted). If they succeed, a loud outcry of "Nasserism" will certainly go up in our countries. If they do not succeed, they will be jailed. Or—if they are from the ruling families—be sent to UN jobs.

Reference is often made to the "revolution of rising expectations" in the Asian countries. Mostly, this is sheer illusion. For the great majority the problem is still survival. But the type of economic development going on in Afghanistan under foreign influence has widened the gap between the poor and the rich. It is not that the foreign experts' villas and way of living are "immoral"; but they have set up a new (and expensive) pattern of life for the Afghan bourgeoisie.

To prevent the foreigners from making their own private enclaves with their own hotels and their own clubs, the Afghans have had modern hotels and restaurants built in Kabul. The policy is to be continued in the provincial cities.

As such, the goal of this policy is to limit the foreigners' influence. But among the poorly paid officials it has brought with it a new need for corruption. Their salaries are low. Life is hard. The Finance Department has opened a cafeteria by the Pashtunistan Place in Kabul. A clean, Italian, well-kept self-service restaurant. There you can eat, drink Coca-Cola and listen to jazz. It has become an important establishment. Its aim is to set a new standard for Afghanistan. And I have also seen how it is kept at the same high level, year after year. Something the foreigners didn't believe who said in 1961,

"These Afghans'll soon muck it up, you see."

The underpaid civil servants go there. They order a Coca-Cola and listen to the music . . . and it swallows a whole day's pay. Nothing is left for the family. Bribes are their only way out. Bribery pays for Coca-Cola; Coca-Colonization and bribes go together.

Black-tent nomads near Adraskan

XLVI

It was south of Herat and northwest of Adraskan. The black tents were old and threadbare. The sun shone in through the faded brown tent blankets, forming patterns on the earth floor.

"Seven wives and eleven sons have died on me," the old man said.

We drank goat's milk, warm from the udder, and they proffered us old long-stored pieces of candy sugar. Through the tent opening I saw how the sand was being whirled up into little dust-devils. It was already afternoon. Hot. Behind me the young women were giggling. Someone called out to them, "If you're ill, drink some goat's milk." And everyone in the tent laughed.

"Our forefathers rode on thoroughbred horses. We were a rich and powerful family of the Durrani tribe. Now all we have left are these few tents. We've lost all our animals. During the hard winter of 1963 four hundred beasts died on us. And since we've no money, and no animals either, we've had to settle down and cultivate the soil. In the old days we used to take our herds over the frontier to Iran. In the spring we went from the plains to the high mountain pastures, and down again to the plains in winter. Now we are settled. Now we're so poor we've had to become farmers. This valley is ours by custom. There's water here. Our herds have gone, but if we work hard the soil yields us a living. We have food to eat."

The great dogs had been tied up with ropes and sacks had been put over their heads. But they scented our presence and growled at the strangers. They were guarding their own people. Inside the tent their puppies were playing. The children dragged their own puppies about after them, carrying the shaggy little dogs about in their arms. The pups' heavy heads were disproportionately large, their ears had already been cropped and their tails shortened. When full-grown they had to be able to protect the herds by tearing wolves in pieces. But there were no more herds. The puppies rolled on their backs in front of me. Shaggy balls of warmth, snapping with their milk teeth and red tongues. The children laughed and the men smiled at the children. I asked whether they produced any grain for market, "No. Never. We eat up everything we produce. Anything that's left over we give to the poor, the hungry. We're free men. When people get into difficulties they must help each other. We don't sell our grain. When we need money, we collect bushes in the desert and sell them for fuel in the bazaars. But money's a curse. In this world money speaks louder than human beings. Money speaks to the Governor in Herat. Money speaks to the King at Kabul. Everything in this life is just money. That's the way of it. And that's how it shouldn't be."

We spoke of Vietnam. The old man, the head of the family said, "Well, that's how the world is; the rich and the powerful torment the poor. They have their airplanes and their bombs. Everywhere it's

243

only money that speaks. The poor man has no friends except his own people and his rifle."

Laughing, the old man, his face pitted with smallpox, held up his rifle. Its butt was inlaid with ivory. The tents were old. The flaps of the felt fluttered in the afternoon wind. It was cool in the tents. We spoke of houses and how to build them.

"Two years we've been living here by the water. Our tents are old, but tents cost money. When we had our herds we had money. Now we've no herds any more. Naturally, we could do with houses, now we're settled. But no trees grow here. If we're to build houses we must buy roof timbers. To get timbers we must have money. The soil here is mediocre. But in the spring there's plenty of water. The harvests are not much to speak of. And if we want to build houses without timbers, then we must build houses with cupolas. Ourselves we don't know the art of building cupolas. For such houses we should have to hire people. And to hire people costs money. In this world everything is money."

We speak of schools. The old man points at the children. Giggling, they hide their faces in their hands.

"Schools would be good for the children. We've nothing against schools. But how will our children get to school? Schools aren't for our children. Schools are for town children."

The nomad culture is no primitive culture. It is specialized. Today it is said to be doomed. At international congresses and in progress reports people say what a good thing settlement is. There's a lot of talk about how the tribes have become settled tillers of the soil, and what a big step forward this is. Yet, poverty has obliged them to settle. And settlement only increases their poverty. In the statistics they are chalked up as the happy outcome of sound policy.

The nomads were herdsmen. They were traders and wandering agricultural laborers. Now the roads are being extended, and others are taking over their trade. The wealthy trading nomads become merchants and money-lenders, and live in the cities.

The experts say the nomads' attitudes must be changed. They must adapt to modern life. But what is modern life? "Money rules the world."

But is there then no way out of poverty, exploitation, oppression, and illness which will allow people to regain their dignity?

244

"The poor man has no friends except his own people and his rifle."

There are people and rifles enough in Asia to make it possible for the poor man to make the world a human one.

Postscript 1971

On May 14, 1872, there was a sharp argument at the meeting of the General Council of the International Working Men's Association. According to the Minutes:

> Citizen *Hales* proposed "that in the opinion of the Council the formation of *Irish* nationalist branches in England is opposed to the General Rules and principles of the Association." He said he brought forward the motion in no antagonism to the Irish members, but he thought the policy being pursued (is) fraught with the greatest danger to the Association . . . The fundamental principle of the Association was to destroy all semblance of the nationalist doctrine and remove all barriers that separated man from man, and the formation of either Irish or English branches could only retard the movement instead of helping it . . .

> Citizen *Engels* said . . . (the motion) was asking the conquered people to forget their nationality and submit to their conquerors. It was not Internationalism but simply prating submission . . .

According to Engels's record of his report at this meeting he further said:

> If members of a conquering nation called upon the nation they had conquered and continued to hold down to forget their specific nationality and position, to sink national differences and so forth, that was not Internationalism, it was nothing else but preaching to them submission to the yoke, and attempting to justify and to perpetuate the dominion of the conqueror under the cloak of Internationalism. It was sanctioning the belief, only too common among the English working men, that they were superior beings

compared to the Irish, and as much an aristocracy as the mean Whites of the Slave States considered themselves to be with regard to the Negroes . . .

That still is the heart of the matter. Thus when President Johnson on March 25, 1965, said:

The United States looks forward to the day when the people and governments of all South-East Asia may be free from terror, subversion and assassination . . .

then the old man in the black felt tent northwest of Adraskan answered:

The poor man has no friend except his own people and his rifle.

We can choose between the internationalism of Hales, of President Johnson, of the B-52 bombers or the internationalism of Engels, of the old man in the black felt tent outside Adraskan, of the rifles.